THE HAMLYN ENCYCLOPEDIA OF
GRANDS PRIX

THE HAMLYN ENCYCLOPEDIA OF
GRANDS PRIX

DAVID HODGES

HAMLYN

Photographic acknowledgements

All photographs supplied by the author except the following:
Allsport 22 (upper), 154 (top), 168 (top); Jeff Bloxham (*Autosport*) 63, 83,
86 (top); Maxwell Boyd 70; Michael C Brown (*Autosport*) 27; Peter Burn 26
(top), 90, 130, 142 (top), 147 (lower), 150 (top); Diana Burnett title spread, 93 (lower),
107 (top), 154 (lower); Camel 99 (lower), 101, 132; Courtaulds 166; DPPI 14
(lower), 127; EDP Photography 110; Embassy 74; Ford 19, 20, 43 (top), 64,
126 (lower), 157 (top), 164; Graham Gauld 122 (lower); Michael R Hewett 29
(lower), 80 (lower), 104, 122 (top), 125, 167 (lower); Louis Klemantaski 167;
LAT 7, 15, 111 (top), 119, 131 (top), 135, 172, 173; Marlboro 93 (top), 107
(top), 136, 145; Tony Matthews 58 (lower); David Phipps 72 (lower); Players
99 (top); Porsche 133; Renault 140; Maurice Rowe 1, 13, 20, 41, 55, 57, 77,
97, 100 (lower), 112, 138, 149, 152, 157 (lower), 158, 163; Nigel Snowdon 22
(lower), 46, 50 (top), 56, 59 (top), 79, 82, 95 (top), 103, 134 (lower), 151,
155, 162 (lower), 171 (lower); Sporting Pictures 118 (lower); Gerry Stream
73; Julius Weitmann 45; Yardley 81, 105.

Published by
The Hamlyn Publishing Group Limited
a division of
The Octopus Publishing Group
Michelin House
81 Fulham Road
London SW3 6RB

and distributed for them by
Octopus Distribution Services Limited
Rushden, Northamptonshire NN10 9RZ

First published in 1988

ISBN 0 600 55785 5

Printed in Italy by Sagdos

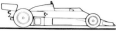

Foreword

It's over twenty years since I started single-seater racing – in a Formula Ford Alexis – and it seems extraordinary that the Formula 1 World Championship began only 17 years before that.

The Grand Prix scene has changed radically since Nino Farina took that first Championship in 1950. The recent technical advances – in chassis design, in aerodynamics, in suspension systems, in engines – are familiar to most followers of motor racing, but this has been a continuing process throughout the history of the Championship. Equally important, maybe, has been the growing professionalism of the team operations and the efforts directed towards driver and spectator safety.

There are those who will tell you that today's F1 racing lacks the romance, excitement and personalities of the old days. That may be so, but with some notable exceptions, Grand Prix racing is very much more competitive than it used to be. You only have to look at the number of times in the last few years that the Championship has not been decided until the last race of the season. The drivers may appear not to be such 'personalities' as their predecessors. This is perhaps because they are more professional; but I can assure you they still enjoy themselves just as much as they used to.

1988 saw the end of the turbo era. Let us hope that this will bring closer, even more exciting racing than we have had for the last few years particularly during the period of transition. Let us also hope that we have another British World Champion soon – it is long overdue.

The Hamlyn Encyclopaedia of Grands Prix takes you from Adelaide to Zolder and most points between. It deals with every aspect of Grand Prix racing including profiles of drivers, constructors and designers with entries on cars, circuits, topics such as aerodynamics, chassis, formula definitions and of course the races. I think it makes an excellent source of reference.

James Hunt

Adelaide circuit

Created for the Australian Grand Prix in 1985, this city circuit was unusual in having fast corners and a 1 km long straight, as well as run-off areas which do not feature prominently at other street circuits. It was made up of uniformly surfaced public roads (bordered by only a few buildings) and a specially constructed 1 km loop in the Victoria Park and racecourse grounds.

Lap distance: 2.35 miles/3.78 km. Lap record: 105.121 mph/169.159 km/h by Gerhard Berger in a Ferrari, 1987.

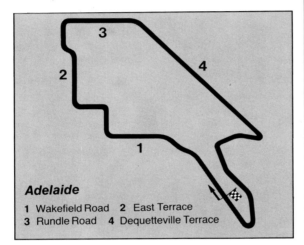

Adelaide

1 Wakefield Road   2 East Terrace
3 Rundle Road   4 Dequetteville Terrace

aerodynamics

Drag or wind resistance increases as the square of a vehicle's speed and this led to the aerodynamics emphasis in road and competition vehicle being on streamlining for about 70 years of automotive history. This applied in the early world championship years, for example with Mercedes-Benz running W196s with full-width bodywork, a streamlined Cooper tried for fast circuits (and rapidly abandoned), Costin's famous Vanwall body, large but smooth and free of the drag caused by small protruberances, and odd unhappy bubble cockpit experiments through to Brabhams as late as 1967. Although full-width bodywork was banned, streamlining has its place, but in the 1960s the aerodynamic emphasis shifted to the positive use of airflow. It took the racing world a long time to recognize the implications of the inverted aerofoil section stub wings in helping to keep Opel rocket cars on the ground in the late 1920s. Swiss designer/engineer Michael May fitted a large wing to a sports-racing Porsche in 1956, only to have it condemned by race officials. In the early 1960s

dragster pilots found that 'wings' helped to keep their contraptions on the straight and narrow and in 1967 the Chaparral sports car team showed how high-mounted wing aerofoils were positive aids to road-holding on circuit cars.

In Formula cars, disregarding ideas which never appeared on cars at circuits, aerodynamic applications came as Ron Tauranac of Brabham and Colin Chapman of Lotus introduced nose winglets to counter lift in 1967. Within a year Brabhams and Ferraris were raced in Grands Prix with rear strut-mounted aerofoils, their loadings balanced by large nose aerofoils. Those rear wings were mounted to the chassis, and thus applied downforce to the complete car, but in 1968 Chapman took the logical step and on the Lotus 49B mounted the aerofoil struts to the rear suspension uprights. At the time he estimated a downforce of 400 lb at 150 mph (181 kg at 240 km/h), which improved traction and adhesion markedly, at the cost of added stresses (for example on transmission components) and some accidents.

Strut-mounted nose aerofoils followed, and then driver-adjustable wings, which could be feathered to reduce drag. Before teams had really started to exploit that line of development, however, in the 1969 Spanish GP the two Team Lotus cars' rear wings failed on a pronounced bump and they crashed heavily and the CSI banned wings. New regulations severely restricted aerofoil positions and dimensions, and the rear wing overhang was to be restricted more and more.

Lotus again led by example in the 72, in which Colin Chapman and designer Maurice Phillippe turned to the wedge shape which had already proved to be aerodynamically efficient in the Type 56 Indianapolis car of 1968. In the 72 the overall wedge was combined with conventional nose aerofoils and various rear aerofoils.

The positive use of the airflow beneath a car came next, again following an example set by Chaparral. But ground effects became extreme and so the sliding skirts that were fundamental to the science were banned for 1981, only to gain an extension until the end of 1982 as a designer came up with a lowering suspension system. For 1983 a completely flat underside within the wheelbase was called for, hence 'flat bottom' regulations.

Despite that, designers still managed to achieve some worthwhile ground effects — at least, the designers of the better-endowed teams with specialist aerodynamicists did ... by no means all of Williams' 1987 success was due to the team's engines.

There is a price to be paid for downforce — drag. 'Movable aerodynamic devices' are banned, so compromise aerodynamic settings

Alfa Romeo 158, 1950

are established in testing and practice sessions. A very shallow angle of attack produces least drag, and therefore higher speeds on a straight, while more aerofoil drag means greater downforce for corners. So the jargon of 'less wing' or 'more wing' can very roughly be equated with higher maximum speed, or faster cornering, or in conjunction with all the other compromises as contributions towards those ends.

AFM

This small German specialist car builder was set up by Alex von Falkenhausen (hence, plus an M for Motorenbau, AFM), initially to build BMW-based specials. AFM became internationally known through a straightforward Formula 2 car, which had a twin-ohc V8 designed by Kuchon. In 1952–53 a works car and some independent entries were run in a few GPs. But AFMs made little impact, and the company was closed down in 1953.

AGS

The French company Automobiles Gonfaronaise Sportive built single seaters for national categories for eight years before their first F2 cars, the JH16 of 1978 and the JH17, attracted attention. Patron Henri Julien took AGS into Formula 1 racing late in 1986 with the turbo powered JH21C Motori Moderni.

Designer Christian Vanderpleyn adapted this for the normally-aspirated class in 1987 as the JH22, using the Cosworth DFZ. It was realistic within the resources of the small team from Gonfaron in southern France – bulky and reliable, although it never appeared competitive until Moreno was sixth overall in the last race. Some resemblances to the later turbo Renaults were attributed to the fact that when Julien bought a redundant transporter from the Régie, there were some RE60 parts still aboard. Philippe Streiff was the team's driver for 1988, with the more compact and competitive JH23.

Ain-Diab circuit

This fast circuit of roads on the outskirts of Casablanca was the venue of the only Moroccan GP to be a championship race, in 1958.
Lap distance: 4.72 miles/7.59 km. Lap record: 117.86 mph/189.64 km/h by Stirling Moss in a Vanwall, 1958.

Aintree circuit

This was an attempt to use Liverpool's famous horse-racing course for motor racing. When opened in 1954 it was an anti-clockwise circuit, but from the second meeting races were run in the conventional direction. The British Grand Prix was first held there in 1955.

The track was flat and as artificial as an airfield circuit, roughly triangular with two reasonable straights, an infield loop and temporary pits, and by British standards it was long.

In the first of five British GPs run at Aintree Stirling Moss headed a Mercedes team 1-2-3-4 in 1955 and also took over Brooks' Vanwall to win in 1957 – the first all-British win in a world championship Grand Prix.

The last GP at Aintree was run in 1962 and by 1964 the circuit seemed lost. However, local enthusiasm revived it for occasional national meetings from 1966, and the 1.64-mile/2.64 km club circuit survives.
Lap distance: 3 miles/4.828 km. Lap record: 93.91 mph/151.1 km/h by Jim Clark in a Lotus, 1962.

Alboreto, Michele *1956–*

Alboreto is a Milanese who became the first Italian to drive for Ferrari for more than a decade when he joined the Scuderia for the 1984 season and – even rarer in recent history – an Italian who won GPs for Ferrari.

Alboreto began racing in local categories (F Monza, then F Italia) single-seaters early in the 1970s and in Formula 3 late in the decade. He was Italian F3 champion in 1979 and European F3 champion in 1980.

In 1981 he raced Tyrrells in ten GPs. He scored his first championship points with a fourth place in Brazil in 1982, and ended that season with a first GP victory, at Las Vegas, and 25 points. He won another GP, at Detroit, with Tyrrell in 1983 before he joined Ferrari. He won one GP in 1984 and two in 1985 before the turbo Ferraris were temporarily eclipsed.

Throughout his career Alboreto has stood out

Michele Alboreto, the most successful Italian driver of the 1980s, in a Ferrari F1/87 at Monaco in 1987

Alfa Romeo 158, 1950

as a stylist, with unusual mechanical sympathy, and aggression coupled with a calm temperament.

World championship races *(to end of 1987): 105 starts, 149½ points, 5 wins: 1982 Caesar's Palace (Las Vegas); 1982 US (Detroit); 1984 Belgium; 1985 Canada, Germany.*

Alfa Romeo

Alfa Romeo's recent Grand Prix ventures failed to live up to the reputation of the Italian marque that was once one of the greatest in racing, with legendary cars in the mid-1920s and the early 1930s, and a model from the late 1930s that was to dominate the early world championship years.

That 158 (*1.5 litri, 8 cilindri*) was designed by Gioacchino Colombo to contest *vetturetta* races, the 1930s equivalent of Formula 2. It had a 1.5-litre straight-8 supercharged twin ohc engine, with a highly conventional chassis and independent suspension.

The cars were hidden during the war and when brought out they complied with the Grands Prix regulations. They were developed by Orazio Satta. More and more power was squeezed from the engines: 275 bhp in 1947,

310 bhp in 1948, 350 bhp in 1950, up to 420 bhp in 1951.

Through those years the gorgeous dark red cars were driven to victory after victory, in 1947 starting on an unbroken run of 26 wins. The total was to be 33, gained by men of great calibre, especially Farina and Fangio, and in an age when there were fewer championship races Alfa drivers amassed 158 points in 1950 and 1951.

The team was withdrawn at the end of 1951, and in a muddled way revived to contest sports car races in the 1960s and 1970s. This programme produced a 3-litre flat-12 engine that was adopted by Brabham for Formula 1 in 1976. Power outputs varied widely between engines, and they were thirsty, so that extra fuel (and weight) had to be carried. Flat-12 configuration was also a handicap in the ground effects period (the cylinder heads obstructed under-car airflow) and a V-12 was developed in 1979.

Meanwhile in 1977 Alfa Romeo's competitions subsidiary Autodelta started work on a GP car, the 177. The return to racing in 1979 showed some promise but there was none of the old glory. For a full programme the 179 was designed by Carlo Chiti, his last complete

The three dark red 158s of the Alfa Romeo team monopolize the front row of the grid for the French GP at Reims in the first championship season, 1950. Fangio in car number 6 took pole with a practice lap almost 8 seconds faster than the best of the two blue Talbots on row 2. Alongside him are the other two members of the 'three Fs' team, Farina and Fagioli. By modern standards the track is ludicrously narrow, trackside protection is negligible and the 3-2-3 grid looks very crowded

design for Alfa. It looked bulky, its V-12 produced more than 520 bhp but needed 25 more litres of fuel than its rivals to complete a race. Not that it often did, despite the best efforts of drivers Bruno Giacomelli and Vittorio Brambilla. In 1980 Giacomelli scored just four points, and Patrick Depailler's death in a test accident was a shattering blow to the team. Andretti joined the team in 1981 for his last full GP season, and disillusionment.

Alfa Romeo joined the turbo ranks late in 1982, with the 182T designed by Gérard Ducarouge. This was modified as the 183T in 1983 and raced by the Euroracing team to the high points of Alfa's recent racing history — second places in Germany and South Africa. Fortunes declined with the 184T and 185T, an inelegant car with 720 bhp on tap from its KKK-turbocharged engine. Its drivers scored no points in 1985, and the programme was wound up. Fiat was soon to take over Alfa Romeo and direct its competitions effort towards saloon racing.

A once-proud Grand Prix line just faded away with the V-8 engines being supplied to the minor Osella team in 1986–88.
Constructors' championship: 1981 8th; 1982 9th; 1983 6th; 1984 8th.

Alliot, Philippe *1954–*

A French driver who carved a niche in the lower echelons of Formula 1 after ten years in racing (*formule Renault* in 1975–78, F3, then F2 in 1982–83 before two seasons with the RAM team), Alliot raced in F3000 in 1986, and in seven GPs with Ligier, scoring his first world championship point in the 1986 Mexican GP. He moved to the new, and happier, Larrouse-Calmels team in 1987 to contest the Jim Clark Trophy 'division' in Lolas. He was competitive, although prone to errors or at least to spinning, and scored points in three Grands Prix.
World championship races (to end of 1987): 49 starts, 3 points.

Alta

Geoffrey Taylor's company built small sports cars and voiturette racing cars at Tolworth in Surrey in the 1930s, then a 1.5-litre supercharged GP design for the first post-Second World War formula. This achieved little, and although the Alta Formula 2 car was also undistinguished, its engine gave up to 150 bhp and was used by the HWM team. For the 2.5-litre GPs Alta built engines for Connaught which gave up to 250 bhp. When Connaught abandoned their GP effort the original Alta company also ceased operations, although the name was briefly revived for a Formula Ford venture in the mid-1970s.

Amon, Chris *1943–*

The abundant talent of Chris Amon was never rewarded with Grand Prix victories although he led many times and was often well-placed. His victories came in other spheres, notably in sports cars and the Tasman series. Amon started racing in New Zealand in 1956 and moved to Europe to drive Reg Parnell's Lolas in 1963, when at 19 he was the youngest driver in Formula 1, then scored his first point in a Tim Parnell Lotus in the 1964 Dutch GP.

In the following seasons he drove a Cooper-Maserati, served Ferrari well through their difficult 1967–69 seasons — he was held in the highest regard by Mauro Forghieri — moved on to March and scored a second among other placings through a season when many felt that if he had stayed with Ferrari he would have won GPs. As with March in 1970, he won a non-championship race with Matra in 1971–72, put in sparkling drives, but won no championship races. Then his career slipped: there were drives in the hopeless Tecno and once in a Tyrrell in 1973, there was the effort on the Amon car that turned out to be wasted in 1974, a couple of BRM outings and in 1975/76 ten starts in Ensigns which brought just one scoring place, fifth in Spain in 1976. He retired that year, returning to New Zealand.
World championship races: 96 starts, 83 points.

Amon

Chris Amon sought to join the ranks of the driver-constructors in 1974, with a Cosworth-engined car financed by John Dalton. The AF1 ('F' for designer Gordon Fowell) had torsion-bar suspension, a slim aluminium monocoque, anticipated a trend (and then a requirement) in carrying its fuel load between cockpit and engine, and apparently had sophisticated aerodynamics.

On the circuits there were component failures and accidents and it started in only the 1974 Spanish GP, when Amon retired it.

Anderstorp circuit

The Scandinavian Raceway, which survives as a flat airfield circuit in the forests of southern Sweden, was the uninspiring setting for the Swedish GP from 1973 until 1978. It comprised a long straight and a sinuous infield section, but despite the apparent simplicity of its lap plan it called for unusual car settings. Some atypical performances were achieved there, for example first and second placings for the six-wheeled Tyrrell P34s in 1976.
Lap distance: 2.5 miles/4.03 km. Lap record: 106.32 mph/171.1 km/h by Niki Lauda in a Brabham BT46B, 1978.

Alfa Romeo 158, 1950

Alfa Romeo failed to recapture the old glories of the early championship days when an Autodelta team entered the Grand Prix arena in the late 1970s, and had little joy in the following years with cars such as this 179B driven by Bruno Giacomelli in the French GP at Dijon in 1981

Andretti, Mario 1940–

Here was a true champion driver, with the temperament for outstanding careers in both Grands Prix and Indycar racing, that started years before the term 'Indycar' came into use. This Italian-born American's early racing was pure USAC (United States Auto Club), on dirt tracks and in the front-engined roadsters during their final years in the mid-1960s. In 1965 he raced in the Indianapolis 500 for the first time, coming third; in 1985 he was second in the 500, but he won it only once, driving a

Hawk in 1969. Yet throughout his European background meant that the pull of the Grands Prix was strong.

Colin Chapman recognized Andretti's talent in the days when Team Lotus meant one driver, Jim Clark. In 1968 Lotus entered Mario for his first Grand Prix, and at Watkins Glen he took pole, and there was little joy in three races with Lotus in 1969. The following year he started in five GPs with an STP-March, scoring his first world championship points with a third place in Spain.

In 1971–72 he had ten races with Ferrari, and a first GP victory, in South Africa in 1971. But partly because he was contracted to Firestone, which withdrew from GP racing, Andretti deserted Formula 1 to concentrate on USAC and US F5000 racing. He drove for Vel's Parnelli Jones team, which in time aspired to GP racing and duly built a car which Andretti drove in the North American GPs in the autumn of 1974 and for a full season in 1975. He scored only five points and while the VPJ4 may have been handsome, it was never properly developed.

After a hesitant start in 1976, and a non-championship race in a Wolf-Williams, Andretti committed himself to Lotus. His partnership with Chapman developed through that year and at its end he won the Japanese GP. Andretti drove the Lotus 78 to win five GPs in 1977, and was disappointed to be only third in the championship. But that season and the car led into 1978 and the Lotus 79. That was a supreme year for Lotus and Andretti. He won six GPs and quite clearly headed the championship.

The highly-rated New Zealander Chris Amon in the Matra team's MS120D in 1972. He drove for several other teams, including Ferrari

The 1979–80 seasons were largely fruitless, 1981 with Alfa Romeo was barren; Andretti returned to Indycars, to win his 50th title race in 1988. He raced in three more GPs, the last two with Ferrari when he took pole at Monza in 1982 and was third in the Italian GP.

World championship races: 128 starts, 180 points, 12 wins: 1971 South Africa; 1976 Japan; 1977 US West, Spain, France, Italy; 1978 Argentina, Belgium, Spain, France, Germany, Netherlands. World champion: 1978.

Argentine Grand Prix

In 1952 a new autodrome at Buenos Aires was used for the Peron Cup races, which had attracted a European entry since they were first run in 1947. This became the venue for the Argentine GP, for many years the first race in the championship season.

Ascari in a Ferrari won the first GP there, as he was winning just about everything at that time, and the great local driver Fangio won the next four. The 1958 result was momentous, as for the first time a rear-engined car won a world championship race: Rob Walker's Cooper-Climax, driven by Stirling Moss.

There was a break from 1961 until 1971, when a non-championship race heralded the return of a full-status Grand Prix in 1972. This was run on the Number 9 circuit of the autodrome, considered cramped for 3-litre cars. The following races went broadly to the dominant teams until 1981, then the event lapsed again.

Winners (world championship GPs)

Year	Driver	Car
1953	A. Ascari	Ferrari
1954	J.-M. Fangio	Maserati
1955	J.-M. Fangio	Mercedes-Benz
1956	J.-M. Fangio and L. Musso	Ferrari
1957	J.-M. Fangio	Maserati
1958	S.Moss	Cooper-Climax
1960	B. McLaren	Cooper-Climax
1972	J. Stewart	Tyrrell-Ford
1973	E. Fittipaldi	Lotus-Ford
1974	D. Hulme	McLaren-Ford
1975	E. Fittipaldi	McLaren-Ford
1977	J. Scheckter	Wolf-Ford
1978	M. Andretti	Lotus-Ford
1979	J. Laffite	Ligier-Ford
1980	A. Jones	Williams-Ford
1981	N. Piquet	Brabham-Ford

Above: Mario Andretti in the 78 he chose to drive at Monaco in 1978, instead of the new and untried 79. His red-topped silver helmet in a black and gold Lotus became familiar in the second half of the 1970s

Inset: Mario Andretti in 1986, looking little older than he did when he won the world championship in 1978

Alfa Romeo 158, 1950

Arnoux, René 1948–

Frenchman Arnoux seems to have been around for a long time – he contested his hundredth GP in 1986. Winning the 1973 *formule Renault*, 1975 European *formule Renault* and 1977 European Formula 2 led to Formula 1 racing, which he started with the one-car Martini operation which failed to last through the 1978 season, and in the North American races that year he drove a Surtees. For 1979 he landed a plum drive, in French terms: the second Renault seat, as that team went into its first full season. That year he scored a useful points total (17) and in 1980 won his first Grands Prix, in Brazil and South Africa. In four seasons Arnoux served Renault well, with four outright victories and 85 points, at the expense of a fairly high accident rate in 1981/82.

He moved to Ferrari in 1983, to win three GPs and achieve his best-ever championship placing of third. The next year was not so good, as he seemed to lose form or motivation, and after the 1985 Brazilian GP he acrimoniously parted company with Ferrari.

In the 1986–87 seasons he shared the ups and downs of the Ligier team, scoring points in 1986 but also building his reputation for being erratic on the tracks. Early in 1987 he also showed his disregard for diplomacy again, when he gave Alfa Romeo the chance to ditch their Ligier contract.

World championship races (to end of 1987): 126 starts, 179 points, 7 wins: 1980 Brazil, South Africa; 1982 France, Italy; 1983 Canada, Germany, Netherlands.

Arrows

The Arrows team was controversial through its first, 1978, season, which it survived to field cars through a decade, sometimes promising to challenge the pace setters but more often middle-of-the-field runners.

The name of this British team is derived from AR for the Italian financier Franco Ambrosio, R for manager Alan Rees, O for Jackie Oliver, W for engineer Dave Wass and S for designer Tony Southgate. The last four left Shadow abruptly to form Arrows in November 1977, and their first car was run in the Brazilian GP in January 1978. However, that FA1 was very similar to Southgate's designs for the Shadow DN9 and after a London High Court case brought by Shadow's Don Nichols it had to be withdrawn.

Its A1 successor was an ineffectual ground effects car, followed by the A1B and the bulky A2. In contrast, 1980's A3 was a handsome car, echoing Williams FW07 lines, but unlike the Williams with inefficient aerodynamics. Southgate left during that season and Wass reworked the A3 to serve through 1981 – the team's

resources were stretched, and for a while it was handicapped by having to run on overweight Pirelli steel-belted radial tyres. Nevertheless Patrese, in his third season with the Arrows, and Mass scored 11 points in 1980; Patrese scored all 10 of the team's points in 1981.

For 1982 there was the A4, and later in the year the A5, which followed Williams FW08 lines very closely. This was a thin season, and so was 1983, with the A6, which was still run in 1984 alongside the A7. The A6 was the last Cosworth-powered Arrows, and in the A7 the team turned to BMW turbocharged engines, initially supplied in a form which complicated designer Wass's task. The car had a fashionable narrow monocoque with a carbon-fibre inner skin and an aluminium honeycomb outer, with half-length side pods for much of the turbo ancilliary equipment; this concentration of weight to the rear added balance problems to a lack of rigidity in the chassis.

That was overcome in the A8, which was stronger and more rigid, and on a longer wheelbase. Mader-prepared BMW turbos were used for the 1985 season, when the cars were reliable and once again Arrows seemed promising – the score in 1985 was 14 points, a vast improvement on 1984's single point. But the team was struggling again in 1986, with the A8 and A9, when once again they achieved only a single championship point.

The 1987 Arrows, the A10, was designed by Ross Brawn, formerly of Williams and Haas, and so it was hardly surprising that it echoed the 1985 Lola (née Beatrice Lola) in some respects. The 'upright' BMW M12/13 engine, renamed Megatron in 1987, gave adequate power and although the A10 never looked a potential race winner Cheever and Warwick picked up championship points with it so that Arrows ended its tenth season in sixth place in the championship. In 1988 Arrows was the only team using Megatron engines, with the same drivers in A10Bs, run from a lavish new base.

Constructors' championship: 1978 9th; 1979 9th; 1980 7th; 1981 8th; 1982 10th; 1983 10th; 1984 9th; 1985 8th; 1986 10th; 1987 6th.

Ascari, Alberto 1918–1955

During this Italian's reign as undisputed king of world championship racing in 1952–53 he set an example of professionalism for a later generation of GP drivers.

Son of one of the outstanding drivers of the 1920s, Antonio Ascari, he raced Maseratis in 1947–48, before moving to Ferrari and winning his first national Grands Prix, (the Swiss and the Italian). In 1948, incidentally, he drove his only GP for his father's old team, Alfa Romeo, placing a 158 third in the French race.

Alberto Ascari in the cockpit of a Ferrari T500 in 1953

Ascari continued with Ferrari until the end of 1953. He won two championship races in 4.5-litre Ferrari 375s, and one of his few 1952 setbacks was a wheel failure when he was running eighth in the Indianapolis 500. In the Grands Prix that year he won every championship race he started, scoring more than twice as many points as the championship runner-up. The 2-litre Ferrari T500 seemed particularly suited to his precise style, and his success with it continued in 1953, when he retained his title.

In 1954 Ascari was released to drive Maseratis (and once a Ferrari) while the Lancia team to which he was contracted prepared its radical D50. He led the last championship race of 1954 in a D50, and the first of 1955, and that season looked promising as he won two non-championship races. Then he became the first driver to crash into the harbour during the Monaco GP. Four days later he tried a sports Ferrari at Monza, and was killed in an unexplained crash. One of Ascari's few weaknesses seemed to be an unwillingness to 'mix it'. But his preference to lead almost clinically highlights his rare talent.

World championship races: 32 starts, 139 gross points, 13 wins: 1951 Germany, Italy; 1952 Belgium, France, Britain, Germany, Netherlands, Italy; 1953 Argentina, Belgium, Netherlands, Britain, Switzerland. **World champion: 1952, 1953.**

Aston-Butterworth

A pair of these novel British F2 cars was built by Bill Aston, and one started in two championship races in 1952, lacking the speed to make an impression. The cars had all-independent suspension and low lines made possible by the flat-four air-cooled Butterworth engine.

Aston Martin

Concentration on a successful sports car programme delayed the first Aston Martin Grand Prix cars since 1922 until the concept they represented had been overtaken. In 1959 the handsome DBR4/250s followed the sports-racing cars in layout, suspension with de Dion rear ends and transmission, and had 6-cylinder engines for which up to 280 bhp was claimed. Roy Salvadori drove Astons to sixth places in the British and Portuguese GPs but the cars were obviously outclassed by rear-engined machines.

A 1960 version was built with independent rear suspension, but this British factory wisely decided to withdraw from the GP field. With 3-litre engines the DBR4/250s enjoyed some success in Tasman racing, and were subsequently prominent in historic events.

Alfa Romeo 158, 1950

Arrows A3 in 1981 driven by Patrese at Dijon. Arrows seemed close to fulfilling promise with this car but never achieved really good results with it

The start of the 1987 Australian GP at Adelaide – Mansell leading from pole, followed by Senna and Piquet, with Prost in McLaren No 1 and destined to clinch the championship in this race

ATS

The first ATS company, Automobili Tursimo e Sport, was set up by a group of Ferrari defectors late in 1961, headed by designer Carlo Chiti and team manager Romolo Tavoni. The aim was a programme on Ferrari lines, with high-performance road and GP cars.

Their 1962 Tipo 100 Formula 1 car had a space frame, independent suspension by wishbones and a twin-ohc V-8 driving through a Colotti gearbox. With the sound pairing of drivers Phil Hill and Giancarlo Baghetti the prospects for 1963 seemed good. However, the opening races showed the venture to be quite hopeless, no points were scored in either championship and ATS did not appear in 1964 as such, although a car substantially rebuilt by Alf Francis was run ineffectually late that year.

ATS

This German team was the creation in 1977 of wheels magnate Hans Gunther Schmid, a capricious autocrat whose whims affected performances on the circuits and caused a high staff turnover through its eight seasons. Presumably Schmid saw a publicity return for the team's 311 appearances in championship races, and the nine points garnered.

A start was made with the erstwhile Penske PC4s in 1977, and Jarier drove one to score a point in the first race. For 1978 Schmid acquired the March F1 equipment (and the March standing in FOCA terms). The Penskes were modified, to become ATS HS-1, while the Gentry-designed ATS D1 was built. That in turn was reworked for 1979, and was to be followed by the Brunner-designed D3 and then the D4s, ground effects cars on Williams FW07 lines.

In 1981 Hervé Guilpin designed ATS HGS-1 and a pair of these modified as D5s served through 1982. That was the team's best season: Winkelhock and Salazar each scored two points.

So far ATS had used Cosworth DFVs, but for 1983 Gustav Brunner designed the D6 for BMW turbo engines. Built around a carbon-fibre monocoque it was an up-to-the-minute design, outwardly neat and compact. However, the team owner's instant circuit decisions did little to improve its racing chances, and unsettled the team. No points were scored in 1983, and just one in 1984 when the D6s and D7s were driven by Winkelhock and Berger in the last season for ATS.

Alfa Romeo 158, 1950

Australian Grand Prix

Although this race did not gain championship status until 1985, it has a longer history than all but six of the other scoring races. It was first run in 1928 over 100 miles/161 km of a 6.4-mile/10.4 km circuit of gravel roads on Phillip Island, off Victoria.

In 1985 the fiftieth Australian Grand Prix was made the last in the year's series of world championship races, run on a new 2.35-mile/3.78 km street circuit at Adelaide (incidentally the 24th venue for the race), and heavily promoted by the South Australian government. The circuit, the general facilities and the race attracted universal praise, at a time when other events on extemporized street circuits were severely criticized.

In that first championship race in Australia Lauda briefly led his last Grand Prix, and Keke Rosberg led the last in which he competed, in 1986. That event was decisive in the battle for the title, made dramatic as leader Nigel Mansell fell out when a rear tyre exploded at around 180 mph and Prost drove through to take both the race and the world title.

Winners (world championship GPs)

1985	K. Rosberg	Williams-Honda
1986	A. Prost	McLaren-TAG
1987	G. Berger	Ferrari

Austrian Grand Prix

Austria had little racing tradition before an F1 race run at Zeltweg in 1961, won by Ireland in a Lotus. A non-championship Austrian Grand Prix in 1963 was won by Jack Brabham from Tony Settember in a Scirocco-BRM.

In 1964 the race became a championship round, then it lapsed until the Osterreichring was established and it was run from 1970 to 1987. It has seen some rare victories: Penske's and Shadow's only GP wins, Brambilla's extraordinary win for March in 1975, de Angelis' narrow victory over Rosberg in 1982 that brought Lotus back to first place on a results sheet for the first time since 1978, and Niki Lauda's only home victory in 1984.

The 1987 race had to be restarted twice, the third start after a ten-car pile up. It was dropped from the 1988 calendar, as changes to the circuit were called for.

Winners (world championship GPs)

1964	L. Bandini	Ferrari
1970	J. Ickx	Ferrari
1971	J. Siffert	BRM
1972	E. Fittipaldi	Lotus-Ford
1973	R. Peterson	Lotus-Ford
1974	C. Reutemann	Brabham-Ford
1975	V. Brambilla	March-Ford
1976	J. Watson	Penske-Ford

The two Arrows A10s driven by Cheever and Warwick in the 1987 Austrian GP, with a background that sums up the splendid Osterreichring

Alfa Romeo 158, 1950

1977	A. Jones	Shadow-Ford
1978	R. Peterson	Lotus-Ford
1979	A. Jones	Williams-Ford
1980	J.-P. Jabouille	Renault
1981	J. Laffite	Ligier-Matra
1982	E. de Angelis	Lotus-Ford
1983	A. Prost	Renault
1984	N. Lauda	McLaren-TAG
1985	A. Prost	McLaren-TAG
1986	A. Prost	McLaren-TAG
1987	N. Mansell	Williams-Honda

Avus circuit

First used in 1921 and venue for the first German GP in 1926, this very artificial circuit has been used for only one world championship race, in 1959. That race was run in two parts, and Ferrari enjoyed a by-then rare 1-2-3 with its tough Dino 246 cars — race winner Tony Brooks put in the fastest lap, the sort of performance still just beyond Climax-engined cars.

At that time Avus still incorporated the steeply banked north bend, linking two parallel straights; there was a new, flat, south curve as the Berlin zonal border cut across the pre-war track. With the north bend, the lap length was 5.15 miles/8.29 km, slightly less from 1967.

*Lap distance: 5.15 miles/8.29 km. **Lap record:** 149.04 mph/239.8 km/h by Tony Brooks in a Ferrari, 1959.*

A non-championship race at Berlin's Avus circuit was arranged as a Mercedes benefit in 1954. It was dominated by the W196 streamliner. The circuit was an oddity, comprising two stretches of autobahn linked by a steep banking at one end and this bend at the south end

Baghetti, Giancarlo 1934–

This self-effacing young Milanese astonished the Grand Prix world in 1961 when he won the first three F1 races he contested and became the first driver to win his debut world championship race since the winner of the first-ever championship race, Farina.

Baghetti started racing in 1956, became serious with a good F Junior season in 1960 and consequently gained the 1961 drives in the Ferrari loaned to FISA, an association of Italian clubs. He drove this car to win the non-championship Syracuse and Naples GPs. In the French GP at Reims he had to battle for every one of its 52 laps. He was second to Dan Gurney in the last corner, beat him to the flag by one fifth of a second, the first Italian to win a grande épreuve since Ascari.

That was the high point of Baghetti's career. When Ferrari was eclipsed in 1962 he made a disastrous move to ATS in 1963, had little joy with a Centro-Sud BRM in 1964 and after that had just three Italian GP drives as his career faded away.

World championship races: 21 starts, 14 points, 1 win: 1961 France.

Balestre, Jean-Marie 1921–

A controversial president of the FIA and FISA, M. Balestre restored authority to motor racing's governing bodies after years when the anarchy of commercial interest threatened to take it over, and that accomplishment offsets some of his odd instant pronouncements and less constructive activities.

Little is known of his early career and his motor sports participation as an amateur, when he was also editor of a motoring journal. His first administrative roles were as clerk of the course at events in France, then as president of the French Karting Association and general secretary to the French Motor Sport Federation (FFSA). In 1973 he was elected president of the FFSA, and held that office through to the 1980s when he was also committed to the international governing bodies.

Balestre was elected vice-president of the CSI in 1975 and resigned in protest at CSI policy in 1976. One outcome of his firm – forceful, even – approach was that he was elected president of FISA, the successor to the CSI, and vice-president of the FIA in 1978.

He sees FISA as the main pillar of the FIA, and certainly it provides a major part of its revenue. One battle Balestre did not win in the following years was for control of the commercial aspects of Formula 1, and eventually he formed an alliance with his adversary of that period, Bernie Ecclestone.

In 1986 Balestre survived a heart operation and resumed his activities, seemingly loath to abandon any of the power and prestige he enjoys through his offices. In 1987 he was re-elected president of the FIA and FISA for another four-year term.

Bandini, Lorenzo 1935–67

Like many Italian drivers of his generation, Bandini started competing in local hill climbs and in the Mille Miglia; unlike most of them, he graduated through Formula Junior to drive for

Ferrari in the Grands Prix.

His F1 career started in 1961 with a Centro-Sud Cooper-Maserati. In the following year he had three Ferrari drives (and won his first championship points with a third place at Monaco) and after starting the 1963 season in an independent BRM he moved to Ferrari.

His only GP win was in Austria in 1964, a year when he was third in Germany and Italy and fifth in Britain. In 1965 he was the dutiful number two to Surtees and in 1966 took over from him in mid-season.

At Monaco in 1967 he was driving hard in second place and obviously tired when he crashed at the harbour-side chicane. He was severely burned and died three days later.
World championship races: 42 starts, 58 points, 1 win: 1964 Austria.

Barcelona circuits

Two of the three circuits in or near the Catalan city have been used for championship races, while the Montmelo autodrome to extend the tradition took shape 15 miles away in 1988.

The Pedrables circuit, used for the 1951 and 1954 GPs, was devised in 1946, using a long wide straight on the Madrid road in the suburbs with a return leg through residential streets in the Pedrables hills district.
Lap distance: 3.92 miles/6.31 km. Lap record: 105.2 mph/169.3 km/h by Fangio in an Alfa Romeo 159, 1951.
The Montjuich Park circuit used roads in a public park in the centre of the city. A hairpin and several other slow corners led downhill from the start-finish line to the only straight of reasonable length, which was followed by four fast curves on the climb back to the pits. There were few natural passing places, while the bumps and camber changes stressed machinery – in 1969 one hump stressed Lotus aerofoils to sudden failure, and both team cars crashed heavily.

Some of the bumps were smoothed when the roads were resurfaced for 1973. Barriers that had been welcomed in 1969, when Hill and Rindt crashed, in 1975 were deemed deficient by drivers who refused to practise. Team mechanics joined local workers to renovate them while officials prevaricated, and eventually one practice session was held. The race started with a chaotic accident, then on lap 26 the rear aerofoil of the leading car, Stommelen's Hill, failed and one of the humps bounced the car onto and partly over the guard rails. Five people were killed. Three laps later the race was stopped, and that was the end of racing on one of the most attractive of all city circuits.
Lap distance: 3.355 miles/3.79 km. Lap record: 101.89 mph/162.84 km/h by Ronnie Peterson in a Lotus, 1973.

Barnard, John *1946–*

Amateur tuning and professional engineering experience with GEC led Barnard to the Lola drawing office in 1968. He started working on F Ford, Vee and Super Vee cars as a draughtsman, but soon had considerable responsibility. He worked on Lola's sports-racing cars but in a search for F1 experience he joined McLaren in 1972, to work on the M23 and USAC cars. Eventually he took Phillippe's place with the Parnelli team.

His first task was to make the VPJ6 a competitive car, and along the way he worked with Weismann on a transverse gearbox. As the Parnelli operation folded he undertook the design of the Chaparral 2K ground effects Indycar. In 1979 he started to develop an F1 proposition for Ron Dennis's Project Four. That led to research on carbon-fibre components, which progressed to a liaison with the Hercules company in the USA, and fortuitously the finance for the project became available (through Marlboro) as McLaren International came into being. Barnard's MP4 for the resurgent McLaren team will stand as an all-time classic, and in refining it he was heavily involved with Porsche on every aspect of the TAG engine that was to power it for much of its career.

The Dennis-Barnard partnership broke up in the summer of 1986, before Barnard's contract expired, as news of his intention to move to Ferrari circulated.

He set up a Ferrari advanced design bureau in a new complex near Guildford in Surrey. The Ferrari F187 had already been laid down, and although Barnard had some influence on its final make-up and refinement through a season that ended so triumphantly for Ferrari, his main task was to design later Grand Prix Ferraris.

Beatrice

This enterprise seemed an extravaganza when Beatrice Companies Inc (claimed to be 'America's largest consumer products company') backed parallel F1 and Indycar teams to be run by Carl Haas. He employed many talented people – too many, and some of the talents were fading a little – and brought the Lola marque back to Grand Prix racing. The car was designed by Neil Oatley and John Baldwin and built by FORCE (Formula One Race Car Engineering Ltd).

The straightforward Beatrice-Lola THL-1 first ran in August 1985 with Hart 415T engines. Alan Jones was persuaded out of retirement to drive it, starting in three late 1985 races, and retiring each time. In 1986 he was joined by Patrick Tambay, and from the third race the

Brabham BT24, 1966

The Beatrice name so boldly emblazoned on this Lola THL-2, driven by Patrick Tambay at Brands Hatch, was seen in racing for a very short time. But Beatrice did bring Lola back to Formula 1

Ford-Cosworth engine was available. By that time the 'Beatrice' element was declining as top management changes brought changes of policy; Team Haas (USA) Ltd saw out the season, gaining six Constructors' Championship points in the name of Lola.

Behra, Jean *1921–59*

One of the last of a generation of French drivers, and a favourite of French spectators, Behra raced French cars until there were none left for him to race, certainly none which matched his capability and tenacity.

He started racing motorcycles, turned to cars in 1950, with an old Maserati, and then to Formula 2 with Gordini in 1951 (he was third in his first race). He stayed with Gordini until the end of 1954. Ironically, when his car did hold together for the duration of one of the French GPs in 1952 and he beat the Ferrari team fair and square it was in the Reims race which was not a world championship event. But that year he did score his first championship points, with third places in Switzerland and Germany.

Behra joined Maserati in 1955, and won two non-championship races, and 1956, when he was number two to Moss, was his best season for points. For the next two years he raced BRMs, winning with them in secondary events. Behra moved to Ferrari, won yet another secondary race (the Aintree 200), then fell out with team manager Tavoni. He turned to his single-seater F2 conversion of a Porsche. In the 1959 Berlin GP for sports cars he spun on the Avus banking and was killed as he was flung from his Porsche.
World championship races: 52 starts, 51 points.

Belgian Grand Prix

The first Belgian Grand Prix for racing cars was run on the magnificent Spa-Francorchamps circuit in 1925. It was a walkover for the Alfa-Romeo team, Antonio Ascari winning in one of their P2s at 74.56 mph/119.96 km/h; when it was last run over the full circuit, in 1970, Pedro

Rodriguez won in a BRM P153 at 149.97 mph/241.3 km/h, then a Grand Prix record.

Fangio and Farina won the first two championship Belgian GPs, which were relatively straightforward, Peter Collins won his first GP at Spa in 1956, Jim Clark won four times in succession (1962–65) although he loathed the circuit, Gurney won the only GP for his Eagle marque in 1967 and McLaren his first for McLaren in 1968. The race was twice run at undistinguished Nivelles, ten times at Zolder, and returned to the new Spa circuit in 1983.

Unhappily, GPs at Spa and Zolder have been marked by accidents: in 1960 Chris Bristow and Alan Stacey were killed and Moss and Taylor were injured, Jackie Stewart's only serious accident was in the wet at Spa in 1966 and Gilles Villeneuve died at Zolder in practice in 1982.

Uniquely, the 1985 race was postponed after the scheduled meeting had begun, for the new track surface at Spa started to break up; the FISA stewards had no option but to cancel, and the race was run later.

Venues and winners (world championship GPs)

Year	Venue	Winner	Car
1950	Spa	J.-M. Fangio	Alfa Romeo
1951	Spa	G. Farina	Alfa Romeo
1952	Spa	A. Ascari	Ferrari
1953	Spa	A. Ascari	Ferrari
1954	Spa	J.-M. Fangio	Maserati
1955	Spa	J.-M. Fangio	Mercedes-Benz
1956	Spa	P. Collins	Ferrari
1958	Spa	C.A.S. Brooks	Vanwall
1960	Spa	J. Brabham	Cooper-Climax
1961	Spa	P. Hill	Ferrari
1962	Spa	J. Clark	Lotus-Climax
1963	Spa	J. Clark	Lotus-Climax
1964	Spa	J. Clark	Lotus-Climax
1965	Spa	J. Clark	Lotus-Climax
1966	Spa	J. Surtees	Ferrari
1967	Spa	D. Gurney	Eagle
1968	Spa	B. McLaren	McLaren-Ford
1970	Spa	P. Rodriguez	BRM
1972	Nivelles	E. Fittipaldi	Lotus-Ford
1973	Zolder	J. Stewart	Tyrrell-Ford
1974	Nivelles	E. Fittipaldi	McLaren-Ford
1975	Zolder	N. Lauda	Ferrari
1976	Zolder	N. Lauda	Ferrari
1977	Zolder	G. Nilsson	Lotus-Ford
1978	Zolder	M. Andretti	Lotus-Ford
1979	Zolder	J. Scheckter	Ferrari
1980	Zolder	D. Pironi	Ligier-Ford
1981	Zolder	C. Reutemann	Williams-Ford
1982	Zolder	J. Watson	McLaren-Ford
1983	Spa	A. Prost	Renault
1984	Zolder	M. Alboreto	Ferrari
1985	Spa	A. Senna	Lotus-Renault
1986	Spa	N. Mansell	Williams-Honda
1987	Spa	A. Prost	McLaren-TAG

Bellamy, Ralph *1938–*

An Australian who almost became a journeyman designer, Bellamy entered the GP field when he worked at Brabham from 1967 before joining McLaren in 1971 and making his mark with the 'Coke-bottle' M19 with its innovative and at that time not entirely successful rising-rate suspension.

A short spell back at Brabham followed before Bellamy was off to Lotus, where the 72 was at its mid-career development stage and its 76 and 77 successors had to be drawn up. He spent a short period with Ensign, undertook some consultancy, and then moved to Lola, where the Larousse-Calmels team LC87 showed typically neat and economic Bellamy lines. He left Lola abruptly early in 1988.

Bellasi

A one-off commissioned by the Swiss independent entrant-driver Silvio Moser when the space-framed Brabham he had raced became obsolete in 1970, this was a Cosworth-engined car built in Italy. It was never competitive and Moser qualified it for only two GP starts.

Bellof, Stefan *1957–85*

Bellof was a driver of the 1980s – German F Ford champion in 1981, followed by two seasons in Formula 2 with Maurer and in the FIA world endurance championship in 1984. That season he drove for Tyrrell and might have scored his first world championship points in his sixth GP, except that his third place on the road at Monaco was disallowed. He scored in Portugal and at Detroit in 1985.

This young German's talents were highly rated and with Ken Tyrrell's team it was expected he would be brought to maturity, with an exciting F1 future. However, he was fatally injured in a Porsche during the 1985 Spa 1000 km endurance race.

World championship races: 20 starts, 4 points.

Beltoise, Jean-Pierre *1937–*

A French driver whose racing career started on motorcycles, Beltoise raced sports cars in 1963 and in 1964, when a serious accident left him with a limp and a permanently weakened arm. Despite this he started a single-seater career with Matra, driving their F3 cars in 1965 (when he scored Matra's first major success, in the Reims F3 race) and 1966 as a lead in to Formula 2. He had a good F2 career, with high points in the F2 class of Grands Prix and the European championship in 1968, when he was already driving Matra's Grand Prix cars.

In these raucous V-12s Beltoise achieved a second placing at Monaco. When the engines were withdrawn for development he spent the 1969 season as number two in Tyrrell's Matra-Ford team, his best in world championship

terms. In 1970–71 he drove for the French team again, coming close to winning with the V-12 in the all-important French GP.

Then came three years with BRM, when he scored his only championship race victory in a very wet 1972 Monaco GP. After that he continued to pick up points-scoring places but his GP fortunes seemed to fade with BRM's in 1973–74. He dropped out of Formula 1, but continued an active racing career in saloons well into the 1980s.

World championship races: 85 starts (4 in F2 category), 77 points, 1 win: 1972 Monaco.

Benetton

The Italian fashion company's multi-coloured scheme had adorned the hapless Alfa Romeos in 1984 and then the Tolemans, before the Toleman team was taken over and run from the Witney base in Oxfordshire, the cars named Benettons from 1986.

Rory Byrne remained and started designing the B186 late in 1985 around the BMW M12/13 power unit. In some areas, particularly the finer areas of aerodynamics, design was not finalized until well into the 1986 racing season, and only then were apparent lapses in cornering qualities set to rights. The B186 was a fast car and in the second half of the season promise was fulfilled when Gerhard Berger won the Mexican GP, on a very bumpy circuit which suited the combination of Benetton and Pirelli tyres very well.

Designer Rory Byrne with the Benetton B188, the latest in a line of cars with well-mannered and effective chassis, and with Ford effort behind the Cosworth DFR engine

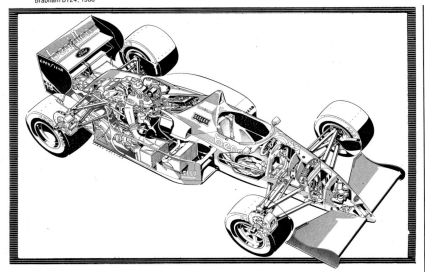

Brabham BT24, 1966

The neat Benetton B187 typified the layout of turbo cars, with a mass of engine/turbo ancillaries packing the side pods, while the V-6 engine itself took up little space. The monocoque is slim, while at the nose designer Byrne has used a double-curvature aerofoil

For 1987 Boutsen took Berger's place along-side Fabi, in B187s. The major mechanical change was in the engine, where the compact Ford V-6 turbo took the place of BMW units. The cars were sometimes very competitive, and good results late in the season placed Benetton fifth in the constructors' championship.

Benetton was a Ford-favoured team, and this led to it using a third engine in as many seasons, when it had the exclusive use of the normally-aspirated 3.5-litre DFR for the Byrne-designed Type 188 in 1988. Boutsen continued with the team with a new partner, Nannini.
Constructors' championship: 1986 6th; 1987 5th.

Berger, Gerhard 1959–

The last two races of 1987 ensured this ex-trovert Austrian his place in Grand Prix history, for he drove Ferraris to win after the marque's longest spell without success.

Berger started his racing career in saloons, drove in Formula 3 in 1983 and raced BMWs very forcefully in the European Touring Car Championship. For his home Grand Prix in 1984 he drove an ATS, and in his next race with it, in the Italian GP, he finished sixth.

His first point to count was scored towards the end of 1985, with an Arrows in South Africa, and there was another top-six finish in Australia. In 1986 his driving matured and he led the Austrian GP, won in Mexico and scored all but two of the Benetton team's points.

With Ferrari in 1987 he increasingly over-shadowed his established team-mate Alboreto – even without his victories in Japan and Australia, Berger would have scored more points than Alboreto. As it was, he was fifth in the cham-pionship table, and emphasized his abilities.
World championship races (to end of 1987): 52 starts, 52 points, 3 wins: 1986 Mexico; 1987 Japan, Australia.

Right: The start of the last Grand Prix run in Switzerland (a Swiss GP was later run in France) with Fangio and Kling in 'open-wheel' Mercedes W196s leading Gonzalez (Ferrari) and Moss (Maserati) away in 1954 at Bremgarten. Berne's Bremgarten circuit was beautiful, but after several serious accidents, involving racing motor cycles, sports cars and Grand Prix cars, it had a sinister reputation.

Berne circuit

The venue of 14 Swiss GPs before racing was banned by the Federal Government in 1955, the Bremgarten circuit was beautiful and exact-ing. Most of it ran through a forest on the outskirts of Berne, which led to problems both in the wet and, because of flickering light and shade, in sunny conditions. It was made up of a succession of fast bends, with no real straights, and into world championship years its varying surfaces included cobbles. Facilities were good, including a pits road that was separated from the circuit itself.

Five world championship GPs were run at the Bremgarten, and in these the fastest lap was set at 101.97 mph/162.56 km/h by Fangio in a Mercedes in 1954.
Lap distance: 4.52 miles/7.28 km. Lap record: 105.4 mph/169.59 km/h, by Bernd Rosemeyer in an Auto Union, 1936.

Berthon, Peter

Close associate of Raymond Mays in the early BRM years, and designer of the over-ambitious and vastly complex Type 15 1.5-litre cars, Berthon redeemed himself to a degree with the championship cars of the early 1960s.

Bms-Dallara

A modest new F1 project in 1988, for Beppe Lucchini's Scuderia Italia, the Bms-Dallara 188 was designed by Sergio Rhinland, and the nominated team driver was Alex Caffi.

BMW

In single-seater racing BMW was the main source of components for several German one-off cars in the early 1950s, was associated with Formula 2 in the late 1960s although the chassis were built by Lola and Dornier, then very much more widely as a supplier of very successful engines. In 1980 designer Paul Rosche set to work on a turbocharged F1 engine, using the standard 4-cylinder block and the cylinder head that had been developed for Formula 2. The Brabham team was given exclusive use of BMW turbo engines for a period.

BMW reputedly got through a lot of engine blocks during development, and Brabham introduced the engine to racing hesitantly in 1982. Then Piquet won that year's Canadian GP in a Brabham-BMW and, despite misgivings about injection and ignition shortcomings, Brabham stuck with the engines from then on.

In 1983 the engines gave up to 570 bhp — quite enough to deal with DFV-powered opponents — and in qualifying trim (first and foremost higher turbo boost) that output was to be virtually doubled by 1985. In 1983, when the engines were also made available to ATS, race power output was 640 bhp (750 bhp for qualifying) with a smooth power band. The drawback for spectators was the very dull sound of those KKK-turbocharged engines!

In 1983 Brabham-BMW won four GPs and Nelson Piquet won the world championship, justifying BMW's investment. During 1984 new standards were set by McLaren's TAG engines and BMW struggled to keep up, a problem compounded as Honda became a Grand Prix power. For 1986 Brabham designer Gordon Murray persuaded BMW to produce an engine to be installed at an angle of 72 degrees (almost flat) in his low-line BT55, and that led to endless problems (there was even a passing mid-season return to upright engines). In 1987 the Brabham-BMW team seemed to lose direction as the engine was generally outclassed, two third placings in GPs being almost a surprise. BMW had in any case already decided to quit.

Meanwhile, the upright M12/13 BMW turbos had been passed to engine specialist Mader, which supplied the Arrows and Benetton

A BMW M12/13 four-cylinder turbo engine in a 1982 Brabham BT50, the year the Brabham-BMW combination started to come good

Gerhard Berger strikes sparks on home territory in Austria in 1987. He was the country's successor to Niki Lauda, and a national sporting hero as he won GPs with Benetton and then Ferrari

Alliot keeps his Lola off the racing line as he is lapped

Thierry Boutsen in the cockpit of a multi-coloured Benetton B187 at Monaco in 1987

Brabham BT24, 1966

teams. By mid-season the Benetton could run with the best, and scored BMW's only win of the year in Mexico. Arrows continued with the dwindling stock of these engines in 1987–88, when the cylinder heads carried the name Megatron. BMW's fairly short Formula 1 foray brought them nine championship victories.

Bonnier, Jo *1930–72*

Joakim Bonnier had a very long and varied racing career, and until Peterson and Nilsson appeared on the GP scene he was Sweden's outstanding driver.

Bonnier competed in rallies in the early 1950s, then in saloon, GT and sports car races before his first GP drives, with Maserati in 1957–58. Late in 1958 he joined BRM, and scored his first points in the Moroccan GP. He was a regular, never prolific, points gatherer through to 1968, in works BRMs in 1959–60, works Porsches in 1961–62, then Walker Coopers in 1963 and Brabhams in 1964–65 before he entered independently. He ran a Cooper-Maserati in 1966–67, a McLaren-BRM in 1968 (when he also had an outing in a Honda), a Lotus 49 which he crashed, and finally he drove a McLaren four times in 1970–71. In that long Grand Prix career his victory in the 1959 Netherlands GP stands out, because it was a first for a Swedish driver and BRM's first world championship race win. He was chairman of the Grand Prix Drivers' Association in the 1960s.

Bonnier was a prominent sports car driver, successful in a variety of cars, always considerate and usually safe, so his death at Le Mans in 1972 was a surprise as well as a shock.
World championship races: 102 starts, 39 points, 1 win: 1959 Netherlands.

Boutsen, Thierry *1957–*

The Grand Prix success expected from this Belgian driver when he moved up out of Formula 2 in 1983 did not come as quickly as predicted, largely because the cars he drove did not match his artistry or his determination.

His first two racing seasons were spent in F Ford, and he followed logically through to an F3 season with a Martini in 1980, to F2 and two victories with March in 1981, and to the Spirit team in 1982.

His first world championship drive was in his native Belgium in 1983 with Arrows, and he stayed with them for three seasons. His first point came with a sixth place in 1984 in Brazil; fortunes were mixed in 1985; he drove hard, sometimes for little reward, sometimes with luck, especially when he was classified second in the San Marino GP, his car running out of fuel in the last corner.

In 1987 he joined Benetton, with a best final placing third in the Australian GP, and continued with the team in 1988.
World championship races (to end of 1987): 73 starts, 32 points.*

Brabham, Sir Jack *1926–*

John Arthur Brabham was one of motor racing's great all-rounders: an outstanding driver, of course, an intuitive technician and practical engineer and a shrewd businessman.

He built a speedway midget at his Sydney car repair workshop in 1947, then started racing in this tough category where he was Australian champion from 1948 to 1951. He moved on to hill climbs, then started road racing with a Cooper-Bristol and was runner-up in the 1953 New Zealand GP. He raced a Cooper-Alta in Britain during the early summer of 1955 and in the British GP of that year drove a rear-engined Cooper-Bristol. For 1956 Brabham mistakenly chose a Maserati 250F, then joined Cooper.

1957 brought few championship points as the team was still using under-size engines, and nine GPs in 1958 produced only three points, scored at Monaco. But Brabham's crouching driving style, adopted in his midget racing days to dodge stones, became familiar.

Jack Brabham relaxed during his third world championship season, 1966

Jack Brabham in the 1966 French GP at Reims, driving his own BT19 towards an historic victory

In 1959 the Coopers had full 2.5-litre engines, and Brabham drove them to win his first Grands Prix, in Monaco and Britain, and the championship. In 1960 he dominated it, winning five consecutive races.

That success meant that Brabham in a Cooper had first use of the Coventry Climax V-8 for the 1.5-litre formula in 1961. He put it through a Nürburgring hedge very early in its first race.

At that same circuit a year later Jack Brabham gave the first Brabham Grand Prix car its debut race – early in 1962 he had raced a Lotus – and in the US Grand Prix he scored the first world championship points by a driver in a car of his own manufacture. That was the product of a venture with fellow-Australian Ron Tauranac, MRD, which initially had to make its way by producing F Junior cars for sale. Jack and Ron usually had a proper idea of priorities, and customer cars to produce income came before the prestige and longer-term rewards of the Grands Prix.

In the Brabham team of the following three years Brabham was partnered by Dan Gurney,

The debut Grand Prix for the Brabham marque, the 1962 German race with Jack Brabham driving the BT3. However, it retired after nine laps, when its throttle linkage failed. It was a typical no-frills Tauranac design

and his own success rate was not very high: seventh, eighth and tenth in the 1963–65 championships. But he was back with a bang in 1966: the first driver to win a championship race in his own make of car in the French GP, followed by victories in the British, Dutch and German GPs to take the title for the third time.

He was perhaps not overjoyed that his number two, Denny Hulme, took the title in 1967, although he was mellowing and references to his taciturn manner were not so common. He still won races, including the French and Canadian GPs that year and scored handsomely to become championship runner-up. Engines let him down in 1968–69, and his team turned to Cosworth power.

His 1970 season, which was to be his last as a driver, started brilliantly with a victory in South Africa. Then there were two extraordinary lapses: at Monaco he was leading into the last corner and ran wide into the safety barrier and while he led the British GP into its last lap, he ran out of fuel and was passed almost within sight of the flag.

Apart from the Grands Prix, Brabham had been successful as a driver in Formula 2, with Coopers in the late 1950s and with his own overwhelmingly superior Brabham-Honda in 1966; he had raced varied sports cars, from Aston Martins to Matras; he had carried the rear-engined gospel from Formula 1 to Indianapolis, quietly placing an under-powered Cooper ninth in the 1960 500.

He sold his interest in the company that carried his name to his partner in 1971 but kept his interest in racing, for example in a company developing engines for lesser formulae and in the careers of his sons Geoff in North America, Gary and David in Britain in 1988, in cars entered by Jack Brabham Racing Team in Britain. He was knighted in 1979.

World championship races: 126 starts, 261 points (253 net), 14 wins: 1959 Monaco, Britain; 1960 Netherlands, Belgium, France, Britain, Portugal; 1966 France, Britain, Netherlands, Germany; 1967 France, Canada; 1970 South Africa. **World champion:** *1959, 1960, 1966.*

Brabham

Jack Brabham was the first successful driver-constructor in Formula 1: the first man to drive a car bearing his own name to victory in a world championship Grand Prix, in the 1966 French event.

Brabham's practical approach had contributed much to the success of the Cooper team, but he decided to go his own way and set up Motor Racing Developments in 1961 in partnership with Ron Tauranac. Their MRD BT1 F Junior car appeared in the late summer of 1961; the MRD initials were soon discarded but the founder partners' initials, BT, used in designations, outlasted their association with the company.

The BT3 F1 car was not ready until late in 1962, and in only three races Jack drove it to score six points. It was an essentially straightforward Climax-powered space frame car, as was the BT7, which followed for the 1963–64 seasons. Dan Gurney drove one to score Brabham's first Grand Prix victory, in the 1964 French event. The BT11, also a 1964 car, was used by several prominent independent entrants, with Climax or BRM V-8s, and it served on through the first two years of the 3-litre formula with enlarged BRM V-8s or Coventry Climax fours.

In 1966 Jack Brabham raced the one-off BT19. It was powered by the Repco 620 V-8, a racing version of an Oldsmobile engine devised by fellow Australian Phil Irving which did not produce great power, but had good torque characteristics and was reliable. It powered Jack to the championship, and was also used in the similar BT20 in which Denny Hulme won the 1967 drivers' championship. Brabham took the constructors' title in both seasons.

The four-cam Repco engines which Brabham used in the following years in BT24 and BT26 were unreliable, and in 1969 both models appeared with DFV engines, when the latter were designated BT26A. These were the last cars in GP racing with space frames, albeit with some stressed panels added by Tauranac to increase stiffness. For 1970 he had to use the monocoque construction imposed by regulations on fuel cells.

As Jack retired to Australia he sold his share in MRD to Ron Tauranac, who in turn sold out to Bernie Ecclestone at the end of 1971. During

the Brabham-Tauranac partnership between 1961 and 1971 Brabham cars won 11 championship races; no more were to fall to the marque until 1974. Tauranac remained for only a short while before leaving to start his own Ralt company, but his assistant Gordon Murray stayed with Brabham, to design a series of innovative and handsome cars.

The first of these was the BT42 in 1973, a small neat car which led to the BT44. In cross-section these featured a 'pyramid' shape, with maximum width (and fuel weight) low down, minimal frontal area and good aerodynamic bodywork, rising-rate suspension and then pull-rod front suspension, and signs of experiments with under-body airflow. Mechanically, of course, the major components came from such familiar sources as Cosworth and Hewland. The finance still came largely from Ecclestone but that was to change.

Reutemann drove BT44s to three GP victories in 1974, Reutemann and Pace to one each in 1975. For 1976 Murray had to design a car for the Alfa Romeo flat 12 engine, which held out some promise of matching Ferrari power units of the same configuration. But in the necessarily bulky BT45, and indeed the cars which followed it, the Alfa engine was unreliable.

An intention had been to run the BT46 with surface coolers along the flanks, digital display instruments, built-in jacks and a six-speed

The BT448B, the last model of Gordon Murray's first series of Cosworth-powered Brabhams, driven by Carlos Pace in 1975, in the then-new Martini livery. The distinctive 'pyramid' cross section shows well, as do the twin nose radiators, slender air box above the engine, and contrasting front and rear tyre sizes. Development of this car was neglected as design work on the Alfa-powered Brabhams took priority

Brabham BT24, 1966

Above: Brabham BT49 at Zandvoort in 1980 – Nelson Piquet won this Dutch GP in it. Marc Surer follows in an ATS D4

Right: The 'low-line' Brabham BT55 of 1986, with lay-down BMW engine and a very low reclined driving position, aimed to achieve minimal frontal area and a clean airflow to the rear aerofoil. It was often revised, but it was never successful – the eighth place gained by Derek Warwick in this car at Brands Hatch was one of the year's better results for the team

Brabham-Alfa gearbox, but BT46s were raced with conventional rads and instruments, and against ground effects Lotus cars. Murray's answer was the BT46B 'fan car'. This had a sealed engine bay with a large horizontal radiator above it. Air was drawn up through this by a large fan (to be exhausted at the rear) and ground effects benefits were substantial. Rival teams protested about the car before Lauda won the Swedish GP with it, and afterwards. The fan was condemned as a 'movable aerodynamic device' and the car only ran again in a Donington demonstration.

Brabhams returned to Cosworth DFVs in the BT49 at the end of 1979. This sleek car, driven by Nelson Piquet, put Brabham back on top in 1980–81. The Brazilian won six GPs in those years, and the championship, while his team-mates contributed little except financial backing.

Piquet's relationship with Murray took the team through another period of development with a new engine in 1982, the BMW turbo in the BT50. By the end of that year the combination was winning, as it had to if the alliance was to survive. At Brands Hatch for the British GP

the Brabham team startled the others by producing all the paraphenalia for a tyre-change and refuelling pit stop. They did not perform one in a race until the Austrian GP when a wheel-change and refuel was completed in 15.6 seconds. A TV-pleasing trend had been set.

The slim and elegant BT52 arrived as ground effects were banned. It had its radiators alongside the engine, where weight helped traction, while the Hewland gearbox was progressively modified by American specialist Pete Weismann. In the BT52B and BT53 carbon-fibre was increasingly used in the monocoque.

The team, and Piquet, had a good 1983 with these cars but in 1984 the BMW engines were unreliable – nine pole positions and two victories was not a good record. The next year looked worse, until Piquet won the French GP in a BT54 (and incidentally gave Pirelli a first GP win since 1957).

In 1986 Murray came up with the BT55, ultra-low but long, with low driving position and 'lay-down' engine, fast on straights, slow in acceleration. Then there was the demoralizing death of de Angelis in testing. The team scored just two points in the season. In that respect 1987 was better – five times better, as de Cesaris and Patrese both managed a third-place finish – but the engines were unreliable and it seemed that as the engine contract ran out, so the team was run down and it was withdrawn from Formula 1 racing in 1988, albeit this was a 'sabbatical' to clear the decks for a fresh start.

Constructor's championship: 1962 7th; 1963 3rd; 1964 4th; 1965 3rd; 1966 1st; 1967 1st; 1968 8th; 1969 2nd; 1970 4th; 1971 9th; 1972 4th; 1973 4th; 1974 5th; 1975 2nd; 1976 9th; 1977 5th; 1978 3rd; 1979 9th; 1980 3rd; 1981 2nd; 1982 5th; 1983 3rd; 1984 4th; 1985 5th; 1986 9th; 1987 8th.

Brambilla, Vittorio *1937–*

In the late 1980s Brambilla would be an anachronism, but in the second half of the 1970s the Grands Prix could still just accommodate an Italian driver in the rugged mould of the between-the-wars era. He always drove hard, sometimes inconveniencing his more sophisticated colleagues, sometimes destructive of machinery.

Brambilla raced March cars from 1974 to 1976, then Surtees for two years, and drove Alfa Romeos in four GPs in 1979–80, the only years when he failed to score points. He could be fast, but lasting a race was problematic; when he finally did so ahead of the field, in the rain-shortened 1975 Austrian GP, he was so elated that he spun his March into the guard rails.

World championship races: 74 starts, 15½ points, 1 win: 1975 Austria.

Brands Hatch circuit

This Kent circuit has a surprisingly long history, for motorcycle grass track races were run there in the 1930s. A short hard-surfaced track which came into use in 1950 was unusual in that races were run anti-clockwise. A loop up the hill to Druids hairpin was added in 1954 to complete the 1.2-mile/1.9 km track short circuit that is still in frequent use (now known as the Indy circuit, after a USAC race in 1978). It has always been popular, not least because spectators in the main grandstand, and nowadays in the hospitality suites that flank it, have excellent views of virtually the whole circuit.

Extensions in 1960 brought the circuit up to an acceptable GP length. It incorporated a reasonably long straight (some stretches called straights, for example Top Straight, or more recently Brabham Straight, past the pits, are not in fact straight), and a mix of challenging corners, some of which have been realigned.

Varied corners, adverse cambers, gradients and dips where cars bottom mean that Brands Hatch is far removed from some clinical modern autodromes, and many drivers like it

The 1986 British GP field streaming down through the exit from the double-apex Paddock Hill Bend at Brands Hatch, one of the most daunting corners on a front-rank circuit. Prost leads, Alboreto's Ferrari is running wide

Brabham BT24, 1966

for that reason alone. Run-off areas have been contrived where it is possible but at some points cannot be fully achieved with the full paraphernalia of gravel traps in a direct line of racing.

The pits are awkwardly situated and the size of the paddock behind them is limited, at least until it is extended into an area that has always been pleasingly clear inside the last bend.

The British Grand Prix was first run at Brands Hatch in 1964, and it became the alternate circuit for the race until 1987, when FISA awarded the race to Silverstone for five years.

Jim Clark won that first GP in Kent, Jo Siffert drove Rob Walker's blue Lotus 49 to the last GP win anywhere for an independent entrant, in 1968, Niki Lauda was involved in two controversies in 1974 and in 1976 when he was declared the winner after his championship rival James Hunt was disqualified. Niki Lauda is one of only two drivers to have won two GPs at Brands Hatch; Nigel Mansell has won a British GP (1986) and a European GP (1985) there.

The Formula 1 Race of Champions was first run at Brands Hatch in 1965 (won by Mike Spence in a Lotus) and appeared fairly regularly on the calendar until 1979; in 1983 Rosberg won the 14th race to carry the title. A non-championship Victory Race was run in 1971, and stopped in sad circumstances after Siffert's fatal accident in a BRM.

*Lap distance: 2.600 miles/4.19 km. **Lap record:** 135.22 mph/217.616 km/h by Nigel Mansell in a Williams, 1986 (2.614 mile/4.206 km circuit).*

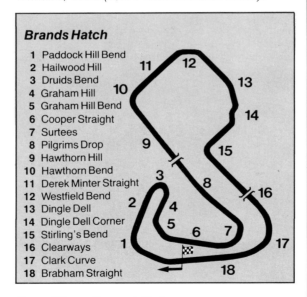

Brands Hatch

1 Paddock Hill Bend
2 Hailwood Hill
3 Druids Bend
4 Graham Hill
5 Graham Hill Bend
6 Cooper Straight
7 Surtees
8 Pilgrims Drop
9 Hawthorn Hill
10 Hawthorn Bend
11 Derek Minter Straight
12 Westfield Bend
13 Dingle Dell
14 Dingle Dell Corner
15 Stirling's Bend
16 Clearways
17 Clark Curve
18 Brabham Straight

Brazilian Grand Prix

The first world championship Brazilian GP was run at the Interlagos autodrome outside São Paulo in 1973, following a successful non-title race won by Reutemann in the 'lobster-claw' Brabham BT34 in 1972. It was staged at Interlagos seven times, but the more modern

Jacarepagua circuit outside Rio de Janeiro has been the favoured venue in the 1980s. The race has gone to Brazilian drivers five times, and Carlos Reutemann and Alain Prost have both won it four times.

Venues and winners (world championship GPs)

1973	Interlagos	E. Fittipaldi	Lotus-Ford
1974	Interlagos	E. Fittipaldi	McLaren-Ford
1975	Interlagos	C. Pace	Brabham-Ford
1976	Interlagos	N. Lauda	Ferrari
1977	Interlagos	C. Reutemann	Ferrari
1978	Jacarepagua	C. Reutemann	Ferrari
1979	Interlagos	J. Laffite	Ligier-Ford
1980	Interlagos	R. Arnoux	Renault
1981	Jacarepagua	C. Reutemann	Williams-Ford
1982	Jacarepagua	A. Prost	Renault
1983	Jacarepagua	N. Piquet	Brabham-BMW
1984	Jacarepagua	A. Prost	McLaren-TAG
1985	Jacarepagua	A. Prost	McLaren-TAG
1986	Jacarepagua	N. Piquet	Williams-Honda
1987	Jacarepagua	A. Prost	McLaren-TAG
1988	Jacarepagua	A. Prost	McLaren-Honda

British Grand Prix

British Grands Prix, or the RAC Grand Prix as it was then titled, were run on a contrived road circuit at the Brooklands autodrome in 1926–27, and although a near-equivalent (in that it attracted main-line teams) was run at Donington in the second half of the 1930s the event lapsed until 1948 when it was revived at Silverstone. This was the venue for the first-ever world championship Grand Prix in 1950 and for the eventful GP the following year, when Gonzalez scored a significant victory, the first for a normally-aspirated car over supercharged cars and Ferrari's first defeat of the Alfa Romeo team that he had once served.

Five Grands Prix were run at Silverstone, which then shared the race with Aintree until 1962 (when Clark started a sequence of four victories in the event). In 1964 Brands Hatch staged the race for the first time and it was the alternate circuit until 1986.

Successive races in the 1970s were controversial – Scheckter triggered a pile-up as the second lap started at Silverstone in 1973, Niki Lauda looked a likely winner at Brands Hatch in 1974 until his return to the track after a pit stop was delayed, in 1975 a downpour at Silverstone caused more than half the cars running to leave the track, in 1976 there was a restart and James Hunt was disqualified after crossing the line first in a spare car.

At wide-open Silverstone or on the near-road circuit at Brands, the race has always been well attended. It is one of only two events to count in every championship year.

Venues and winners (world championship GPs)

1950	Silverstone	G. Farina	Alfa Romeo
1951	Silverstone	F. Gonzalez	Ferrari
1952	Silverstone	A. Ascari	Ferrari
1953	Silverstone	A. Ascari	Ferrari

Brabham BT24, 1966

1954	Silverstone	F. Gonzalez	Ferrari
1955	Aintree	S. Moss	Mercedes-Benz
1956	Silverstone	J.-M. Fangio	Ferrari
1957	Aintree	C.A.S. Brooks/S. Moss	Vanwall
1958	Silverstone	P. Collins	Ferrari
1959	Aintree	J. Brabham	Cooper-Climax
1960	Silverstone	J. Brabham	Cooper-Climax
1961	Aintree	W. von Trips	Ferrari
1962	Aintree	J. Clark	Lotus-Climax
1963	Silverstone	J. Clark	Lotus-Climax
1964	Brands Hatch	J. Clark	Lotus-Climax
1965	Silverstone	J. Clark	Lotus-Climax
1966	Brands Hatch	J. Brabham	Brabham-Repco
1967	Silverstone	J. Clark	Lotus-Ford
1968	Brands Hatch	J. Siffert	Lotus-Ford
1969	Silverstone	J. Stewart	Matra-Ford
1970	Brands Hatch	J. Rindt	Lotus-Ford
1971	Silverstone	J. Stewart	Tyrrell-Ford
1972	Brands Hatch	E. Fittipaldi	Lotus-Ford
1973	Silverstone	P. Revson	McLaren-Ford
1974	Brands Hatch	J. Scheckter	Tyrrell-Ford
1975	Silverstone	E. Fittipaldi	McLaren-Ford
1976	Brands Hatch	N. Lauda	Ferrari
1977	Silverstone	J. Hunt	McLaren-Ford
1978	Brands Hatch	C. Reutemann	Ferrari
1979	Silverstone	C. Regazzoni	Williams-Ford
1980	Brands Hatch	A. Jones	Williams-Ford
1981	Silverstone	J. Watson	McLaren-Ford
1982	Brands Hatch	N. Lauda	McLaren-Ford
1983	Silverstone	A. Prost	Renault
1984	Brands Hatch	N. Lauda	McLaren-TAG
1985	Silverstone	A. Prost	McLaren-TAG
1986	Brands Hatch	N. Mansell	Williams-Honda
1987	Silverstone	N. Mansell	Williams-Honda

Above: A BRM driven by Graham Hill leads John Surtees (Lola) and Dan Gurney (Porsche) in their race-long German GP battle in 1962. They finished in this order

Left: BRM's best Grand Prix victory was scored by Jean-Pierre Beltoise at Monaco in 1972 with this P160

Brabham BT24, 1966

The start of a classic British Grand Prix, in 1969. Jochen Rindt leads off from pole in a Lotus 49. He and Jackie Stewart – alongside him at the start in a blue Matra MS80 – battled for three-quarters of the race, when a pit stop delayed him and Stewart won unchallenged. The other driver starting from the front row is Hulme in a McLaren M7C.

The grid stretched back round Silverstone's Woodcote Corner, then one of the fastest in racing, unencumbered with the chicane that was added in 1975 or slowed by a sharp left-right on the run-in introduced in 1987

BRM

British Racing Motors, or BRM, was the brain-child of Raymond Mays and Peter Berthon (responsible for the very successful ERA voiturettes of the 1930s). Its concept was well suited to the new post-war British enthusiasm for motor sport and British industry's need for a prestige flagship, and their first BRM was completed in 1949. This car had taken shape very slowly with a straightforward chassis and a very advanced but fearfully complex centrifugally-supercharged 1.5-litre V-16. This was very powerful, its best output of 485 bhp at a shattering 12,000 rpm being 319 bhp per litre, but the type of supercharger restricted the effective revs range. The car was so complex that the small BRM team never made it raceworthy for the Grands Prix for which it was built. It did not come to a grid until 1950 and only started in one championship race. In that 1951 British GP Parnell and Walker drove BRMs heroically to fifth and seventh places.

Under the control of industrialist Alfred Owen, BRM turned to simplicity in the P25 for the 2.5-litre formula. This was a pretty car, with a 4-cylinder engine and once some oddities in the suspension and braking systems were abandoned, it was effective. Painfully the team groped towards competitiveness, the great breakthrough coming in the Netherlands in 1959, with a Grand Prix pole position and then a drive to victory by Jo Bonnier. These cars then became the basis of a rear-engined BRM (P25s were converted to the new layout).

As the 1.5-litre formula came into force BRM was under threat of closure by its patron, and the team rose to the challenge. Berthon designed the handsome P57, a rear-engined car with a tubular space frame and a high-revving V-8, which had the then-novel transistorized ignition and fuel injection. BRMs became reliable under chief engineer Tony Rudd; in 1962 Graham Hill drove P57s to victory in four championship races. Through the remaining years of the formula BRM was a respected team, with the P57 and the monocoque P261 introduced in 1964. During the 1.5-litre years Hill won ten GPs in BRMs and in Italy in 1965 Jackie Stewart won his first in a P261.

The V-8 was enlarged to 2 litres as a stand-in power unit for the first season of 3-litre GPs,

1966, while a full-size engine was built. This proved to be a monumental folly, effectively two 8-cylinder units, one above the other to form a complicated and heavy H-16.

Fortunately BRM had also laid down a V-12, for sports car use, although this was not available to the team until 1968. The P126 in which it was used in 1968 was an unusual BRM: it was designed and built away from BRM's headquarters at Bourne, and it also used a Hewland gearbox (BRM had never been a 'kit-car' constructor, like Ferrari making all the major parts used on its cars). The P126 was not outstanding, nor was the similar P133, nor the cars which followed in the late 1960s, in part because the V12 did not match the Cosworth DFV in output, even in its 48-valve form.

However, there was promise in the P153 designed by Tony Southgate, and although this car was not a winner in 1970 it led to the P160, which was, although not always reliable. Southgate used a 'bathtub' monocoque, bulbous low on the flanks where the fuel load was carried. The cars were fast and handled well, and the team had two first-class drivers in Rodriguez and Siffert.

Jean-Pierre Beltoise drove a P160 to win the Monaco GP in 1972, but by that time BRM was already a lost cause. Control had been assumed by the husband of Jean Stanley, of the Owen Organization's governing family. He had grandiose ideas about running large teams to please sponsors, and the dedicated executives and mechanics could not keep up, and inevitably began to leave. Southgate's P180 was not a success, nor was Mike Pilbeam's P201 of 1974, in part because the V-12 was lagging further and further behind.

In 1975 the team became Stanley-BRM, and struggled on with P201s, almost disappearing in 1976. Then in 1977 Stanley introduced the last BRM, and the team's last sponsor. The P207, designed by Len Terry, turned out to be very bulky, and hopeless as several drivers tried to qualify it to start in races.

The remnants of this once-proud team were auctioned at Bourne.

Constructors' championship: *1958 4th; 1959 3rd; 1960 4th; 1961 5th; 1962 1st; 1963 2nd; 1964 2nd; 1965 2nd; 1966 4th; 1967 6th; 1968 5th; 1969 5th; 1970 6th; 1971 2nd; 1972 7th; 1973 6th; 1974 7th.*

BRM had an Indian summer in 1971 with the P160, which was fast and reliable and a race winner in the hands of Rodriguez, Siffert and Gethin

Brabham BT24, 1966

Brooks, Tony 1932–

C.A.S. Brooks was an outstanding natural driver, with a smooth style that was well suited to the last generation of front-engined GP cars. He started racing in club events with a Healey in 1952 and his motor sport future seemed to lie in sports car racing until he raced a single-seater, an F2 Connaught, for the first time in 1955. Within weeks, and still virtually unknown, he started in his first race outside Britain, in the Syracuse GP in Sicily.

He drove a Connaught to defeat the Maserati works team and make his name overnight. That success led to a BRM contract, followed by a very nasty accident at Silverstone, and little reward. He moved to Vanwall in 1957, scored his first championship points at Monaco and then shared the winning car in the British GP with Stirling Moss. In 1958 he won three GPs in Vanwalls, then joined Ferrari to win the 1959 French and German GPs and finish second in the world championship.

The Coopers of the Yeoman Credit team hardly matched his talents in 1960, nor did the interim BRMs of 1961, although he did place one third in his final Grand Prix, in the USA. At the end of 1961 this quiet man slipped quietly out of racing.
World championship races: 38 starts, 75 points, 6 wins: 1957 Britain; 1958 Belgium, Germany, Italy; 1959 France, Germany.

BRP

The British Racing Partnership was launched in the 1950s as a team to enter cars for Stirling Moss, whose personal contracts meant that he could not drive for some main-line teams. In 1963 BRP became a minor constructor, building monocoque cars powered by BRM V-8s. Innes Ireland scored BRP's only F1 victory, in a 1964 non-championship event, and the team's best GP scoring results were two fifth places (by Innes Ireland in Austria and Italy in 1964). BRP then undertook an Indianapolis project for 1965 (the cars failed to finish in the 500), nothing came of a one-off 3-litre F1 project in 1966 and the venture was closed down.

Brundle, Martin 1959–

Short-oval saloon racing and hot rods led Martin Brundle straight into the British Saloon Car Championship with a Toyota at the age of 17. His first single-seater drives were in F Ford 2000 in 1979.

He fought a season-long battle for the British F3 title in 1983, when he won nine races in a Ralt RT3, was second in 11 races, yet lost the championship to Ayrton Senna. He made his Grand Prix debut in the 1984 Brazilian race. He finished fifth, but those points were annulled, as were the six for his splendid second place at Detroit, as part of the Tyrrell team's penalty for using allegedly irregular fuel.

He did not gain any points until 1986 at Rio de Janeiro. At the end of the year Brundle decided to move to Zakspeed. He scored their first-ever points, in the San Marino GP, but at the end of the year decided not to take up his option to continue, committing himself to Jaguars for 1988.
World championship races (to end of 1987): 54 starts, 10 points.

Brunner, Gustav

Brunner designed original cars that were never developed, for ATS in 1980, stepped aside from F1 to undertake the innovative F2 Maurers, came back to ATS and to Alfa/Euroracing for brief spells and was then given a free hand by RAM, producing the small and cleverly neat O3 that was to be let down by its systems in 1985. By that time he was on his way to Ferrari, to the team that designed the F187 that was eventually to bring the team victories after a long break. When those races were won, Brunner had already moved again, to design the compact Rial ARC1 for Gunther Schmid's new Rial team.

Buenos Aires circuits

The Autodromo Almirante Brown featured several circuits, the Circuito No 9 being used when the Argentine Grand Prix returned to the championship calendar in 1972, and the longer No 12 from 1974.

Both shared the pits and other facilities; the major difference was in longer straights, so in terms of speed the long circuit was faster. Its two main straights were linked by the long fast Curvon, and at the end of the second a hairpin led onto an intermediate gear infield section, which incorporated another short straight before a hairpin led back to the start/finish line.
Lap distances: 2.12 miles/3.41 km (No 9), 3.708 miles/5.968 km (No 12). Lap records: 105.08 mph/169.07 km/h by Fittipaldi in a Lotus, 1973 (No 9); 126.8 mph/204.059 km/h by Piquet in a Brabham, 1981 (No 12).

Bugatti

Bugatti is widely proclaimed to have been enormously successful in main-line racing in the 1920s and 1930s, but in fact when other main-line teams were around Bugattis were usually beaten out of sight. The reputation seemed to carry over to 1956, when the name fleetingly returned to GP racing as the factory produced two cars to an advanced design by

Cooper T53, 1960

Colombo. This comprised a space frame, de Dion axles front and rear, and a straight eight mounted transversely behind the driver.

One of these Type 251s was entered for the French GP, when Trintignant qualified it 17th (of 19) and ran as high as 13th in the race before retiring after 18 laps. The cars were never raced again, but make an interesting 'might-have-been' exhibit in the French national automobile museum at Mulhouse.

Byrne, Rory *1944–*

This South African designer became known through his Royale F Ford cars in the mid-1970s, after he had moved to England to help a friend in racing. In 1976–77 the Toleman team ran Royales in F Ford and F Ford 2000 and this led Byrne to join Toleman when the team moved into Formula 2. He was given the go-ahead to design and build the first Toleman cars, for F2 racing in 1980.

Within three years his cars dominated the championship, and Toleman took the next step, into Formula 1 – logical, perhaps, but bold as the team had no experience at this level.

By 1984 the Tolemans had an excellent reputation, especially for the handling qualities of the TG184 and the TG185, the 1985 car that was largely produced in house. Problems with tyre suppliers and sponsors led to Benetton taking over the team in 1986, when Byrne continued to produce chassis that were never less than first rate – uniquely among the designers of GP-winning cars, he has only worked for the one constructor, and his B188 was his fourth new car in as many years.

Canadian Grand Prix

First run as a sports car race in 1961, the Canadian GP became a Formula race and a world championship round in 1967. It was run eight times at Mosport Park, which was rated a challenging drivers' circuit in the 1960s but by the end of the next decade was considered less than adequate, and twice at picturesque St Jovite. From 1978 it was run on the Ile Notre Dame at Montreal, on the circuit that was named after local driver Gilles Villeneuve in 1982.

The early Canadian GPs provided good racing, and in 1973 the rare sight of a pace car out in a Grand Prix. Scheckter won the last Mosport race in a Wolf, in Walter Wolf's adopted home country. In 1979 Niki Lauda's abrupt retirement after the meeting had started

almost overshadowed the race, and Jones beat Villeneuve in a great race in 1982. Riccardo Paletti was killed in a startline accident in 1982. The 1987 race was dropped from the calendar and this led to legal action by sponsors Labatt, which in turn was dropped as the race was restored in 1988.

Venues and winners (world championship GPs)

1967	Mosport	J. Brabham	Brabham-Repco
1968	St Jovite	D. Hulme	McLaren-Ford
1969	Mosport	J. Ickx	Brabham-Ford
1970	St Jovite	J. Ickx	Ferrari
1971	Mosport	J. Stewart	Tyrrell-Ford
1972	Mosport	J. Stewart	Tyrrell-Ford
1973	Mosport	P. Revson	McLaren-Ford
1974	Mosport	E. Fittipaldi	McLaren-Ford
1976	Mosport	J. Hunt	McLaren-Ford
1977	Mosport	J. Scheckter	Wolf-Ford
1978	Montreal	G. Villeneuve	Ferrari
1979	Montreal	A. Jones	Williams-Ford
1980	Montreal	A. Jones	Williams-Ford
1981	Montreal	J. Laffite	Ligier-Matra
1982	Montreal	N. Piquet	Brabham-BMW
1983	Montreal	R. Arnoux	Ferrari
1984	Montreal	N. Piquet	Brabham-BMW
1985	Montreal	M. Alboreto	Ferrari
1986	Montreal	N. Mansell	Williams-Honda

Capelli, Ivan *1963–*

This Italian driver with a convincing style – a hint of flamboyance coupled with overall steadiness – made his name in F3000.

As reigning European F3 champion, he contested the 1985 F3000 series with the shoe-string-funded Genoa Racing team. Late that year he had his first F1 drives, for Tyrrell. He crashed in the European GP at Brands Hatch, but made up for that in Australia, when despite limited practice he achieved fourth place.

In 1986 he returned to F3000, scoring two outright victories in a March and winning the championship. His F1 experience was scarcely extended by two AGS drives to two retirements, but in 1987 Capelli was the fledgling Leyton House March team's driver in the 'atmo' class of Grands Prix. This turned out to be very competitive; Capelli won the Jim Clark Cup category twice, and scored a championship point in the Monaco GP.

World championship races (to end of 1987): *19 starts, 4 points.*

Cevert, François *1944–73*

Parisian Cevert started his racing on motor cycles but soon turned to cars and won the Volant Shell prize for 1966, an F3 car. That Alpine provided no more than experience, but in 1968 Cevert won the French F3 championship with a Tecno. The move up to Formula 2 with Tecno was natural in 1969 and when Johnny Servoz-Gavin retired after the start of the 1970 season Tyrrell recruited Cevert to

replace him in his Elf-backed March team. He scored his first championship point in Italy that year.

The next three seasons were spent as number two to Jackie Stewart in the Tyrrell team, with Gardner's cars that he found sympathetic to his style. In 1971 he was third in the championship, with two second placings to his credit and then a fine end-of-season victory in the USA.

In the early 1970s Cevert was the leading French driver, thoroughly schooled in Formula 1 racing by Ken Tyrrell and apparently destined for success.

He seemed off form in 1972, when his best results were two second places, but in 1973 he was second in no fewer than six Grands Prix.

Stewart was to retire at the end of that year and Cevert was to succeed him as Tyrrell number one, but in practice for the US Grand Prix he crashed and was killed instantly.

World championship races: 46 starts, 89 points, 1 win: 1971 USA.

Chapman, Colin *1928–82*

A legendary innovator, Colin Chapman is remembered for his many clever designs, for his enormously successful Grand Prix team, his road cars that were never quite as successful, and for his many business interests. Chapman introduced the monocoque form of construction into modern single-seater racing with the

Colin Chapman, in a cheerful mood during one of the later downbeat periods for Team Lotus

25 in 1962, brought Ford into Grand Prix racing and along the way laid the ground plan for the Cosworth DFV engine, brought sponsorship into the Grand Prix world, and while he did not invent 'wings' he very quickly forced the aerodynamic pace. He was ruthless in some of his business, utterly charming at times, very convincing when putting the Lotus case or introducing a new car and often contemptuous of authority. His achievements in the field of Grand Prix racing are without parallel.

He could also have been a very good driver, as was evident from his sports car racing on British circuits. He was entered in a Vanwall in the 1956 French GP, only to have a coming-together with Mike Hawthorn in practice. His racing career ended when he was beaten at Brands Hatch in 1958 by Jim Clark.

Chapman's first GP cars were cleverly packaged front-engined machines, and if Team Lotus had even a chance to make them reliable they could have been outstanding. As it was, Chapman had to follow the Cooper lead before he tasted Grand Prix success. That first came at the end of a decade which Chapman had started as a salary-earning construction engineer with the British Aluminium Company. He turned full-time car constructor in 1952. The next decade was supreme.

The death in 1968 of Jim Clark, with whom he had had an outstanding rapport, was a great blow, but Hill helped pull Team Lotus through and although Rindt and Fittipaldi drove Chapman's very original 72s to win the title, neither had Clark's close and trusting relationship with him. That rapport came again with Mario Andretti in the 1970s, and to a degree with Ronnie Peterson – many doubted his wisdom in pairing Andretti and Peterson in 1978, but he probably knew better than track-side cynics that Ronnie would honour the agreement that Mario was to be world champion.

The cars they drove were the ground effects machines towards which Chapman had worked for a couple of years, apparently abandoning suspension development as his principal concern. Ground effects had a profound influence on racing car designers, but Chapman again outran his invention – in trying to steal another advantage, he lost his way.

Ever a man to sail close to the wind where regulations were concerned, he came up with the twin-chassis concept in the 88, which was banned. For the first time he seemed to lose the will to fight.

A revival did come, with the fairly straightforward 91. A Chapman car won again, in Austria in 1982. By that time he was testing active suspension, which was to come to the GP circuits in 1987, as another Chapman legacy.

Colin Chapman died after a heart attack in 1982.

chassis

As the world championship period opened chassis were generally simple constructions of two main tubular side members, cross-braced, which provided some rigidity in some directions only. More tubes were introduced, leading to the space frame, a three-dimensional structure of small tubes stressed to give maximum rigidity – ideally, no tubes in the triangulated structure should be subjected to bending loads. This type of chassis was most fully developed by British constructors, ironically with Lotus in the forefront, for in 1962 Colin Chapman introduced the monocoque (literally single shell) chassis to single-seater cars. In that monocoque sheet metal was formed into an integral unit, with the advantages of lightness and rigidity, and as techniques developed with considerable safety advantages for drivers. Chapman's first monocoques used side pontoons linked by the floor and the bulkheads, but soon much more integrated monocoques came into use. Over-simplified, the basis of these was folded light-alloy sheets, riveted along the 'seams' and reinforced at loading points. In a search for strength, and then as designers needed slim monocoques for ground effects cars, 'sandwich' materials or aerospace-type honeycomb lightweight panelling was increasingly used. Fuel tank protection regulations in 1970 meant that monocoque construction became universal in Formula 1.

In the 1980s carbon-fibre composite moulded monocoques became the norm, with McLaren leading the way. The composites comprise strands of carbon fibre, which are individually strong in tension, in thin layered sheets with the 'strands' in each layer at an angle to those of the adjacent layer. Metal plates are laminated into the structure for attaching components. Carbon-fibre monocoques are very light, very stiff, immensely strong and withstand accident impacts very well.

Cheever, Eddie 1958–

An American with the background of a home in Italy, Cheever has been driving GP cars since 1978, sometimes in a number two role with top teams, sometimes in grid fillers.

He was a kart champion before turning to F Ford and F3 in 1975. Three seasons in F2 and saloon drives with the BMW Junior team followed, then in 1978 he had a one-off drive in a Hesketh in the South African GP.

In his first Grand Prix of his first season as a full team member he crashed his Osella in the same event in 1980. The year brought just one finish to set against four failures to qualify and nine retirements. Ken Tyrrell nevertheless took him on in 1981, and his first race brought

points, with fifth place at Long Beach.

He had two impressive races with the Matra-engined Ligiers in US events in 1982 and joined Renault in 1983 for his best season for points (22) with the principal results a second place in Canada and three third placings. Then came two frustrating seasons with the Euroracing Alfas, and a year with only one GP drive.

He was back in GP racing full time in 1987–88 with Arrows.

World championship races *(to end of 1987): 102 starts, 58 points.*

Chiti, Carlo *1924–*

Chiti's ample figure really belongs to the great days of Italian racing when artistry and flair rated high, and computers were alien. He graduated in aeronautical engineering but started his professional career with Alfa Romeo, moving on to Ferrari in 1957 to work on racing engines, then and for too long afterwards the be-all and end-all of Ferrari designs. His best-known F1 power units were the 65- and 120-degree V-6s for the first year of 1.5-litre GPs in 1961. Chiti left, with others, to form the hapless ATS team in 1962, but later rejoined Alfa Romeo and master-minded their return to Grand Prix racing. When Euroracing took over the race team Chiti was ousted, and with Piero Mancini he set up Motori Moderni, and quickly came up with a turbo F1 engine, used by minor teams, which enjoyed little success.

Cisitalia

This small Italian company wildly over-reached resources in building a remarkably advanced racing car to a design by Ferry Porsche in 1949 (hence a designation Porsche Typ 360). It had a space frame, a supercharged flat-12 engine mounted behind the cockpit, all-independent suspension and a two- or four-wheel drive option. Money ran out, and Piero Dusio of Cisitalia took the car to Argentina, where it ran once, very briefly, as an Autoar. Porsche later retrieved it to preserve it as one of the great might-have-beens of racing – if raced, it could have enormously influenced the early championship years – while parts for a second car were acquired for the Donington racing car museum.

Clark, Jim *1936–68*

Jim Clark had abundant natural talent, which he applied equally to racing a Lotus-Cortina saloon, a NASCAR stocker, a mulish Lotus 30 sports-racing car or one of Colin Chapman's outstanding Grand Prix creations. His entire Grand Prix career was spent in Lotus cars and he drove them to win 25 times from 72 starts in championship races, a better than one-in-three success rate. Beyond that, he was the first European driver for 45 years to win the US Indianapolis 500, in 1965.

Clark started his motor sport career in local driving tests and rallies around his home in the Scottish Borders, and he raced for the first time in 1956, in a Sunbeam and a DKW. He moved on to a Porsche, and then to wider experience with a Border Reivers Jaguar D-type and a Lister-Jaguar. His first single-seater race was in a Formula Junior Gemini at the end of 1959; in

1960 he drove for Lotus in F Junior, F2 and very soon in the Grands Prix. Clark's Grand Prix debut was in the Dutch race that year, and he scored his first points in the Belgian GP at Spa, a circuit which he came to loathe and where he was to win four times.

In 1961 he won his first F1 victories, in the non-championship but long-established Pau Grand Prix driving a Lotus 18, and in South Africa in a Lotus 21.

The monocoque Lotus 25 arrived in 1962 and Clark drove it to three GP victories. He narrow-ly lost the 1962 drivers' championship to Graham Hill, but won it in 1963, when he scored seven victories and his points total was greater than the combined scores of the joint runners-up. He lost the title in 1964, regained it in 1965, lost it in 1966, although still showing his ability and adaptability in drives in the Lotus 43 with its great lump of BRM H-16: he was the only man to win a championship race with that engine.

In 1967 he drove the Lotus-Ford 49, and once its teething troubles were over he won

The incomparable Jim Clark

four championship races in it. With this car and the close partnership with Chapman, Clark promised to reach new heights. However, after a successful Tasman season and a 25th world championship victory, in South Africa, Clark was killed in an unimportant Formula 2 race at Hockenheim. The sense of loss in racing circles has seldom been more intense.

World championship races: 72 starts, 255 (net) points (274 gross), 25 wins: 1962 Belgium, Britain, USA; 1963 Belgium, Netherlands, France, Britain, Italy, Mexico, South Africa; 1964 Netherlands, Belgium, Britain; 1965 South Africa, Belgium, France, Britain, Netherlands, Germany; 1966 USA; 1967 Netherlands, Britain, USA, Mexico; 1968 South Africa. **World champion: *1963, 1965*.**

Clermont-Ferrand circuit

This track looped around two of the Auvergne foothills nowadays seems an improbable venue for the French GP, but the race was held on the narrow and sinuous circuit as recently as 1972. It boasted one straight, a 1 km climb up from the start/finish line, gradients as steep as 10 per cent and 51 varied corners; in places the ground alongside the track fell away steeply, and elsewhere there were rock faces on the outside of some corners.

The GP was run there for the first time in 1965, when Jim Clark lapped at 98.59 mph/ 145.791 km/h, and the race was also held there in 1969, 1970 and 1972.

Lap distance: 5 miles/8.055 km. **Lap record:** *103.62 mph/166.751 km/h by Chris Amon in a Matra, 1972.*

Colin Chapman Cup

This championship within the world championship series was run for normally-aspirated cars in 1987. The outcome was quite clear cut, Tyrrell's two-car team winning it with 169 points, from the single-car Lola and AGS teams (50 and 41 points respectively).

Collins, Peter *1931–58*

Collins was a leading member of the new wave of British drivers who became so prominent in Grand Prix racing in the 1950s. He came out of the forcing house of the 500 cc Formula 3, and in 1952 was driving F2 HWMs in Grands Prix, his debut being in the Swiss GP. He went on to race Vandervell's 4.5-litre Thinwall Special very successfully in *formule libre* events which led to two GP drives in the early Vanwall in 1954. He raced in only two GPs in 1955, driving the Owen Organization's Maserati 250F, run to keep the team's hand in while the 2.5-litre BRM was built.

Collins moved to Ferrari, where he spent the rest of his career, in 1956. He scored his first points that year at Monaco, and his first championship victory in Belgium, and by the Italian GP the drivers' championship could have gone to him or to Fangio, the team leader. The Argentinian retired early, Collins handed over his healthy car in a remarkable selfless gesture, and Fangio drove it to second place in the race to clinch the title.

In 1957 Collins was joined at Ferrari by his great friend Mike Hawthorn, but it was a down beat season for the Scuderia Ferrari and he won only two non-championship Italian provincial F1 races. He had two particularly pleasing Silverstone victories in 1958, in the International Trophy and the British Grand Prix. He was killed in his next race, the German GP.

World championship races: 32 starts, 47 points, 3 wins: 1956 Belgium, France; 1958 Britain.

Colombo, Gioacchino *1903–77*

A genius among Italian automotive designers, Colombo worked in the industry for more than 30 years, from the 1920s to 1956, when he produced a highly original design for the last Grand Prix Bugatti.

In 1937 Alfa Romeo seconded him to Ferrari at Modena to design the Alfa Romeo 158 for voiturette racing, a car that dominated the first world championships. Before the 158 even reached its prime, Colombo had laid down the first Ferrari V-12, and after that he moved to Maserati where with Massimino he was responsible for the F2 cars of the 1952–53 world championship period (the car which Fangio drove to win the 1953 Italian GP was incidentally the last Grand Prix winner with a live rear axle).

Coloni

A new Grand Prix contender which appeared towards the end of the 1987 season, the FC187, was designed for Enzo Coloni by Robert Ori. It was an attractive and entirely conventional car, with a normally-aspirated Cosworth DFZ engine. Nicola Larini failed to qualify to start in the Italian GP and so gave the car its race debut in Spain. Gabriele Tarquini was the one-car team's driver in 1988, with the 188.

computers

'On-board' computers to look after engine management systems, or in the case of the 1987 Lotus active suspension, became an accepted part of Grand Prix cars in the 1980s. In the late 80s CAD/CAM (computer aided design/computer aided manufacture) became a buzz term, although by no means all designers, or design teams, were fully committed to it.

Connaught

This British constructor came tantalizingly close to real GP success, and indeed was the first to win in Formula 1. Connaught was founded in 1950 by designer Rodney Clarke with engineer Mike Oliver.

Their first single-seater was the 1950 F2 A-type, which was raced in minor British events by Connaught's financial backer, Kenneth MacAlpine. The A-type used a Lea-Francis engine in a tubular chassis, with independent front suspension and a de Dion rear end. More cars were built when Formula 2 became the world championship category in 1952–53, and drivers of the calibre of Salvadori showed that the car lacked nothing in road holding but quite a lot in power.

The B-type followed, with a 2.5-litre 240 bhp Alta engine for the formula that came into effect in 1954, although it was not ready for that season. In its first guise its ladder frame carried a handsome all-enveloping body, but this was heavy and vulnerable, and hardly practical, so it was abandoned in favour of normal open-wheel bodywork. Connaught's 1955 record was hardly encouraging until Tony Brooks won in Sicily. Clarke and Oliver still had to operate the team on a shoestring budget, and so activities tended to be concentrated on British events and servicing customers' cars.

In the only championship rounds Connaught entered in 1956 Fairman placed a works car fourth in the British GP, and Flockhart and Fairman were third and fifth in the Italian GP.

The last race for a Connaught works team was the 1957 Monaco GP, when another talented new driver, Stuart Lewis-Evans, finished fourth in a car dubbed 'toothpaste tube'.

By that time MacAlpine had withdrawn his support, and in 1957 Connaught ceased operations. Two of the B-types were bought by Bernie Ecclestone, to run in Tasman races; the single C-type space-frame car was completed (to appear in a US GP, then modified and supercharged, entered unsuccessfully at Indianapolis in 1962), and an advanced rear-engined monocoque-chassis design never took shape in the metal. In a later age of commercial sponsorship the outcome for such an enterprising little outfit could well have been different.

Connew

Peter Connew displayed outstanding optimism in undertaking this project, for when the age of one-off specials in GP racing had passed this Briton built a straightforward Cosworth-engined 'kit car' in a private garage with the help of friends, and there was even a Connew PC1B (or PC2). Migault failed to qualify the first for the 1972 British GP when the suspension failed, but the second ran for more than a third of the Austrian GP – a Connew's only GP start.

The Connaught B-type driven by Jack Fairman in the 1956 British GP at Silverstone.

Constructors' championship

This was instituted in 1958 to complement the drivers' championship, which has remained much more widely known. Some such as Enzo Ferrari claim that the constructors' title is more significant. Recently it has carried tangible benefits, as early-season points have been a qualification for admission to the teams' travel expenses pool in a following season.

Broadly, the scoring system has followed the drivers' championships': the first five cars scored 8, 6, 4, 3 and 2 points between 1958 and 1960 and the first six have scored 9, 6, 4, 3, 2 and 1 points since 1961. However, only the highest-placed car of a marque scored until 1979, and only the best results from a specified number of races counted (for example, in the 1970s, the season was split for scoring purposes, with the best results in each 'half' counting). Since 1979 all points scored by the first six in all races have counted.

Winners and runners-up

1958   Vanwall, 48; Ferrari, 40; Cooper-Climax, 31
1959   Cooper-Climax, 40; Ferrari, 32; BRM, 18
1960   Cooper-Climax, 48; Lotus-Climax, 34; Ferrari, 26
1961   Ferrari, 45; Lotus-Climax, 35; Porsche, 22
1962   BRM, 42; Lotus-Climax, 36; Cooper-Climax, 29
1963   Lotus-Climax, 54; BRM, 36; Brabham-Climax, 28
1964   Ferrari, 45; BRM, 42; Lotus-Climax, 37
1965   Lotus-Climax, 54; BRM, 45; Brabham-Climax, 27
1966   Brabham-Repco, 42; Ferrari, 31; Cooper-Maserati, 30
1967   Brabham-Repco, 63; Lotus-Ford, 44; Cooper-Maserati 28
1968   Lotus-Ford, 62; McLaren-Ford, 49; Matra-Ford, 45
1969   Matra-Ford, 66; Brabham-Ford, 49; Lotus-Ford, 47
1970   Lotus-Ford, 59; Ferrari, 52; March-Ford, 48
1971   Tyrrell-Ford, 73; BRM, 36; Ferrari, 33
1972   Lotus-Ford, 61; Tyrrell-Ford, 51; McLaren-Ford 47
1973   Lotus-Ford, 92; Tyrrell-Ford, 82; McLaren-Ford, 58
1974   McLaren-Ford, 73; Ferrari, 65; Tyrrell-Ford, 52
1975   Ferrari, 72½; Brabham-Ford, 54; McLaren-Ford, 53
1976   Ferrari, 83; McLaren-Ford, 74; Tyrrell-Ford, 71
1977   Ferrari, 95; Lotus-Ford, 62; McLaren-Ford, 60
1978   Lotus-Ford, 86; Ferrari, 58; Brabham-Alfa, 53
1979   Ferrari, 113; Williams-Ford, 75; Ligier-Ford, 61
1980   Williams-Ford, 120; Ligier-Ford, 66; Brabham-Ford, 55
1981   Williams-Ford, 95; Brabham-Ford, 61; Renault, 54
1982   Ferrari, 74; McLaren-Ford, 67; Renault, 62
1983   Ferrari, 89; Renault, 79; Brabham-BMW, 72
1984   McLaren-TAG, 143½; Ferrari, 57½; Lotus-Renault, 47
1985   McLaren-TAG, 90; Ferrari, 82; Williams-Honda and Lotus-Renault, 71
1986   Williams-Honda, 141; McLaren-TAG, 96; Lotus-Renault, 60
1987   Williams-Honda, 137; McLaren-TAG, 76; Lotus-Honda, 64

Cooper, John *1923–*

Charles Cooper and his son John were improbable revolutionaries, but they changed the face of racing.

Charles Cooper was involved in motor sport in the 1920s, and John became an apprentice toolmaker, and later took charge of his father's garage in Surrey when Charles was injured. That became the base for Cooper's racing ventures.

With his father, John built a car to the then-new half-litre regulations that were to become the first Formula 3, mounting its JAP engine behind its cockpit. In 1947 Coopers built a batch of cars, and from then on the Cooper marque took off.

John Cooper continued to compete, for fun maybe, but not without success until the end of 1952. That year front-engined Cooper cars started running in world championship races. Coopers soon reverted to their well-established layout, and Jack Brabham came into their world. While Charles Cooper resisted change, Jack Brabham persuaded John that some Cooper ways should be altered. But the whole equipe was friendly, and in today's terms it was astonishingly economic – the Coopers ran their Formula 1 team in 1959–60 on an annual budget of £50,000, and income from trade bonuses, start monies and prizes exceeded that.

John Cooper knew that those days would not continue and in the early 1960s he was away from the circuits for some time, recovering from a serious accident in a twin-engined Mini, and Charles Cooper died late in 1964. John Cooper sold the racing organization to Jonathan Sieff. He continued with it, into an age when he was out of sympathy with the Grand Prix business and the frictions within the team seemed more deep-rooted than the noisy rows of the old days of Charles Cooper.

The team folded when Sieff withdrew. John Cooper moved quite happily to a garage in Sussex. He still appeared at occasional race meetings, to watch GP cars on the lines he had empirically laid down, still the friendly outgoing man of years past.

Cooper

Coopers were not the first to essay rear-engined Grand Prix cars in the post-1945 era, but they were the first to win GPs with them, and soon every constructor had to follow the lead of the Surbiton *garagiste*. The influence of Charles and John Cooper was out of all proportion to the size of their company, or their teams, and was also oddly at variance with their own natural conservatism.

Cooper had entered Formula 2 with outwardly conventional cars, and started contesting world championship races in 1952. The normal F2 cars were the T20 Cooper-Bristol with a box-section chassis and the tubular-framed T23. Both had transverse leaf spring suspension front and rear; this has been disparaged but at that time it gave the effect of independent suspension, and the road-holding qualities of these Coopers helped to compensate for a power shortcoming. Variants included Cooper-Altas (a Moss car having coil spring ifs, a dc Dion rear and disc brakes).

A one-off run in the 1955 British GP by Jack Brabham had a 2-litre Bristol engine mounted behind the cockpit (in a sports car chassis) and this pointed Cooper back towards the familiar layout. For the Formula 2 that came into effect in 1957 Coventry-Climax-engined Coopers (T41, T43 and T45) became the pace setters, and they were rear-engined. They had simple tubular frames and Cooper's transverse leaf rear suspension, and minimal development adapted them to run in Grands Prix with enlarged Coventry-Climax FPF engines. In 1958 Rob Walker entered a T43 with a 1.96-litre engine in the Argentine GP when Stirling Moss drove it to a historic victory – the first in a world championship race for a mid-engined car. Maurice Trintignant then drove the same car (with a 2.1-litre engine) to win the next Grand Prix, at Monaco.

The following season Cooper ran a full works Grand Prix team, using T51s with 240 bhp FPF engines, and independent cars appeared with BRM, Ferrari and Maserati engines (a major Italian constructor was apparently interested to find out about cars with mid-mounted engines). The team used reliable Cooper-Knight transaxles with Citroen-based gearboxes. The Climax engine might have produced substantially less power than rival BRM and Ferrari units, but the Coopers were light, had good traction and a low frontal area to compensate.

Jack Brabham won the works team's first Grand Prix at Monaco and also won the British GP. Stirling Moss in Walker's car won in Portugal and Italy and Bruce McLaren won his first GP at Sebring. Coopers took the constructors' championship by a healthy margin.

The team was completely dominant in 1960, with the T53. It was still a relatively simple car, but it had low lines, a new multi-tubular space frame, and coil spring and wishbone independent suspension – gone at last, at Brabham's insistence, was the transverse-leaf arrangement, which had tended to make for 'rear wheel steering'.

The five years of the 1.5-litre formula were not so good for Cooper–Brabham left after the first season and a firm trend towards sophistication set in. Cooper's only 1.5-litre championship victory was McLaren's in the 1962 Monaco GP in a T60.

Blunt Charles Cooper died in the autumn of 1964, and in the spring of 1965 the Cooper Car Company was bought by the Chipstead Motor Group, which had strong links with Maserati. Jonathan Sieff (Chipstead's chairman) and Roy Salvadori took on executive roles, while John Cooper remained in charge of technical affairs. Then Bruce McLaren, Cooper's number one driver after Brabham left, built a pair of Coopers to be run in the Tasman series by Bruce McLaren Motor Racing. That venture resulted

The Maserati-engined Cooper T81 of 1966 being driven by Jochen Rindt to third place in the 1966 German GP. It was not an elegant piece of machinery, but in the hands of top-rank drivers such as Rindt it was effective through the opening phase of 3-litre championship racing

Jack Brabham, characteristically crouched in the cockpit of a Cooper T53 in 1960, the second championship-winning year for team and driver

in only one victory, in the Australian GP (significant as it was Firestone's first victory in this type of racing) but it signalled Bruce's departure.

Maserati provided Cooper with a bulky and heavy V-12 for the 3-litre formula that came in 1966. In mid-season John Surtees joined Cooper, which looked a strong team again. Surtees and Pedro Rodriguez both won races with the Maserati-engined T81, but the car was soon outclassed. Cooper's last F1 victory was scored by Rodriguez in the 1967 South African GP. After an abortive effort with BRM V-12-powered T86s in 1968 – Cooper was sixth in the constructors' championship – the team faded away.

Constructors' Championship: *1958 3rd; 1959 1st; 1960 1st; 1961 4th; 1962 3rd; 1963 5th; 1964 5th; 1965 5th; 1966 3rd; 1967 3rd; 1968 6th.*

Coppuck, Gordon

This British designer followed Robin Herd from the National Gas Turbine Establishment to McLaren and with Jo Marquart took over from him in 1968. Soon Coppuck was chief design engineer, with responsibility for CanAm and USAC cars, and from 1973 took on the design of the F1 cars.

His first F1 car was the M23 for 1973, in which he followed through the wedge theme from the M16 track car, aiming for maximum aerodynamic efficiency (which includes minimum drag) and safety, with only a few elements, primarily in the suspension, carried over from Bellamy's M19. The M26 which

followed was less successful, and the M29 and M30 were failures. The bulky M30 of 1980 was his last McLaren, and his projected all-new follow-up did not happen: there was no place for him in McLaren International as new boss Ron Dennis brought in John Barnard.

After a spell with March, Coppuck continued in Formula 2 with John Wickham in the Spirit team, which moved briefly into F1 with the first Honda turbo engine. For 1987 Coppuck designed the March 871, which was produced very quickly and proved an ideal instrument for the new Leyton House team to race in its first season.

Cosworth

Cosworth Engineering Limited was set up by Keith Duckworth and Mike Costin in 1958 and by the early 1960s had a solid reputation for its Ford-based racing engines and a sound relationship with Ford of Britain (Ford contributed to the development costs of the Cosworth SCA Formula 2 engine based on the Cortina 116E block).

The withdrawal of Coventry Climax in 1966/7 caused enormous problems for the British constructors who had come to rely on their engines, and they cast about for 3-litre power units. Colin Chapman approached two senior executives of Ford, Walter Hayes and Harley Copp, who saw the potential in a Grand Prix engine carrying Ford's name. The powerful Ford Policy Committee backed the project, which was commissioned from Cosworth in two stages, a production block-based F2 engine

and an F1 engine; the cylinder head, which Duckworth regarded as all-important, would be common to the four-cylinder F2 FVA and the V-8 DFV for Formula 1 – the Four Valve A-series and the Double Four Valve. For the DFV Cosworth had to venture into areas such as cylinder block production for the first time.

The first DFV was completed five months after work started. It was compact and neat, simple and light, and thus met Chapman's requirements. The initial power output just exceeded the target of 400 bhp. There were to be some problems through the engine's life, for example with valve gear, but none were very serious.

Jim Clark won first time out with the brand new combination of Lotus 49 and Cosworth DFV engine, in the 1967 Dutch Grand Prix.

In 1968 teams were offered (at £7,500!) a 90-degree V-8 engine with four valves per cylinder. Bore and stroke were 85.74×64.77 mm/ 3.37×2.55 inches giving a capacity of 2,993 cc/ 182.64 cu in. Lucas fuel injection and transistorized ignition was used. It was 54.48 cm/

Above: After a flirtation with a turbocharged V-6, Ford and Cosworth turned back to naturally-aspirated engines with the DFZ of 1987 and this DFR for 1988 and following seasons. In its first year the specification of the DFR varied, for example with four or five valves per cylinder

Left: An outstanding combination – a Ford-Cosworth DFV engine in the back of a Lotus 49, with Jim Clark in its cockpit talking to engine designer Keith Duckworth. Clark was waiting for a practice session at Zandvoort in 1967, and in the Dutch GP he drove the Lotus-Ford to a stunning debut victory

21.45 inches long overall and weighed about 168 kg/370 lb. In 1967 it was rated at 410 bhp at 9,000 rpm (with an initial revs limit of 9,200, although components such as valvegear were safe to 11,500 rpm).

In the early 1980s the engine was substantially unchanged – indeed, some parts were interchangeable with early DFVs. Ports and valves had been redesigned, some components modified, and weight reduced to about 152 kg/ 340 lb. The rev limit was up to 11,000 rpm and maximum power as the DFV entered its last front-line season was 495–500 bhp. From the initial production batch of five engines the number increased to over 400 in 1986 and as most teams used DFVs through the 1970s Cosworth authorized seven other companies to do overhaul and rebuild work.

Cars powered by DFV engines won 154 championship races between 1967 and 1983. The last was Rosberg's at Monaco, although Alboreto's win in the 1983 Detroit GP in a Tyrrell powered by the DFY derivative can be added. By chassis, 'double-figure' winners with DFVs were Lotus with 47, McLaren 30, Tyrrell 22, Williams 17 and Brabham 15. Emerson Fittipaldi made most, 143, GP starts with DFVs behind him and Ford calculated that he covered 21,164.4 racing miles with DFVs.

There were of course numerous successes for DFV-powered cars in non-championship races, as well as for the DFL (sports car) and turbocharged DFX (CART/USAC) derivatives. The short-stroke (90×58.8 mm) DFY was produced for Formula 1 and for 1983 rated at 520 bhp at 11,000 rpm. For years Keith Duckworth had resisted the idea of turbocharged F1 engines, but in the 1986 San Marino GP his very compact 120-degree V-6 turbo bearing the Ford name made its race debut in a Lola. This time there was no instant success, and there were to be no victories before development was abandoned. For the normally-aspirated category in the Grands Prix of 1987, however, Cosworth came back strongly with the DFZ. This 3.5-litre 90-degree V-8 was rated at 580 bhp at 11,000 rpm in that year, when it powered all the normally-aspirated contenders.

The DFR is another V-8 deriving from the DFV and carrying the Ford name. The specification of this varied throughout 1988, for example with four-valve heads or normally-aspirated 3.5-litre V-8 five-valve heads (three inlet and two exhaust per cylinder) which were designed in conjunction with Yamaha. A direct Ford contribution was the EEC IV computerized engine management system, previously used on the turbo V-6. For 1988 the 600 bhp DFR was supplied exclusively to Benetton, and then made available to other teams in 1989.

In 1969 Keith Duckworth and Robin Herd designed an advanced four-wheel drive Grand Prix car, almost in a laboratory spirit. It had a one-off magnesium DFV, 'reverse-mounted' in the chassis, with Cosworth transmission and a very unconventional aerodynamic body by Herd. The Cosworth was never raced; the single car that ran on test is in the Donington racing car museum and parts for another exist as a museum exhibit.

Courage, Piers *1942–70*

Courage spent conventional British *ab initio* years in club racing, moved on to Formula 3 with little success in 1964, then found his feet in this class in 1965–66 with Charles Lucas' team, driving Brabhams and Lotus 41s. This brought him to the attention of BRM, and he was run in a kind of competition with Chris Irwin in the Tasman series. That led to only two GP drives in 1967, but Tim Parnell ran him through a full season with his independent BRMs in 1968, when he scored points in France and Italy.

Meanwhile, Courage had also driven in Formula 2 for Frank Williams, who entered him in the 1969 Tasman races. A developing partnership between razor-keen entrant and fast-maturing driver followed in 1969. Courage scored two second places (at Monaco and Watkins Glen) in William's Brabham BT26.

Williams ran the works de Tomaso F1 entry in 1970. The Dallara-designed Cosworth kit car was hardly competitive, but Courage drove the 308s hard, and was placed third in the Silverstone International Trophy, but scored no points. Courage was running seventh in the Dutch GP when he crashed, and seemingly was dead before his car erupted in flames.

World championship races: 28 starts, (one in an F2 category), 20 points.

Coventry Climax

Readily-available and practical major components were essential to the rise of the British racing car industry, and in Formula 1 few suppliers were more important than Coventry Climax, whose engines were in the forefront between 1957 and 1967.

Under the name Coventry Climax the company dated from 1917, and during the 1920s and 1930s supplied engines to numerous car manufacturers. The first post-1945 Climax racing engine was a 1,097 cc sports car unit, the FWA, based on the FW ('Featherweight') fire pump engine designed by Hassan and Mundy. It was followed by the 1460 cc FWB for F2 and for the twin-ohc FPF, which was the mainstay of British teams through the period of that Formula 2. Its origins were in a Formula 1 project, for the FPF in effect stemmed from one

bank of the 2,477 cc light-alloy FPE ('Fire Pump Engine', nicknamed Godiva). This V-8 produced 264 bhp in its early tests in 1953 and was abandoned as inadequate, although in fact it would have matched the much-vaunted Mercedes engine. The connaught, HWM and Krieft chassis built for it also had to be discarded (four FPE engines surfaced in 1966, having been acquired by Paul Emery).

In 1957 some FPF engines stretched to 1,960 cc for F1 use initially produced 176 bhp, then 180 bhp on 100-octane fuel in 1958. For 1959 a new crankcase facilitated an increase in capacity to 2,462 cc, to give 239 bhp. This engine powered Jack Brabham to two world championships in Coopers.

For the 1.5-litre Formula that began in 1961 a 1,498 cc FPF developing 152 bhp was introduced as a stopgap, while the FWMV V-8 was developed. This was rated at 174 bhp when it first appeared in the summer of 1961 and at 210 bhp in 1965, and from 1962 until 1965 it was the most successful engine of the formula.

During this period Coventry Climax built the prototypes of a most exciting power unit, the FWMW flat-16, to meet a threat from Ferrari and Honda V-12s. In bench tests it gave 220 bhp, but it was never raced. In 1962

Leonard Lee of Coventry Climax had also announced his intention to take the company out of racing; the principal customers agreed to a substantial price increase, and Climax carried on. However, the decision not to contest 3-litre Grands Prix from 1966 was firm, although Chapman persuaded Lee to build a 2-litre 245 bhp version of the FWMV, as another stopgap.

Between 1957 and 1967 Coventry Climax-engined cars started in 95 world championship races, and won 40 – if the 16 starts in the first two 3-litre years are discounted, the success rate is better than 50 per cent – a quite remarkable record.

crashes

By its nature Grand Prix racing is hazardous yet compared with most other 'dangerous' sports it has an excellent safety record. The single-car risks are greatest when track conditions suddenly change or mechanical failure leads to loss of control; multiple accidents are obviously more likely at starts or during the opening laps of a race when cars are bunched.

In terms of cars eliminated, the largest accidents were at Monaco in 1950, when nine cars

Driver Hans Herrmann has been thrown clear, to watch his BRP-entered BRM self-destruct after its brakes failed at the end of the long straight leading into the Sudkehre at Avus during the second part of the 1959 German GP. Herrmann was not seriously injured

Cooper T53, 1960

were involved as drivers came on an unexpected wet patch where sea water had splashed onto the road, and at Silverstone in 1976 when Jody Scheckter lost control of his McLaren at the start of the second lap and nine cars were eliminated in a chain reaction accident. A sudden downpour at Silverstone in 1975 accounted for 12 cars in the British GP, but most of these were really individual accidents. Five of the ten cars involved in a start accident in Italy in 1978 were eliminated and so were five in three separate accidents in the first corner of the 'new' Nürburgring at the start of the 1984 European GP. Four were eliminated in a first-

corner crash at Monaco in 1980.

Two restarts were called for in Austria in 1987 after multiple collisions but although several cars were damaged beyond immediate repair only one was not replaced with a spare for the race.

More top-rank drivers have been killed in sports cars than in Formula 1 cars and almost as many have been fatally injured in test or practice accidents as in races. The modern racing car is immensely strong and drivers have survived very high-speed accidents little injured, and this list of fatal accidents in F1 cars is not long, lamentable though it may be:

At Hockenheim in 1986 Johannson's Ferrari (28) had been knocked sideways by a car which is out of shot and in turn has rammed Fabi's Benetton, spinning it through 180 degrees and knocking a rear wheel awry

1954, Onofre Marimon (Maserati), German GP practice; 1957, Eugenio Castellotti (Ferrari), testing at Modena; 1958, Luigi Musso (Ferrari), French GP; Peter Collins (Ferrari), German GP; Stuart Lewis-Evans (Vanwall), Moroccan GP. 1960: Harry Schell (Cooper) testing at Silverstone; Chris Bristow (Cooper) and Alan Stacey (Lotus), Belgian GP. 1961, von Trips (Ferrari), Italian GP; 1964, Carol Godin de Beaufort (Porsche), German GP practice. 1966, John Taylor (Brabham), German GP; 1967, Lorenzo Bandini (Ferrari), Monaco GP; Bob Anderson (Brabham), testing at Silverstone. 1968, Jo Schlesser (Honda), French GP. 1969, Gerhard Mitter (Brabham) F2 category of German GP; 1970, Piers Courage (Brabham), Dutch GP; Jochen Rindt (Lotus), Italian GP practice. 1971, Jo Siffert (BRM), non-championship race at Brands Hatch. 1973, Roger Williamson (March), Dutch GP; Francois Cevert (Tyrrell), US GP practice. 1974, Peter Revson (Shadow), testing at Kyalami, Helmuth Koinigg (Surtees), US GP. 1975, Mark Donohue (Penske), Austrian GP warm-up. 1977, Tom Pryce (Shadow), South African GP. 1978, Ronnie Peterson (Lotus), Italian GP. 1980, Patrick Depailler (Alfa Romeo), testing at Hockenheim. 1982, Gilles Villeneuve (Ferrari) Belgian GP practice; Ricardo Paletti (Osella), Canadian GP. 1986, Elio de Angelis (Brabham) testing at Paul Ricard.

The first Grand Prix accident with deaths to spectators was at Monza in 1928, when 28 people died, and Monza was also the scene of the worst accident in world championship racing, when von Trips' Ferrari crashed into the crowd in 1961 and 13 spectators died. Nine spectators were killed when Farina (Ferrari) crashed in Argentina in 1953, five officials or photographers when Stommelen (Lola) crashed in Spain in 1975, two by Villeneuve's Ferrari in Japan in 1977 and one by Gurney's BRM in the Netherlands in 1960. A marshal was killed by a wheel from Ginther's BRM at Monaco in 1962.

Dallas circuit

This circuit in the grounds of Dallas Fair Park was contrived to take the place of Long Beach and Las Vagas as a venue for a GP in western USA. It was a 16-corner street circuit which promised to be fast and interesting but turned out to be inadequate in most respects for the United States Grand Prix (Dallas) run on it in 1984. Rosberg won that 162 mile/261 km GP at 80.283 mph/129.203 km/h.

*Lap distance: 2.42 miles/3.89 km. **F1 lap record:** 82.83 mph/133.302 km/h by Niki Lauda in a Brabham, 1984.*

DB

Frenchmen Charles Deutsch and René Bonnet enjoyed some success with small sports cars through the second half of the 1940s and the 1950s, less with their single-seaters for the 500 cc Formula 3 and the Monomill *ab initio* one-model racing class. These cars gave rise to an odd F1 essay, when two Monomills were fitted with Roots-supercharged 750 cc versions of the flat-twin engine to qualify them for F1.

The cars were run in the 1955 Pau GP, when they were so obviously outclassed that the project was abandoned before they were entered for a world championship race. But as a little footnote to racing history, these were the only front-wheel drive supercharged Formula 1 cars.

de Angelis, Elio *1958–86*

In an earlier age Elio de Angelis might have been rated a gentleman driver, although he was a talented professional and no amateur. In his early days he was indeed labelled a 'rich Italian kid' but he proved himself in racing. He started on karts, progressed to Formula 3 in 1977 and when he won the Monaco F3 race in 1978 he had already moved on to Formula 2.

In 1979 he joined Shadow, to drive one of the oldest cars in Formula 1 and score his first points with a fourth place in the US Grand Prix. That led to a Lotus contract for 1980 and he stuck with the team as its fortunes recovered from a low and then fluctuated: in a 1982 high point he won by inches in Austria, in 1983 he scored just two points. In the following two seasons he scored with admirable consistency, but he left Lotus at the end of 1985 as he felt

Elio de Angelis in a Renault-powered Lotus 94T in practice for the 1983 GP d'Europe. He was faithful to Lotus for most of his F1 career

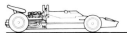

that he had been passed over for the number one seat. He joined Brabham, another struggling team.

Elio de Angelis was fatally injured during a test session at Paul Ricard in May 1986.
World championship races: *108 starts, 122 points, 2 wins: 1982 Austria; 1985 San Marino.*

de Cesaris, Andrea *1959–*

Through much of his racing career de Cesaris has enjoyed the advantages of a silver spoon (from his father's business connections) and has coupled this with an ability to drive fast laps, if not to complete races.

A Roman, he raced karts in 1977 and in the British F3 championship in 1978–79, with some success in 1979. He drove in a Project Four F2 March in 1980, scoring a late-season win at Misano before he had two drives with Alfa Romeo in Formula 1.

In 1981 the thread of Marlboro backing continued as de Cesaris drove for McLaren, crashing at six GP meetings and scoring a single point, in the San Marino GP, before returning to Alfa Romeo in 1982–83. He came second in the German and South African GPs in 1983. Two years with Ligier followed, the second being cut short at 11 races, following a high-speed end-over-end accident that was spectacular even by his standards, in the 9th race.

He returned to the Grands Prix in 1986 with Minardi, recording 14 retirements to set against one finish. De Cesaris then filled the second Brabham cockpit in 1987, with one rather lucky points-scoring finish, third in Belgium. In 1988 he drove the promising new Rial.
World championship races *(to end of 1987): 104 starts, 31 points.*

Dennis, Ron *1947–*

A one-time engineering apprentice, Cooper mechanic, then personal mechanic to Jack Brabham, Ron Dennis became one of the sport's leading entrepreneurs in the 1980s.

He left Brabham in 1970 to set up Rondel with Neil Trundle, to run F2 cars for drivers such as Hill, Reutemann and Scheckter. He formed Project Three in 1975, to run F2 and F3 cars, then Project Four on similar lines in 1979, when it also ran Lauda in the Procar series.

In 1980 Project Four 'merged' with McLaren Racing to create McLaren International, with Dennis and Teddy Mayer as joint managing directors, in fact a takeover that salvaged a sinking team. Mayer soon departed, to leave Dennis to confirm his standing as a talented and ambitious – and successful – racing manager. He built McLaren up as a major enterprise with outstanding facilities and associations, notably with Philip Morris (Marlboro) and Honda.

Depailler, Patrick *1944–80*

One of the wave of French drivers who came to the fore in the late 1960s and early 1970s, Depailler had to work harder for his place in a Grand Prix team than most, and he was yet another who at least in part owed that place to the talent-spotting acumen of Ken Tyrrell. Depailler started competing on motor cycles in 1963, turned to cars and for a while worked as a mechanic with the Alpine F3 team before getting an F3 drive for 1967. His F3 career peaked with the French championship in 1971.

He drove for John Coombs in Formula 2 in 1973, and made his F1 debut on his 'home circuit' of Clermont-Ferrand, in a Tyrrell. While he continued in F2 in 1974, winning the European championship in a March, he also drove a full F1 season with Tyrrell. He won a world championship point from his first GP of that year, and in Sweden he became the first French driver to start a Grand Prix from pole position since 1950. With Tyrrell increasingly seemed a good number two, until he won at Monaco in 1978.

For the next year he switched to Ligier, won the Spanish GP but put himself out of racing after seven GPs, while he recovered from injuries in a hang-gliding accident. He returned to racing in 1980, with Alfa Romeo, only to be killed in a test accident at Hockenheim.
World championship races: *93 starts, 141 points, 2 wins: 1978 Monaco; 1979 Spain.*

de Tomaso

For the 1.5-litre formula the Italian, one-time amateur driver Alessandro de Tomaso built space-frame cars with a production-based Conrero Alfa engine or an OSCA unit for sale in 1961 while developing a version with a 'pure' flat 8. Neither project progressed far on the circuits (three retired from the 1961 Italian GP).

The 1970 F1 programme was more serious, for to support the image of the road cars a one-car Grand Prix team was to be run by Frank Williams for Piers Courage. Dallara designed the de Tomaso 308 on 'Cosworth kit car' lines, coming up with a monocoque machine that was becoming competitive when Courage was killed in the 1970 Dutch GP.

After Courage's death the little team completed the season half-heartedly; de Tomaso withdrew and Williams ran a March in 1971.

Detroit circuit

A Motown venue seems so right for a Grand Prix, but compliments about the Detroit street circuit have been hard to find since its inaugural race in 1984. Much of it is hemmed in with concrete, there are numerous right-angle cor-

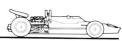

De Tomaso 308, 1970

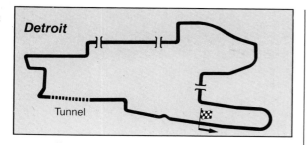

ners and short linking straights, and since some corners were slightly eased after the first race little possibility remains of further improvement within the layout. Lap speeds are very low, and that tends to show Formula 1 in a poor light.
Lap distance: 2.56 miles/4.12 km. Lap record: 89.586 mph/144.171 km/h by Ayrton Senna in a Lotus, 1987.

Dijon-Prenois circuit

This circuit was an attractive alternate venue for the French GP, offering contrasts with Paul Ricard much as Brands Hatch does with Silverstone – the one hilly and sinuous, the other fast and flat – until in the mid-1980s the autocrats of motor racing gave preference to the fast flat circuits in both countries.

In hilly Burgundy country some ten miles north of Dijon, the track has a variety of fast and slow corners – a long curve leading into the climb up to the main straight is particularly dramatic.

The first Grand Prix at Dijon was run in 1974, when the lap length was a mere 2.04 miles/ 3.29 km, but for the next GP, in 1977, it was extended. Dijon-Prenois was the venue for the 1982 Swiss Grand Prix, enjoying a one-year revival as a championship race.
Lap distance: 2.361 miles/3.8 km. Lap record: 133.246 mph/214.432 km/h by Alain Prost in a McLaren, 1984.

Donohue, Mark *1937–75*

American Mark Donohue was a vastly accomplished driver, a total professional whose career was closely linked with Roger Penske, and a quiet modest man. He raced sports cars to Sports Car Club of America titles in the early 1960s, then at an international level and in CanAm, and also in TransAm series. He first ran at Indianapolis in 1969, finishing fourth, and he won the 500 in 1972. He also gained single-seater road racing experience in Formula 5000.

In 1971 Donohue had a one-off Formula 1 race in a hired McLaren M19 in the Canadian GP, and finished third. In 1973 he retired from racing, but was tempted back to drive for Penske in Formula 1. The first Penske car was not competitive so Penske bought a March 751

to provide comparative experience and maintain the race programme.

In the warm-up for the 1975 Austrian Grand Prix the March crashed heavily after a tyre failure and Donohue died two days later.
World championship races: 14 starts, 8 points.

Drivers' championship

The World Championship for Drivers was instituted in 1950. The first and last races in that year's seven-race series were the British and Italian GPs, appropriately as they are the only races that have counted in all subsequent championships. Between 1950 and 1988 24 races have been scoring events, including the Indianapolis 500 until 1960. The number in a season has been as low as seven (1950 and 1955), and as high as 17 (1977), settling in the 1980s at 16.

The championship is decided on a points scoring system, which is open to criticism in that it favours consistent finishing rather than victories. Before the Concorde agreement in 1981 the points scored in a specified number of a season's races counted, and drivers who scored in more had to discard their lowest scores (hence references to gross and net points). The first five finishers in a race scored 8, 6, 4, 3 and 2 points in the first 11 championships, and until 1959 a point was also awarded for the fastest race lap. Since 1961 the first six places have scored 9, 6, 4, 3, 2 and 1 points. Half points were awarded for shared drives until 1957, and for shortened races such as the 1975 Spanish and Austrian GPs. Drivers can score nowadays only if registered with a team at the start of a season.

Champions and runners-up

	Driver	Car	Wins	Points	Runners-up
1950	Farina	Alfa Romeo	3	30	Fangio; Fagioli
1951	Fangio	Alfa Romeo	3	31/37	Ascari; Gonzalez
1952	Ascari	Ferrari	6	36/52½	Farina; Taruffi
1953	Ascari	Ferrari	5	34½/46½	Fangio; Farina
1954	Fangio	Maserati and Mercedes	6	42/57	Gonzalez; Hawthorn
1955	Fangio	Mercedes	4	40/41	Moss; Castellotti
1956	Fangio	Ferrari	3	30/33	Moss; Collins
1957	Fangio	Maserati	4	40/46	Moss; Musso
1958	Hawthorn	Ferrari	1	42/49	Moss; Brooks
1959	Brabham	Cooper	2	31/34	Brooks; Moss
1960	Brabham	Cooper	5	43	McLaren; Moss
1961	P. Hill	Ferrari	2	34/38	von Trips; Moss
1962	G. Hill	BRM	4	42/52	Clark; McLaren
1963	Clark	Lotus	7	54/73	Hill; Ginther
1964	Surtees	Ferrari	2	40	Hill; Clark
1965	Clark	Lotus	6	54	Hill; Stewart
1966	Brabham	Brabham	4	42/45	Surtees; Rindt
1967	Hulme	Brabham	2	51	Brabham; Clark
1968	Hill	Lotus	3	48	Stewart; Hulme
1969	Stewart	Matra	6	63	Ickx; McLaren
1970	Rindt	Lotus	5	45	Ickx; Regazzoni
1971	Stewart	Tyrrell	6	62	Peterson; Cevert
1972	Fittipaldi	Lotus	5	61	Stewart; Hulme
1973	Stewart	Tyrrell	5	71	Fittipaldi; Peterson
1974	Fittipaldi	McLaren	3	55	Regazzoni; Scheckter

The start of the 1987 United States Grand Prix at Detroit. To the left of the grid, some teams have marked the pits road as guidance for their drivers making stops. The pits are very makeshift

Lotus designer Gérard Ducarouge concentrates as Ayrton Senna makes a point

1975	Lauda	Ferrari	5	64½	Fittipaldi; Reutemann
1976	Hunt	McLaren	6	69	Lauda; Scheckter
1977	Lauda	Ferrari	3	72	Scheckter; Andretti
1978	Andretti	Lotus	6	64	Peterson; Reutemann
1979	Scheckter	Ferrari	3	51/60	Villeneuve; Jones
1980	Jones	Williams	5	67/71	Piquet; Reutemann
1981	Piquet	Brabham	3	50	Reutemann; Jones
1982	Rosberg	Williams	1	44	Watson; Pironi
1983	Piquet	Brabham	3	59	Prost; Arnoux
1984	Lauda	McLaren	5	72	Prost; de Angelis
1985	Prost	McLaren	5	73/76	Alboreto; Rosberg
1986	Prost	McLaren	4	72	Mansell; Piquet
1987	Piquet	Williams	3	73/76	Mansell; Senna

Ducarouge, Gérard *1942–*

This Parisian designer played a vital role in restoring Lotus to the front rank, and in maintaining its reputation for innovative cars, as Team Lotus technical director.

Ducarouge trained as an aeronautical engineer. He started his career with Nord Avia-

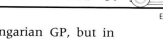

tion, then joined Matra-Sports and became involved in the sports-racing car programme. When Matra withdrew he moved to Grand Prix racing with the Ligier team. He designed his first GP car (the JS5, on Matra lines) and established his reputation with cars that won seven Grands Prix. He was sacked from Ligier in mid-1981, and took up the challenge of designing Alfa Romeo's turbo cars, staying only until 1983, unable to strike up a rapport with the Euroracing people who ran the Alfa team. He was fired on a dubious pretext and moved to Lotus, another floundering team with uncompetitive cars, which at the time used Renault engines.

Within five weeks the team had the 94T, which Ducarouge designed around a modified 91 chassis rather than spend time and effort trying to make the 93T a competitive car. His lighter and smaller 95T for 1984 was a more cohesive design, and led into the 97T and 98T which won five races between them. He stayed with Lotus in the forefront of Grand Prix technology through 1987 when the yellow Lotus-Honda 99T was decidedly avant-garde and 1988 with the ultra-slim 100T.

Dumfries, Johnny *1960–*

The Earl of Dumfries is a talented driver often thwarted by inadequate backing.

He started racing karts in 1980, turned to F Ford in 1981, and to a part-season of F3 racing in 1983. That was followed by success in the 1984 British F3 championship, driving a BP-backed, VW-engined, Dave Price-run Ralt. He did test work for Lotus and spent the 1987 F1 season with the team as number two to Ayrton Senna. Dumfries scored his first world championship points in the Hungarian GP, but in 1987 had to turn to sports cars.
World championship races: *15 starts, 3 points.*

Eagle

All-American Racers was formed in 1965 by Dan Gurney and Carroll Shelby, with backing from Goodyear, anxious to end Firestone's reign at Indianapolis. Shelby soon left, and as Gurney was keen to extend his Grand Prix career as a constructor, the initials AAR were applied to a parallel operation, Anglo-American Racers, based in Sussex, next door to Weslake.

Designer Len Terry's Eagle T1G had a push-rod ohv 4.2-litre Ford V-8 for USAC racing, while the T2G to the same basic design was initially powered by 2.75-litre Coventry Climax FPF four-cylinder engines as a stopgap while the Gurney-Weslake V-12 was completed. In the French GP Gurney scored the first points for Eagle in one of these interim cars.

The basis of the cars was a light-alloy monocoque, and with distinctive 'beak' nose piece and partial engine covers, they were very handsome. Suspension was conventional and, inevitably in those days, a Hewland gearbox was used. The V-12, a twin-ohc unit designed by one-time BRM engineer Aubrey Woods, was hardly raceworthy for the last three events of 1966 and although reliability was achieved in 1967, consistency was not. Late in 1966 it produced 364 bhp, and while some of the engines may have given the claimed 417 bhp in

Dan Gurney in one of his handsome blue and white Eagle T1Gs. The Gurney-Weslake V-12 in this car has 'Eagle Weslake' on its cam covers. Deep cockpit sides are noteworthy, as is the high-quality finish of the whole car

Eagle T2G, 1967

1967 others failed to produce 400 bhp, perhaps reflecting the 'one-off' nature of Weslake production.

The 1967 season started well, when Gurney drove an Eagle to win the Race of Champions at Brands Hatch and then took the Belgian GP, the first 'all-American' victory in a full Grand Prix since 1921. In the rest of that season, though, the best result was a third place, in Canada.

In 1968 Gurney set up an independent engine facility, but the pace set by Cosworth-powered cars was intimidating; the Eagles appeared in only five events, with no success. This was a sad end for a venture that had started with such enthusiasm, but at least the USAC side had 'come good', with a first championship race win in 1967 and a 1-2 at Indianapolis in 1968.

Constructors' championship: 1966 6th; 1967 7th.

East London circuits

The first races at this South African port and resort were run in 1934 over a long road circuit, very much in the old tradition of road racing, and a shorter 11-mile/17.5 km version was used in 1936–39. In 1959 a circuit on the outskirts of the town was inaugurated, and a Formula 2 South African Grand Prix run in the following year (won by Paul Frère in a Cooper).

Three world championship South African GPs were run on the circuit, between 1962 and 1965, after which Kyalami supplanted it.

Lap distance: 2.43 miles/3.92 km. Lap record: 100.1 mph/161.091 km/h by Jim Clark in a Lotus, 1965.

Ecclestone, Bernie *1936-*

Londoner Bernard Ecclestone became one of the most powerful men in motor racing as president of the Formula One Constructors' Association (FOCA) in the 1970s, a position he consolidated when he became a vice-president of FISA (the international governing body of the sport) in 1987.

He had been involved in motor racing since his teens, as a motor cycle racer who moved to cars with a 500 cc F3 Cooper at the age of 19. After an accident at Brands Hatch he retired from driving. In 1957 Ecclestone bought the Connaught team, to run its cars in the Tasman series and in Europe in 1958. After the death of Stuart Lewis-Evans he withdrew from the sport again, only to re-appear in the 1960s, guiding Jochen Rindt's business affairs. That led to an invitation to run the Lotus F2 team when Rindt joined Lotus in 1969. Ecclestone therefore had a solid background in motor racing when Ron Tauranac invited him to take a business interest in MRD (Brabham). In 1971 Ecclestone bought control of the complete company.

He soon abandoned Brabham's customer car activities to concentrate on the GP team, and while resources were only adequate he was not averse to rent-a-drive second strings. But he kept Brabham in the forefront, encouraging designer Gordon Murray. Much responsibility devolved on his staff, notably his lieutenant Mike Blash and Murray, as other interests demanded their shares of Ecclestone's attention. Apart from finance and property companies, these included FOCA, and running that led him to limit his Brabham activities (to the point where the GP team was withdrawn in 1988).

FOCA flexed its muscles in the 1970s, while the commercial side of the world championships was developed on a very sound footing, and took on FISA in a feud that lasted for most of the decade. The armistice in 1987 left Balestre as titular head, to enjoy the prestige of being president of the FIA as well as FISA, while Ecclestone controlled the commercial aspects, and was thus the real power in F1.

If Bernie Ecclestone achieved nothing else, he dragged the Grands Prix out of the age of amateurism.

Emeryson

Paul Emery was a prolific British special builder who produced straightforward space-frame Formula 1 cars in the early 1.5-litre days of the early 1960s. The most serious racing effort with them was by Equipe National Belge with a Maserati-engined pair, which achieved little. Two years later the space frames and other Emeryson parts formed the basis of the BRM-engined Scirocco cars.

Ensign

One-time sports car and Formula 3 driver Morris Nunn (hence N-sign) became a constructor in 1971, and in 1972 ran a pair of successful F3 cars for Rikki von Opel. By that time Nunn was looking towards the Grands Prix, and von Opel funded the N173 F1 car, which he first raced in the 1973 French GP. This was a good Cosworth-engined 'British kit car', with handsomely original and aerodynamically effective glass-fibre bodywork.

Von Opel left in 1974 and Hong Kong entrepreneur 'Teddy' Yip took on the team. In 1975 the Dutch HB Bewaking company sponsored the British Ensign, primarily for Wunderink, then for van Lennep who drove N175 (or MN04) to score Ensign's first championship point, in the German GP. This N175 was a typically neat design, but it was lost to Nunn as the HB association fell apart and the Dutch company took it to race as a Boro.

Ensign enjoyed mixed fortunes with the

Ferrari 156, 1961

Dave Baldwin-designed N176 in 1976, Chris Amon's fifth place in the Spanish GP being offset by accidents. A reasonable budget (Tissot and Castrol) and the N177s, which Regazzoni drove for Nunn and Tambay for Yip in 1977 brought the high point for Ensign and tenth place in the constructors' championship. These cars served no fewer than seven drivers in 1978, including Nelson Piquet for his first GP drive (in the German GP) and Derek Daly, who scored the team's only point. Qualification, rather than points, became the target in 1979, with an extemporized wing car. A design by Ralph Bellamy and Nigel Bennett gave Ensign credibility in 1980, but the season turned to ashes as Regazzoni crashed heavily at Long Beach. In 1981 Marc Surer scored four points in an uprated N180B, and Eliseo Salazar another to carry Ensign into its last year, 1982. N180B and N181 served Roberto Guerrero, but there were no successes and at the end of 1983 Yip and Mo Nunn abandoned the Grands Prix.

The Ensign story was one of survival, often with more achieved on miniscule budgets than some more pretentious teams managed with generous sponsorship.

Constructors' championship: 1977 10th.

ERA

Aged British ERAs, looking every inch mid-1930s racers were driven to honourable finishing places in late-1940s events while efforts were made to get the later E-type to finish a race, with little success until 1949. A new Formula 2 car, designated G-type, was built for 1952, when it could have been a championship contender. However, after starts in minor events and the Belgian and British GPs the project was abandoned, the car being used as the basis of Bristol sports-racing cars.

Estoril circuit

The Estoril autodrome in Portugal has an advantage over some of the kind in not being flat. It was laid down on a plateau in the foothills some four miles from Estoril in 1972 and considerably overhauled for its first Grand Prix in 1984.

It has one long straight past the pits and main grandstands, with a mix of tight corners and very fast bends in the linking section of its lap. Paddock and pits facilities are good, so is viewing from natural slopes as well as from stands.

Lap distance: 2.703 miles/4.35 km. **Lap record:** *122.737 mph/197.526 km/h by Gerhard Berger in a Ferrari, 1987.*

EuroBrun

This new team started in Formula 1 in 1988, marking Walter Brun's entry into the premier category and the return of Euroracing, with conventional slim carbon-fibre monocoque cars built in Paolo Pavnello's workshops near Milan, to a design by Mario Tolentino and Bruno Zava. Mader-prepared Cosworth engines were specified for the 188 and drivers were Oscar Larrauri and Stefano Modena.

European Grand Prix

Through the first two decades of the world championship additional status was conferred on one Grand Prix in each season with the imposing title Grand Prix d'Europe. Thus the 1955 Monaco GP was the European Grand Prix. This provided no extra prize money or championship points, and the practice lapsed until 1983. The title was then used for a second championship race in a country.

Venues and winners (world championship GPs)

1983	Brands Hatch	N. Piquet	Brabham-BMW
1984	Nürburgring	A. Prost	McLaren-TAG
1985	Brands Hatch	N. Mansell	Williams-Honda

Fagioli, Luigi *1898–1952*

Luigi Fagioli's career began in 1925 and culminated when he drove for the all-conquering Alfa Romeo team in 1950–57. In a full 1950 championship season he was third in the championship; in 1951 he started in only one GP, and although during the French race he had to hand over his car to team leader Fangio he was nevertheless credited with a victory, and gained his niche in racing history as the oldest driver to win a world championship race (at the age of 53 and one month).

Fagioli continued racing in sports cars, placing a Lancia third in the Mille Miglia in 1952 but a few weeks later he was fatally injured in an accident during practice for the sports car Monaco GP.

World championship races: 7 starts, 32 (gross) points (28 net), 1 win: 1951 France.

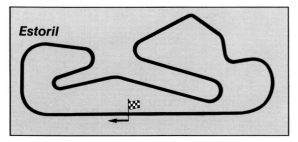

Estoril

Mo Nunn's first and very distinctive F1 Ensign, MNO1, driven by patron Rikki von Opel in the little team's fourth Grand Prix, the 1973 Italian race at Monza

Fangio, Juan-Manuel 1911–

Legends of the great Argentine champion are supported by very solid facts: he contested only 51 world championship races, starting from pole position 28 times and winning 24, or 47 per cent of his championship races. And although he was not a flamboyant man, he has a personality to add to the legends, so that he still attracts crowds when he appears at a function or in a paddock. Fangio's first experience of racing was as a riding mechanic in road races and point-to-point road races in the 1930s. In 1948 he drove a European thoroughbred single-seater for the first time, when he raced one of the Maserati 4CLs the Argentine Automobile Club bought to give local drivers experience of competing against European aces.

With club and government backing he was sent to Europe in 1949; he won six regional GPs, driving a Maserati, once a Gordini and once a Ferrari, and he retired from his *grandes épreuves*, Belgium and France.

He was invited back to Europe in 1950 by Alfa Romeo, scored his first championship victory in his second race with the 158, and won three of the six in which he started. He won three again in 1951, and the first of his five world championships.

After a minor race with BRM in Northern Ireland in 1952 Fangio drove overnight to race a Maserati at Monza in northern Italy the following day, where he crashed and broke his neck.

Fangio returned to racing in 1953, and in the Italian GP at the end of the year he beat the previously all-conquering Ferraris in a

Maserati. He started 1954 with Maserati, then when the Mercedes-Benz team to which he was contracted had its W196 ready he made its reputation by winning races in it – incredibly, much of the credit nowadays seems to be awarded to the W196. He drove the German cars again in 1955, and clinched his second successive title in them.

Fangio then drove one season for Ferrari, gaining his fourth title before happily returning to Maserati in 1957. The Old Man could judge tactics to a nicety, and still drive very hard, as he showed Hawthorn and Collins in a legendary German Grand Prix that year. That was his last GP victory, in his last championship season.

Fangio raced in Grands Prix twice in 1958, the last time to honour an obligation, finishing fourth in a Maserati in the French GP (early in the year he won the non-championship Buenos Aires GP, his last F1 victory). Then he retired, to become a successful businessman, an outstanding representative for the car and component manufacturers shrewd enough to contract him, and a superb ambassador for the

The first two world champions, Italian Nino Farina (left), who won the first title, in 1950, and Juan-Manuel Fangio from Argentina, who won it in 1951 and then four times, 1954–57

Fangio in full flight in a Maserati 250F, driving towards his last championship victory, in Germany in 1957. This was perhaps his greatest drive, for he started knowing that he would have to stop for a rear tyre change while Hawthorn and Collins in Ferraris could race through non-stop. So he made a tactical virtue of necessity, also starting with half-full fuel tanks and thus a lighter car. He broke the Nürburgring lap record ten times, caught the British pair and beat Hawthorn to the flag by 3.6 seconds

sport as through to the late 1980s he occasionally appeared at circuits around the world.

World championship races: 51 starts, 277½ points (245½ net), 24 wins: 1950 Monaco, Belgium, France; 1951 Switzerland, France, Spain; 1953 Italy; 1954 Argentina, Belgium, France, Germany, Switzerland, Italy; 1955 Argentina, Belgium, Netherlands, Italy; 1956 Argentina, Britain, Germany; 1957 Argentina, Monaco, France, Germany.
World champion: 1951, 1954, 1955, 1956, 1957.

Farina, Giuseppe *1906–66*

Dr 'Nino' Farina was the first world champion driver and although never the greatest driver of his period was one of the leading figures in racing through to the 1950s. He was an Italian professor of law who started racing in the early 1930s and gained a reputation as a classic stylist. After the Second World War Farina drove with the Alfa Romeo team in 1946, raced Maseratis and Ferraris 1948–49, then drove for Alfa Romeo in 1950–51. In the first of those seasons he won three championship races, including the first-ever, at Silverstone. After that he tended to be overshadowed by men like Fangio and Ascari, but he continued racing and scored two more championship victories, while in sports cars his career was marked by successes and crashes. Injuries lingering from one of these, at Monza in 1954, eventually forced his retirement from the Grands Prix. He started in three early-1955 GPs after pain-killing injections, and in spite of this he managed to finish second in the 1955 Argentine GP. And third in that race as well, for on an intensely hot day the Ferrari team swapped drivers around several times! The Belgian GP that year, when he was third, was his last, although he later made abortive attempts to qualify at Indianapolis.

Farina died in a road accident on his way to the 1966 French GP.

World championship races: 33 starts, 128⅓ (gross) points (116⅓ net), 5 wins: 1950 Britain, Switzerland, Italy; 1951 Belgium; 1953 Germany.
World champion: 1950

Fédération Internationale de l'Automobile (FIA)

This is the international governing body of motoring, based in Paris, which succeeded the AIACR (Alliance Internationale des Automobile Clubs Reconnus) in 1946, and delegated sporting matters to the Commission Sportive Internationale (CSI) until 1978 and subsequently to the Fédération Internationale du Sport Automobile (FISA).

That re-organization came about largely as a result of the activities of FIA's president Jean-Marie Balestre, and a power struggle with the Formula One Constructors' Association (FOCA) followed. At times this threatened to split the racing world, with the so-called grandee teams (notably Ferrari and Renault) in FIA's camp and the other prominent teams (Brabham, Lotus, etc) and most of the small fry dedicated to FOCA, while that organization to all intents and purposes took over the running of some events.

The rifts were healed with a very firm reconciliation between Balestre of the FIA and FISA and Bernie Ecclestone of FOCA in 1987.

Ferguson

Project 99 was built at Coventry in 1960 to show off the Ferguson four-wheel drive system and in appearance was a conventional front-engined car with a Coventry Climax power unit. Apart from its four-wheel drive, it had inboard brakes all round, and the Dunlop Maxaret anti-lock braking system. Jack Fairman started the P99 in its only Grand Prix, the 1961 British event, and Stirling Moss took it over during the race (it was to be disqualified). Moss later drove it to victory in the Oulton Park Gold Cup to record a first victory for four-wheel drive in an F1 road race, and the last for a front-engined car. The P99 was later raced in Tasman events and used in hill climbs in 1964.

Ferrari, Enzo *1898–*

The patriarch of Grand Prix racing, Enzo Ferrari has devoted his every effort to high-performance cars, especially Grand Prix cars, for more

Enzo Ferrari

years than most other people in the sport have been alive. He is an Italian autocrat, sometimes a benevolent one and he expects the loyalty due a man whose active involvement continued into old age and whose influence is still considerable.

Ferrari raced a little in the 1920s but his organizational talents were of greater value, primarily to Alfa Romeo. In 1929 he founded Scuderia Ferrari, to run Alfa Romeos that included the quasi-works team of the 1930s. This arrangement fell apart in 1938, when Ferrari moved towards building his own cars.

The company turned to machine tool manufacture during the Second World War, and was moved from Modena to Maranello, where the factory remains today. There is a test track at nearby Fiorano where Ferrari sees his cars in action – he has not attended races for many years, although into the early 1970s he visited Monza on an Italian GP practice day, and he watches races on television.

The Ferrari Grand Prix team has remained his passion. It still makes all its own major components, and during the feuds of the late 1970s and early 1980s Ferrari tended to be scathing about the kit-car teams.

He can devote himself to his racing team freed of other worries, for Fiat, which baled his company out when in normal commercial circumstances it would have gone to the wall,

underwrites the team and the road-car operation. If the racing world wants to involve Ferrari in its deliberations, it goes to Maranello, and his was one of three signatures on the 1987 document intended to stabilize Grand Prix racing into the 1990s. So he is as central to racing as it has been to his life for almost 70 years.

Ferrari

There was a Ferrari team in the first world championship season in 1950, although not in the very first race, and in 1986 a Ferrari team contested the marque's 400th championship race. Ferrari entered cars in every season, although occasionally races were missed, for

Below: Dominant pairing of the 2-litre championship seasons, Albert Ascari in a Ferrari T500, in the 1952 German GP

Bottom: Burly Froilan Gonzalez forcing his 4.5-litre Ferrari onto the pits straight at Silverstone in the 1951 British GP. Protective clothing was then unheard of, but although crash helmets did not become compulsory in FIA-sanctioned races until the following year most drivers wore them

Right: The last effective traditional front-rank car, the 1960 Ferrari Dino 246, being flung by Phil Hill through Thillois corner at Reims in a vain pursuit of the rear-engined devices that had made it, and the concept it represented, quite obsolete. The car's nose was dented when Hill made contact with Brabham's Cooper in an early-race attempt to take the lead

Opposite: Gilles Villeneuve qualifying a Ferrari 126CK at Silverstone, where he crashed early in the 1981 British GP. The 126CK was the team's first turbo car, fast but thirsty, heavy and with a reputation for evil handling. Luck, and a certain skill in preventing overtaking attempts, were on Villeneuve's side when he drove them to win two GPs

Right: A Ferrari classic: the 312T was one of the outstanding cars of the era before ground effects in the mid-1970s. The engine was a four-cam flat-12, the water radiators were behind the front wheels and the oil radiators ahead of the rear wheels. A transverse five-speed gearbox neatly fitted within the wheelbase

example when Enzo Ferrari wanted to make a 'political' point. Technically, Ferrari was never avant-garde, and generally in the forefront only with engines: in areas such as aerodynamics his team often lagged behind.

It is greatly to his credit that Ferrari regularly fielded a team of cars, even when they were sadly outclassed. Ferrari became much more than just a team – it became an indispensable core, and without Ferraris a grid could seem threadbare, although the cult of sports personalities diluted that a little in the 1980s. Nevertheless, Ferrari cars have always been more important than their drivers and the marque has always been very strongly identified with its founder.

When Enzo Ferrari entered Grand Prix racing in his own name his target was to defeat Alfa Romeo. The car designed by Gioacchino Colombo, almost inevitably had a V-12 engine, was the 125 Gran Pemio in 1948, when Farina gained the first Ferrari F1 victory in a secondary event at Garda. Ferrari abandoned supercharged engines and for 1950 a new designer, Aurelio Lampredi, started work on an unsupercharged V-12. This first appeared in 3,322 cc form in a 275F1 in the 1950 Belgian GP, when Ascari placed one fifth. A little later in the season a 4.1-litre version appeared, and at the

end of the season Ascari took second place in the Italian GP with a 375F1, which had a 4,498 cc V-12. Gonzales drove one to victory in the 1951 British GP to end the long reign of the Alfa Romeo 158/159.

For the next two years the world championship races were run for 2-litre unsupercharged Formula 2 cars. Ferrari's Tipo 500 for this category was a very straightforward car, with a tubular frame and a twin-ohc 4-cylinder engine (90 × 78 mm, 1,985 cc). It had been raced in

Below: Ferrari spent two years without victories before Gerhard Berger won the last two races of 1987 to end the longest 'drought' in the marque's history. He won in Japan and in Australia, where he headed the field from the start

Ferrari 156, 1961

1951 and so was fully developed for the championship races of 1952–53, in which it was beaten only once, in the 1953 Italian GP. Ascari won two championships, and Farina, Hawthorn and Taruffi all won races with T500s.

The Ferrari 625 and 555 Squalo were generally outclassed in 1954–55. Hawthorn did win the 1954 Spanish GP in one, but only as faster cars retired. The 1955 Super Squalo had an improved chassis, but a worse race record, and both types were withdrawn when Lancia's near-collapse brought the Lancia GP cars to Ferrari.

These Jano-designed cars were campaigned as Ferraris, and increasingly modified as the team fought a rearguard action against the maturing British teams.

Fangio led the team in 1956, driving the Lancia-Ferraris to win four championship races, while his young team mate Peter Collins won two, but in 1957 Fangio drove Maseratis, and Ferrari did not win a championship race.

During that year, however, the first Dino engines came into use, in Formula 2. These were named Dino after Ferrari's son, who had a hand in their design; in F2 form the V-6 was further designated 156, in customary Ferrari nomenclature denoting capacity (15) and the number of cylinders (6), so the F1 version of late 1957 was the 246, and there was a 256 in 1958. These were used in the last effective Grand Prix cars with front-mounted engines, and the V-6s were the most satisfactory component in them for some 295 bhp was produced by the 256 in 1958. That year Mike Hawthorn and Peter Collins each won a race in one, and Hawthorn accumulated sufficient points to take the world championship.

The cars were uprated, with disc brakes in 1959, and the de Dion rear suspension gave way to wishbone independent rear suspension in 1960 – but successes were few: Brooks won on two fast circuits in 1959 and Phil Hill scored the last GP victory for a front-engined car in 1960. By that time a rear-engined Ferrari was running.

The team was ready for the first year of 1.5-litre Grands Prix in 1961, and gratifyingly engine power was decisive. In road-holding and handling the rear-engined 156 was not in the same league as the British cars, but its V-6 engines (two types were used) gave up to 180 bhp in 1961, which the British teams could not match. Phil Hill drove them to win the drivers' title, and Ferrari won the constructors' championship for the first time.

Dissent split the team in 1962, designer Chiti and other key personnel left, and British cars dominated GP racing. Mauro Forghieri took over as chief engineer and made an immense contribution through the next twenty years. More immediately, he struck up a rapport with

the team's new number one driver, John Surtees, who won the 1964 championship. Ferrari produced a new V-8, and for 1965 a 235 bhp flat-12, and followed the Lotus lead to monocoque chassis construction fairly rapidly.

Ferrari was again well prepared when the 3-litre regulations came in in 1966 with a V-12, which late in 1966 had a 260 bhp output in a 36-valve version. By mid-season, however, internal politics had driven Surtees away from the team, and the drivers' championship was lost to Brabham by default.

In the following seasons Ferrari V-12 cars were increasingly outclassed by British cars with the generally lighter and better-mannered chassis and the Ford-Cosworth DFV engine. In 1968 the team was sometimes reduced to one entry, for the highly-regarded Chris Amon, but in 1969 a 48-valve 410 bhp engine promised better. Just one victory was scored and the effort seemed to fade again, in part because Ferrari still tended to contest too many classes.

Fiat had supported Ferrari since 1955, when it bailed out Lancia and handed over that company's GP team, plus backing for a continuing Ferrari GP effort. In the mid-1960s Fiat stepped in to thwart a Ferrari-Ford liaison, and Fiat interest became more active with another Ferrari financial crisis and in the 1970s Fiat pressed for results to justify expenditure.

For 1970 there was an all-new Ferrari, with a new flat-12 engine (78.5 × 51.5 mm, 2,991 cc) producing up to 460 bhp. This played a load-bearing role and was mounted under a backbone which projected from the back of the semi-monocoque chassis. The 312B was an unusually well integrated design; it suffered teething troubles, but during the 1970 season it came good. Ferrari won four GPs, and with a highly professional new manager, Peter Schetty, prospects were promising. But the 312B was a winner only twice in 1971, and the team slipped further in 1972.

Chassis development problems continued, as a first car with the deformable structure that became mandatory in 1973 failed. Forghieri was again 'exiled' to other project work (soon he had to be recalled to the racing team). Eventually the 312B2 monocoques were built by John Thompson in England. 1973 was a season best forgotten, and the team was reorganized for 1974. Luca de Montezemolo took over team management, Forghieri was in charge of technical development, and drivers Lauda and Regazzoni were equipped with revamped 312B3s. Almost suddenly, Ferrari won races again.

For 1975 the 312T brought Ferrari back to dominance. In many respects it was a refinement of the 312 family, with the 'T' referring to the famous *trasversale* – transverse – gearbox, installed at right angles to the normal to keep its

weight within the wheelbase. With up to 500 bhp available, and good if 'nervous' handling, Lauda and Regazzoni won six championship races with it, and brought the constructors' title back to Ferrari for the first time since 1964.

In 1976 Ferrari again won six races and the constructors' title. The hat trick was completed in 1977, with four outright GP victories. On the down side, Lauda left the team before the end of the season. In 1978 the cars were successfully adapted for a switch from Goodyear tyres to Michelin radials and Reutemann and Villeneuve won five GPs. Scheckter and Villeneuve won three championship races each in 1979, and the team took another constructors' title. However, by then ground effects had arrived, to pose problems in the chassis department, and with the flat-12 engine, for its cylinder heads protruded into space crucial for ground-effects airflow.

Ferrari worked towards a turbo car, after testing a BB Comprex supercharged unit; a V-6 with KKK turbochargers was preferred. In the first 126C this engine (81 × 48.4 mm, 1,496 cc) gave 540 bhp, but it was installed in an ineffectual chassis. Courage and talent brought two victories for Villeneuve.

Dr Harvey Postlethwaite was brought in to design a new chassis for 1982, and the 126C2 had a much stiffer chassis which combined with suspension revisions during the season to transform the car. Villeneuve's fatal accident in Belgium was a dreadful setback, followed by an accident to Pironi, yet Ferrari still won the constructors' championship, the first turbo team to do so.

The 'flat-bottom' season of 1983 opened with Ferrari using modified 126Cs, while the 126C3 was readied. This had a carbon-fibre monocoque but a switch to Goodyear rubber that year complicated circuit-to-circuit comparisons and late in the year the Ferrari effort seemed to falter again, although they won another constructors' championship.

That run could not last. The 1984 126C4 was outwardly a smoother car than others in the 126 'series', with vastly improved handling. But in a season when the McLarens were dominant, Ferrari enjoyed only one victory, the first by an Italian driver in a Ferrari since 1966. The 156/85 for 1985 was a thoroughly modern car, but unusually among Ferraris it had a power disadvantage compared with its front-line rivals. Alboreto won in Canada and Germany, but there were no more Ferrari wins until the end of 1987.

Forghieri was put out to grass and John Barnard of McLaren appointed technical director. He chose to work in England while Postlethwaite attended to aerodynamic research and J-J His looked after the engine side. Postlethwaite's aerodynamic work eventually bore fruit in an area long neglected by Ferrari and one where most catching-up was needed. The F187 with its new 90-degree V-6 was designed by a team including Gustav Brunner. It was reliable in the second half of the season, at the end of which Ferrari was back on top with Berger winning the last two races. Meanwhile, John Barnard was completing designs for its successors as 88C versions were first used in 1988.

Constructors' championships: *1958 2nd; 1959 2nd; 1960 3rd; 1961 1st; 1962 5th; 1963 4th; 1964 1st; 1965 4th; 1966 2nd; 1967 4th; 1968 4th; 1969 5th; 1970 2nd; 1971 4th; 1972 4th; 1973 6th; 1974 2nd; 1975 1st; 1976 1st; 1977 1st; 1978 2nd; 1979 1st; 1980 10th; 1981 5th; 1982 1st; 1983 1st; 1984 2nd; 1985 2nd; 1986 4th; 1987 4th.*

Fittipaldi, Emerson 1946–

The most gifted natural driver of the first Brazilian wave to make an impact on the Grand Prix world and the youngest world champion when he first took the title in 1972, Fittipaldi seemed almost to throw his career away for an odd mix of patriotism and a reputedly enormous fee.

A brooding Emerson Fittipaldi in 1975, his second season as a reigning champion after he had taken the 1974 title with McLarens

Ferrari 156, 1961

Son of a motor sports journalist, Emerson climbed a conventional ladder – karts, GT cars and saloons and then Formula Vee in Brazil leading to England in 1969. He took a quick course with Jim Russell to 'acclimatize', and swiftly scored in F Ford, and F3.

That set him up to move into Formula 2 with Lotus in 1970, and after half a season at that level he made his Grand Prix debut in an ageing Lotus 49 in the British race. In his next GP, in Germany, he scored his first points, and he won his fourth Grand Prix, the US race.

After those two breathless seasons a road accident in 1971 checked his career, for he did not win a single GP and was sixth in the championship. But in the next season he won five Grand Prix victories in Lotus 72s and the world championship by a wide margin.

This winning streak continued through the early races of 1973, but in the summer incidents and accidents relegated him to second place in the championship. He switched teams, to McLaren to drive the M23 to three GP victories and to take the championship narrowly from Regazzoni. He lost the title to Niki Lauda in 1975, when he was at the centre of a protest about safety measures at the Spanish GP.

At the end of 1975 he surprised the racing world when he joined his brother's Copersucar team. He persevered with generally uncompetitive cars – Copersucar or Fittipaldi – for five seasons, virtually half his Grand Prix career, winning 37 championship points, fewer than he had scored in any of the 1972–75 seasons. His high point was a second place in the Brazilian GP in 1978. He was involved in business enterprises, but insisted he was just the team's driver, worrying about mechanical problems and so on.

He turned his back on the Grand Prix world except for some test laps in a Spirit early in 1984, but in the 1980s he became a regular Indycar competitor. He was still a winner and a championship contender in the late 1980s.

World championship races: 144 starts, 281 points, 14 wins: 1970 USA; 1972 Spain, Belgium, Britain, Austria, Italy; 1973 Argentina, Brazil, Spain; 1974 Brazil, Belgium, Canada; 1975 Argentina, Britain.
World champion: 1972, 1974.

Fittipaldi

Wilson Fittipaldi set up as a constructor to build an F1 car to race in 1975, with backing from the Brazilian national sugar marketing board, Copersucar, after which the car was named. It turned out to be a 'Cosworth-Hewland kit car' on conventional lines penned by one-time mechanic Richard Divila, with notably sleek bodywork. It was not effective and Wilson Fittipaldi was not a very talented driver so the FD01–03 failed to make an impact on GP racing.

In the F5A the Fittipaldi team had a reasonably competitive points-scoring car, although the only time it might have been rated a potential winner was when Emerson placed it second in the opening race of 1978. It had to be brought out again in 1979, as its planned successor flopped

Ferrari 156, 1961

More could be expected of the FD04, outwardly a less striking design, but driven by Emerson Fittipaldi in 1976. He failed to qualify once, but partly offset this by finishing three races in sixth place, making Fittipaldi eleventh in the constructors' championship – although Copersucar was the prime sponsor, the name was now hyphenated with Fittipaldi.

The F5 was designed by Dave Baldwin, and echoed his sensible and practical Ensign design. It first raced in mid-1977, and served on through 1978, developed as the ground-effects F5A by Caliri. Three were built at the team's Reading base, for realism had led to a British headquarters.

The F5/F5A produced better results and in 1978 Emerson gained the highest placing ever achieved in a Fittipaldi car, second in his home Grand Prix at Jacarepagua.

In the next year the F6A was a failure, then, ironically as the Copersucar decals disappeared, the future seemed brighter. Fittipaldi Automotive absorbed some of the assets of the Wolf team, notably designer Harvey Postlethwaite and team manager Peter Warr, as well as the Wolf cars (which became Fittipaldi F7s). The 1981 F8 served on through 1982.

Meanwhile, Emerson finished third in an F7 at Long Beach in 1980, and Rosberg was third in the Argentine GP. At the end of the year, though, Emerson retired from GP driving, Postlethwaite went to Ferrari, and the team slid.

Neither driver (Rosberg and Serra) scored, because the cars were under-developed and the team under-financed. In 1982 Chico Serra managed just one finish 'in the points'.

A single F9 was completed. Fittipaldi could join the turbo ranks only with a sponsor as benificient as Copersucar, and the state of the Brazilian economy in the early 1980s meant that was unlikely for simple prestige. The team quietly folded after Serra had failed to qualify the F9 to start in the last race of 1982.

Constructors' championship: *1977 9th; 1978 7th; 1980 7th.*

Expressive gestures were normal for Mauro Forghieri in pit lanes, but he was the gifted engineer behind Ferrari teams for two decades. Niki Lauda, in his first GP season with the team, listens intently

Forghieri, Mauro

Until 1987 the Italian Mauro Forghieri appeared the complete Ferrari man, the volatile chief engineer – designer and much more – of the Grand Prix cars that scored 55 victories during his reign of more than 20 years. Son of a technician in Ferrari's Alfa Corse team in the 1930s and an engineering graduate, Forghieri joined Ferrari as assistant to the excitable Carlo Chiti in 1959, taking over from him in 1961. He was responsible for the cars driven by champions from Surtees to Scheckter, most notably perhaps the flat-12 'boxer' 312Ts driven to success after success by Niki Lauda in the 1970s. Forghieri was never a disciple of the 'British way' in GP technology, and the Ferrari team consequently floundered during the ground effects era. He then laid down the '126' line of turbocharged V-6 cars, which was cruelly set back in 1982 by accidents to drivers Villeneuve and Pironi.

The 1984 season was his last in charge of the Ferrari GP team, and he was moved to head the company's advanced development department. John Barnard took over racing car design; but the racing world was nevertheless surprised when Forghieri joined Lamborghini, to run a

Ferrari 156, 1961

Gas turbine haze shimmers behind the unique Lotus 56B, driven by Reine Wisell in the 1971 British GP. The Swede suffered throttle problems in this race, and although he finished he covered insufficient laps to be classified. Chapman's wedge shape shows clearly, as does a feature common to 4-wd cars, equal size wheels and tyres all round

new competitions and advanced projects department, with a Formula 1 engine high on his list of priorities.

formula

The term is used to define road racing's major categories: Formula 1, except for 1952–53 the Grand Prix formula, to which world championship races are run; Formula 2, the world championship formula in 1952–53, then apart from a period in the early 1960s the second-level category until 1984 when it gave way to Formula 3000; Formula 3, the third-level category except for a period in the early 1960s when Formula Junior in effect took the places of F2 and F3.

Principal regulations
Formula 1

1948–53	max engine capacity 1.5 litres (supercharged engines) or 4.5 litres (normally aspirated engines).
1954–60	max engine capacity 750 cc supercharged or 2.5 litres normally aspirated. 'Commercial' fuel, defined as 100 octane Avgas, obligatory from 1958.
1961–65	max engine capacity 1.5 litres, minimum 1.3 litres, both normally aspirated. minimum weight 450 kg/992 lb including oil and water.
1966–85	max engine capacity 1.5 litres supercharged or turbocharged or 3 litres normally aspirated. minimum weight 500 kg/1102 lb.

1966–85 (cont)	Principal changes:
1969	on-board fire extinguisher required. Dimensions and positions of aerofoils ('wings') severely restricted during season.
1970	minimum weight 530 kg/1168 lb. Bag fuel tanks stipulated, so monocoque construction became necessary.
1972	minimum weight 550 kg/1212 lb. Engines with more than 12 cylinders barred.
1973	minimum weight 575 kg/1268 lb. Deformable structure fuel tank protection required, with max 250-litre fuel tank capacity.
1974	rear aerofoils further restricted: overhang limited to 1 m/39 inches behind centre line of rear wheels.
1976	high engine air intakes (airboxes) banned. Further restrictions on overhang of front and rear aerofoils. Max overall car width 215 cm/84.7 inches; max height above lowest sprung part of car 85 cm/33.5 inches; max tyre width 21 inches (c. 53 cm), max rear wheel diameter 13 inches (c. 33 cm).
1977	max overall height 95 cm/37 inches.
1978	single 250-litre fuel cell.

1979   overall car length 5 m/198 inches.

1981   minimum weight 585 kg/ 1290 lb. Sliding skirts banned, and 6 cm/2.36 inch ground clearance required.

1982   minimum weight 580 kg/ 1279 lb. Survival cell cockpit stipulated.

1983   minimum weight 540 kg/ 1190 lb. Flat bottom requirement (to ensure ground clearance, and cut out 'lowering suspension' devices). Further restrictions on aerofoil sizes and overhang at rear. Four-wheel cars stipulated, thus ruling out six-wheelers.

1984   fuel cell capacity restricted to 220 litres/48.39 imp gallons/ 58.11 US gallons, and refuelling during races banned.

1985   small ancillary aerofoils ('winglets') at rear banned. Crash-tested nose box required.

1986   turbocharged engines only, max capacity 1.5 litres. Fuel cell capacity 195 litres/42.89 imp gallons/51.51 US gallons.

1987–88   max engine capacities 1.5 litres turbocharged or 3.5 litres normally aspirated, respective min car weights 540 kg/1190 lb and 500 kg/ 1102 lb. Turbo engine max boost restricted to 4 bar in 1987, 2.5 bar in 1988 (4- and 2.5-bar meaning 4 or 2.5 times ambient barometric pressure, enforced by use of FISA 'pop-off' valves); turbo fuel capacity 150 litres/33 imp gallons, multi-stage or liquid cooled turbo intercoolers banned.

1988   requirement that drivers' feet are behind front axle line.

1989   max engine capacity 3.5 litres. Normally aspirated engines only.

Formula 2

1948–53   max engine capacity 500 cc supercharged or 2 litres normally aspirated.

1957–60   max engine capacity 1.5 litres.

1964–66   max engine capacity 1 litre.

1967–71   max engine capacity 1.6 litres.

1972–75   max engine capacity 2 litres; production-based engines stipulated.

1976–84   max engine capacity 2 litres; specialist racing engines permitted.

Formula 3000

1985–   max engine capacity 3 litres, with engine speeds restricted to 9000 rpm by electronic rev limiter/cut-out

device common to all cars. Flat-bottom cars, one make of tyres stipulated from 1986.

Formula Junior (national class in Italy in 1958, international formula from 1959).

1959–63   max engine capacity 1 litre or 1.1 litre, depending on car weight.

Formula 3 (national class in some countries from late 1940s).

1950–60   max engine capacity 500 cc normally aspirated.

1964–70   max engine capacity 1 litre.

1971–73   max engine capacity 1.6 liters, power output limited by restriction on engine air supply.

1974–   max engine capacity 2 litres, flat-bottom cars stipulated from 1985.

Formula One Constructors' Association (FOCA)

This organization of Grand Prix entrants grew up in the 1970s and flexed its muscles at the obduracy of the international governing body FISA late in that decade and in the first half of the 1980s.

The strength of FOCA was in the so-called kit-car teams, although some of them practised more advanced technology than the 'grandee teams' such as Ferrari and Renault, which backed or accepted authority. The clash of interests came to the surface over turbo cars which were being actively promoted by FISA. At times a real split seemed imminent, but Concorde agreements patched things up and in the second half of the 1980s FOCA figureheads were careful to demonstrate a new unity between FISA and FOCA.

four-wheel drive

This failed to live up to its theoretical promise in Grand Prix racing. In the world championship period the first four-wheel drive (4-wd) car to race was the Ferguson P99, run in the 1961 British GP. It then made a very strong impression when Stirling Moss drove it to win the Oulton Park Gold Cup, on a wet Cheshire track. BRM built and tested their P67 in 1964, but did not race it, or pursue that line of development in 1969 when Lotus, McLaren and Matra all raced 4-wd cars. By that time tyre technology, suspension design and aerodynamics had advanced to the points where any gains in those areas (especially traction) were offset by the additional weight and complexity of 4-wd. Only the simplest of these cars, the space-frame Matra MS84 with its Ferguson system, seemed promising.

There remained only one more abortive effort, by Lotus with the gas turbine-engined 56B in a few 1971 races.

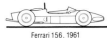

Frazer Nash

An abortive F2 essay carried the name of this old British company into the GP lists in 1952, when the conventional Bristol-engined machine was not competitive.

French Grand Prix

This is the oldest of all national Grands Prix, first run in 1906 as an assertion of France's then-dominant position in the automotive world – the autocrats of the Automobile Club de France just could not comprehend that their country's entry in the inter-nations Gordon Bennett Trophy should be no larger than any other, and so set up this Grand Prix for manufacturers' teams. As a racing car event it retained its pre-eminence until 1921, when the first Italian GP was run, and it was the year's most important event for just a little longer.

That first race was run over 770 miles/1239 km and won by Renault 'works' driver Ferenc Szisz, then it fell to Fiat, Mercedes and Peugeot before Jimmy Murphy won in an American Duesenberg in 1921 and Segrave in a British Sunbeam in 1923.

It has been run on six circuits during the world championship era. Continuity has been broken once, when the 1955 race was cancelled in the wake of disaster at Le Mans.

Generally, it has conformed to the championship series pattern of each season, but some races stand out. Among these are the 1953 race, when Mike Hawthorn beat the great Fangio by a second after 2¾ hours' racing; Mercedes' return to GP racing in the 1954 event; Fangio's fourth, and still unequalled, victory in that race; Giancarlo Baghetti's first and only GP victory in the first championship race he contested, in 1961; Porsche's only GP victory in 1962; the Brabham team's first, scored by Gurney in 1964, and Jack Brabham's first in a car bearing his name in 1966; Ferrari's tenth victory in this race (and the last to date) in 1975; Renault's second, and the first anywhere for a turbo car, in 1979.

Venues and winners (world championship GPs)

1950	Reims	J.-M. Fangio	Alfa Romeo
1951	Reims	L. Fagioli/J.-M. Fangio	Alfa Romeo
1952	Rouen	A. Ascari	Ferrari
1953	Reims	J. M. Hawthorn	Ferrari
1954	Reims	J.-M. Fangio	Mercedes-Benz
1956	Reims	P. Collins	Ferrari
1957	Rouen	J.-M. Fangio	Maserati
1958	Reims	J. M. Hawthorn	Ferrari
1959	Reims	C. A. S. Brooks	Ferrari
1960	Reims	J. Brabham	Cooper-Climax
1961	Reims	G. Baghetti	Ferrari
1962	Rouen	D. Gurney	Porsche
1963	Reims	J. Clark	Lotus-Climax
1964	Rouen	D. Gurney	Brabham-Climax
1965	Clermont Ferrand	J. Clark	Lotus Climax
1966	Reims	J. Brabham	Brabham-Repco
1967	Le Mans	J. Brabham	Brabham-Repco
1968	Rouen	J. Ickx	Ferrari
1969	Clermont Ferrand	J. Stewart	Matra-Ford
1970	Clermont Ferrand	J. Rindt	Lotus-Ford
1971	Paul Ricard	J. Stewart	Tyrrell-Ford
1972	Clermont Ferrand	J. Stewart	Tyrrell-Ford
1973	Paul Richard	R. Peterson	Lotus-Ford
1974	Dijon	R. Peterson	Lotus-Ford
1975	Paul Ricard	N. Lauda	Ferrari
1976	Paul Ricard	J. Hunt	McLaren-Ford
1977	Dijon	M. Andretti	Lotus-Ford
1978	Paul Ricard	M. Andretti	Lotus-Ford
1979	Dijon	J.-P. Jabouille	Renault
1980	Paul Ricard	A. Jones	Williams-Ford
1981	Dijon	A. Prost	Renault
1982	Paul Ricard	R. Arnoux	Renault
1983	Paul Ricard	A. Prost	Renault
1984	Dijon	N. Lauda	McLaren-TAG
1985	Paul Ricard	N. Piquet	Brabham-BMW
1986	Paul Ricard	N. Mansell	Williams-Honda
1987	Paul Ricard	N. Mansell	Williams-Honda

Fuji International Speedway

Dating from the early 1960s, this circuit is some 40 miles/64 km from Yokohama, and Mount Fuji dominates the skyline. It was the stage for the final dramatic act of the Hunt v Lauda championship battle of 1976.

In plan the shorter circuit used for the 1976–77 GPs is a distorted 'D' with one long straight. The first corner swings the circuit through 180 degrees and towards three faster bends. The last corner is deceptively long and fast until it tightens before its exit onto the straight. *Lap distance: 2.709 miles/4.359 km. Lap record: 131.235 mph/211.203 km/h by Jody Scheckter in a Wolf, 1977.*

Gardner, Derek *1931–*

Most designers move around the racing car industry, but Derek Gardner worked for only one team, and for a relatively brief period when he introduced cars that were highly successful, or revolutionary. As a transmission designer, he first met Ken Tyrrell when he was involved with the Matra MS84 and Tyrrell soon invited him to design a Formula 1 car.

This had to be done in great secrecy in a converted bedroom at Gardner's home, and the mock-up was built in his garage. When the car appeared, on schedule in the late summer of 1970, it seemed to follow Matra lines, although outwardly Gardner would have preferred to put more accent on the wedge shape that

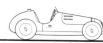

showed in 001's side elevation. This theme was developed through to the most familiar of the early Tyrrells, 003 with its tubby 'Coke-bottle' lines, run in 1971–72.

Gardner's second-generation cars (005–006) met drivers' requirements and the regulations for deformable side sections. The 007 was developed throughout its career, for example with in-line radiators. Through 1976 Gardner was developing his six-wheeled project. This put into practice his theories about aerodynamic penetration and better cornering and braking from larger tyre 'contact patches'. These theories might have been fully proved if work in other areas, notably tyre development for the small front wheels, had kept pace. The P34 was Gardner's last Formula 1 car and at the end of 1977 he returned to transmission engineering.

gas turbines

A Rover-BRM's performance at Le Mans in the mid-1960s suggested that the gas turbine had a future as a road-racing power unit, an impression reinforced by track cars, notably the Lotus 56 at Indianapolis in 1968. One of the four cars Lotus laid down for that event was a spare, and for 1971 it was built up as a 56B, with its Pratt & Whitney turbine modified to equivalency with a 3-litre piston engine.

Although this four-wheel drive car was heavy, and had to carry a weighty fuel load, it promised to be competitive in certain conditions – where there were long straights or in wet weather, for example. Drivers had to adjust to a two-pedal technique (there was of course no gearbox), and the accelerator had to be depressed when braking to avoid severe throttle lag and sluggish initial acceleration, so very large brakes and brake pedal were fitted.

Fittipaldi, Walker and Wisell raced it in 1971, the Brazilian getting it through to the end of a world championship race, placing it eighth in the Italian GP, and then going on to take second place with it in its last race, a secondary event at Hockenheim. The car was essentially a one-off and the development possibilities were not pursued. Interest in gas turbines, for competition cars or road cars, died away.

German Grand Prix

First run in 1926 on the Avus track in Berlin, the German Grand Prix became a world championship race in 1951, when it was held at the Nürburgring.

Ferrari won the first four post-1945 German GPs, followed by a German victory in 1954. That Mercedes may not have been outstanding but was driven by an outstanding driver, Fangio, who also won the race for Ferrari in 1956 and outstandingly for Maserati in 1957.

Relatively poor attendances at the Nürburgring were cited as the reason for running the 1959 race at Avus, and heats had to be arranged to spare machinery and tyres. In 1960 it was a non-championship F2 race. In both years there were 'political' reasons.

Stirling Moss drove a virtuoso race to win in Rob Walker's 'outclassed' Lotus in 1961, Clark pushed the Nürburgring lap record above 100 mph as he won in 1965 and Jackie Stewart put in an astounding drive in vile conditions to win by a wide margin in 1968.

The race was run at Hockenheim for the first time in 1970, then it was back at the 'Ring until 1976, when Niki Lauda survived a terrible accident and the safety lobby had a justified field day. So the race went back to Hockenheim, where it has been run ever since, except for 1985 when Alboreto won on the new Nürburgring autodrome circuit.

Venues and winners (world championship GPs)

1951	Nürburgring	A. Ascari	Ferrari
1952	Nürburgring	A. Ascari	Ferrari
1953	Nürburgring	A. Ascari	Ferrari
1954	Nürburgring	J.-M. Fangio	Mercedes-Benz
1956	Nürburgring	J.-M. Fangio	Ferrari
1957	Nürburgring	J.-M. Fangio	Maserati
1958	Nürburgring	C. A. S. Brooks	Vanwall
1959	Avus	C. A. S. Brooks	Ferrari
1961	Nürburgring	S. Moss	Lotus-Climax
1962	Nürburgring	G. Hill	BRM
1963	Nürburgring	J. Surtees	Ferrari
1964	Nürburgring	J. Surtees	Ferrari
1965	Nürburgring	J. Clark	Lotus-Climax
1966	Nürburgring	J. Brabham	Brabham-Repco
1967	Nürburgring	D. Hulme	Brabham-Repco
1968	Nürburgring	J. Stewart	Matra-Ford
1969	Nürburgring	J. Ickx	Brabham-Ford
1970	Hockenheim	J. Rindt	Lotus-Ford
1971	Nürburgring	J. Stewart	Tyrrell-Ford
1972	Nürburgring	J. Ickx	Ferrari
1973	Nürburgring	J. Stewart	Tyrrell-Ford
1974	Nürburgring	C. Regazzoni	Ferrari
1975	Nürburgring	C. Reutemann	Brabham-Ford
1976	Nürburgring	J. Hunt	McLaren-Ford
1977	Hockenheim	N. Lauda	Ferrari
1978	Hockenheim	M. Andretti	Lotus-Ford
1979	Hockenheim	A. Jones	Williams-Ford
1980	Hockenheim	J. Laffite	Ligier-Ford
1981	Hockenheim	N. Piquet	Brabham-Ford
1982	Hockenheim	P. Tambay	Ferrari
1983	Hockenheim	R. Arnoux	Ferrari
1984	Hockenheim	A. Prost	McLaren-TAG
1985	Nürburgring	M. Alboreto	Ferrari
1986	Hockenheim	N. Piquet	Williams-Honda
1987	Hockenheim	N. Piquet	Williams-Honda

Gethin, Peter *1940–*

Londoner Peter Gethin led parts of only three laps in Grand Prix racing, but he won the 1972 Italian GP, in one of the closest finishes ever seen in world championship racing, by 0.01 seconds.

He was however, more successful outside Formula 1 – in small sports cars, in F3 and eventually in F2 where he beat a very good field at Albi in 1968 before turning to F5000.

That was with the works McLaren, and he moved into the McLaren F1 team following Bruce's death, scoring his first point when he came sixth in Canada. He continued with McLarens through to the summer of 1971, then moved to BRM, and that great moment at Monza.

He had few rewards in a season with BRM in 1972, then after two more F1 drives he went back to F5000. Later his short jaunty figure was familiar around the circuits as a team manager at a secondary level, with his own F2 team in 1978, then with the Onyx team and in 1985 back in the GP world as Toleman's manager for a season.

World championship races: 30 starts, 11 points, 1 win: 1971 Italy.

Ghinzani, Piercarlo *1952–*

Ghinzani is an Italian driver who seemingly deserves greater success than the score sheet records, for he has spent much of his F1 career with teams sustained by hope. He was prominent in Formula 3 (European champion in 1977, Italian champion in 1979) and also raced sports cars. He joined Osella in 1981 and drove his first GP in Belgium that year. He survived a serious accident in South Africa in 1984, then scored his first points with a fifth place at Dallas. He continued with Osella to mid-1985, then moved to Toleman, but was back in the uncompetitive Osella team in 1986. A move to Ligier must have seemed to promise better things, but Ligier in 1987 was a confused team and Ghinzani left to join Zakspeed for 1988, hoping for better times.

World championship races (to end of 1987): 65 starts, 2 points.

Giacomelli, Bruno *1952–*

Giacomelli's early races were in F Ford and F Italia, then one of the more colourful middlemen of racing in the 1970s, Sandro Angeleri, arranged for him to drive for March in the 1976 British F3 series. He won eight races, and the championship. After winning three F2 races in 1977 Giacomelli completely dominated the 1978 championship in a March, winning 8 of the 12 races; his points score for that year remains unequalled.

He had already experienced Formula 1, in the third McLaren run in the 1977 Italian GP and five times in McLarens in 1978. Then he committed himself to Alfa Romeo as the team ran itelf in with the heavy old 177 in 1979. Prospects looked good for the next season

when Giacomelli scored in the Argentine race, but he achieved only one other fifth place all year. He passed up other opportunities and loyally stayed with Alfa until the end of 1982, which hardly improved his career prospects. Nevertheless, there was a Toleman drive in 1983, with a team where he was obviously happy but scored only one point. Giacomelli somehow failed to get the right breaks in Formula 1 and became another Italian ex-F1 driver, racing in lesser categories.

World championship races: 69 starts, 14 points.

Gilby

Syd Greene's Gilby Engineering company was by no means the first to turn out a GP car from a London garage, and this 1960 one-off looked the part. It was followed by a Climax-engined car, designed by Len Terry on quite straightforward space-frame lines but with distinctive bodywork.

Keith Greene drove it to good placings in secondary events, and to one GP finish, 15th in the British race. The design was modified for a BRM V-8 in 1962, but Greene achieved little and it was sold to Ian Raby for 1963, when it was again well placed in non-championship races but made no impression in its only GP.

Ginther, Richie *1930–*

An outstanding development driver as well as a better-than-average racer, Paul Richard Ginther came out of American West Coast sports car racing to join the Ferrari sports car team, then the F1 team in 1960. His first Grand Prix was at Monaco, where he was the first driver to race a rear-engined F1 Ferrari – a daunting maiden occasion, but he placed sixth.

He had only two more GP drives in 1960. He continued with Ferrari through 1961, a high point being his duel at Monaco with Stirling Moss, who won by three seconds.

Ginther then spent three seasons with BRM as number two to Graham Hill, and when he was runner up to Hill in the 1963 drivers' championship he finished in every race. In 1964 he joined Honda, played a role in bringing their first transverse-engined car to the forefront, and drove one to his only GP victory, at Mexico City in the last 1.5-litre Grand Prix in 1965.

After an interlude with a Cooper-Maserati early in 1966 he drove the big new Honda, and survived a bad accident at Monza in Italy, before joining Dan Gurney's Eagle team for 1967. He failed to qualify at Monaco, and during qualifying at Indianapolis decided to quit racing.

World championship races: 52 starts, 107 points (102 net), 1 win: 1965 Mexico.

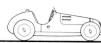
Gordini 2 litre, 1952

Gonzales, José Froilan *1922–*

A prominent member of a group of Argentine drivers who made a considerable impact in the early world championship years, 'Pepe' Gonzales made his name when he drove a Ferrari to win the 1951 British Grand Prix, and thus end Alfa Romeo's long reign.

Races in Argentina earned him a trip to Europe in Fangio's footsteps, and in his first GP he drove a Maserati at Monaco in 1950. He started the next season with a Talbot, then when Taruffi was injured he took his place in the Ferrari team. He got one of the 4.5-litre V-12s up to second place in his first race, at Reims, then had to hand it over to team leader Ascari. The next race was the British, when he hurled the Ferrari round Silverstone to score an historic victory, and earn another nickname, Il Cabezon or Pampas Bull. His five Grands Prix with Ferrari in 1951 earned him third place in the championship, but the next two seasons with Maseratis were largely unrewarding. In 1954 he was back with Ferrari, battling hard to win the British GP again and with top-six finishes in five more GPs to end the season second in the championship.

A sports car crash put him out of action for much of 1955 and, plump to the point of being overweight, he came to a grid for only one more race in Europe, at Silverstone in 1956 when the transmission of his Vanwall broke at the start. After that his racing was confined to Argentina.

World championship races: *26 starts, 77 points (72 net), 2 wins: 1951 Britain; 1954 Britain.*

Gordini

In the 1950s French hopes for Grand Prix success largely rested with the frail cars of Amédée Gordini, although he was given negligible support as he struggled on with inadequate resources. He entered the voiturette class in 1946 and the new Formula 2 in 1948. These were simple cars, and underpowered with 1,433 cc engines giving no more than 105 bhp. But they handled well and achieved good results in the regional GPs then common, when they were driven by men of the calibre of Sommer, Wimille and Fangio, who drove his first race in Europe in a Gordini at Reims in 1948.

A Wade-supercharged version of the engine made the Simca-Gordinis Grand Prix cars in all but performance in 1950. A new model in 1951 had a new engine, a twin-ohc 1986 cc (75 × 75 mm) straight six, which was mounted in a parallel-main tube frame, with independent front suspension and the live rear axle with torsion bars then considered normal.

These cars were competitive in Formula 2

The neat little Gordinis of the 1951 team, which in this 1.5-litre supercharged form showed some signs of speed but few signs of reliability. The 2-litre Formula 2 cars for the following seasons were outwardly similar and had similar performance characteristics

Gordini 2 litre, 1952

and became Grand Prix cars in 1952, when they were the only serious challengers to the Ferraris. However, unreliability dogged *le Sorcier's* team, and although the cars were fast they seldom lasted a race. One did, for one main-line event, when Jean Behra trounced the full Italian works teams in one of that year's Grands Prix de France series, at Reims. Gordinis did not get near the Italian cars in 1953.

The engine was enlarged to 2,475 cc (82 × 80 mm) to give 220 bhp for the 2.5-litre Formula 1, but even that modest power was too much for the light chassis. Very occasional top-six placings in 1954 were followed by none in 1955.

Gordini adapted his sports-car straight-eight for Formula 1 (75 × 70 mm, 2475 cc), but when this appeared late in 1955 its output was no more than 230 bhp. It was mounted in a beefy new chassis, with torsion-bar independent suspension all round and Messier disc brakes, and sleek bodywork. The one Gordini advantage, lightness to compensate (to a degree) for lack of power, was lost. The old six-cylinder cars had to be brought out again in 1956 and 1957. They did not have drivers who could wring a respectable performance out of them, however, and after the Monaco GP in 1957 there were no more top-six placings for Gordinis.

The marque just faded away as Amédée Gordini undertook development work for Renault, where his name was applied to 'tuned' versions of the Dauphine saloon.

Gugelmin, Mauricio *1963–*

Many enthusiasts thought this Brazilian driver's Grand Prix debut, in a Leyton House March 881 in the 1988 Brazilian race, was long overdue. Before this he had won Brazilian kart and F Fiat championships, the RAC British F Ford title in 1982, the European F Ford 2000 title in 1984 and the prestigious British F3 championship in 1985. Two good seasons in F3000 followed, and in 1987 Gugelmin undertook F1 test work which confirmed his ability.

Gurney, Dan *1931–*

One of the select band of leading drivers who successfully made the transition to constructors, Dan Gurney came out of American West Coast sports car racing in 1958 to drive sports Ferraris in major European events. In mid-1959 Ferrari ran him in Grands Prix, first in the French race and then in the German GP, where he won his first points with a second place.

For his first full F1 season he drove BRMs,

Dan Gurney

with no success, and he moved to Porsche for the opening 1.5-litre season of 1961. He was third in the championship that year and although he dropped to fifth in 1962 during that year he won his first GP – and Porsche's only championship GP – in France.

That year he ran at Indianapolis for the first time, and in 1963 he persuaded Colin Chapman to visit the Speedway, and Ford, an outing that had far-reaching consequences for it led to European victories in the 500 and the end of the long roadster era. Meanwhile, in the Grands Prix Gurney spent three seasons with Brabham, winning in France and Mexico in 1964, the Rouen victory being the first for Brabham in a Grand Prix.

For 1966 Gurney's Eagle programme was under way, and he drove his cars to score four points that year. In 1967 he had a non-championship win at Brands Hatch, and much more importantly won the Belgian Grand Prix in one of his own cars. After that the Eagle F1 team went into a decline. Gurney drove a Brabham once in 1968, drove McLarens in the three North American GPs that year, and until clashing commitments ended the association he came out again for McLaren in 1970, taking Bruce's place. Gurney scored his last championship point with a sixth place in the 1970 French GP. Late that year he retired from driving to concentrate on his Eagle team in Indycar racing.
World championship races: 86 starts, 133 points, 4 wins: 1962 France; 1964 France, Mexico; 1967 Belgium.

Hailwood, Mike *1940–81*

Mike Hailwood was a hero, and a British driver whose ability in Formula 1 was perhaps not fully recognized in his time. He came to motor racing as one of the greatest racing motor cyclists – eventually winner of ten world championships on two wheels – and had a couple of tentative GP outings in 1963. The following year he drove in nine GPs, once in a Lotus-Climax (at Monaco, where he scored his first point) but usually in one of the Lotus-BRMs run by Tim Parnell.

He still raced bikes, and largely disappeared from the GP scene for seven years, from 1965–71, coming back to four-wheeled racing in sports cars and Formula 5000. At the end of the 1971 season he drove two races for John Surtees, leading his comeback GP in Italy, and then he raced two full seasons with Team

Surtees. Although he won the European F2 championship in 1972 he had bad luck in GP racing, coming closest to a victory in Italy in 1972. In 1974 he moved to McLaren, to the Yardley-backed car that was perhaps less favoured by the team than the Marlboro-sponsored M23s.

In South Africa that year he rescued Clay Regazzoni from his blazing BRM after their cars had collided, and in recognition was awarded the George Medal. He crashed in the German GP that year and his severe leg injuries ended his racing career. He was killed in a road accident in March 1981.
World championship races: 50 starts, 29 points.

Hart, Brian

One-time British aerospace engineer, successful club-level driver in 1959 and eventually a tenacious F2 driver, Brian Hart became an engine specialist by the early 1970s, first with the iron-block Ford BDA, then with his alloy-block derivative. The 420R F2 engine came into use in 1977 and in 1980 it powered the Tolemans that dominated the championship.

Toleman commissioned Hart to produce a turbocharged engine for their entry into Formula 1 in 1981. His four-cylinder 415T (88 × 61.5 mm, 1,496 cc) initially had two Garrett AirResearch turbochargers and was rated at a modest 490 bhp.

It was to be developed through five years, and the small RAM and Spirit teams turned to it, as Lola (née Beatrice) did initially. However, 415T power outputs varied between units, and were seldom adequate – 760 bhp was quoted in 1986. Garrett turbos gave way to Holset units and a fixed-head version of the engine was introduced.

Hart 415Ts were last raced in Lolas; in 1986 Hart joined forces with Cosworth.

Hawthorn, Mike *1929–1959*

Mike Hawthorn was the first British driver to win a world championship Grand Prix and was Britain's first world champion. The pipe-smoking blond who raced wearing a bow tie remains the popular image. He was at once a throwback to the 1930s and in the forefront of a new wave of British drivers.

He raced Riley sports cars in 1950–51, then drove an F2 Cooper-Bristol so effectively in 1952 that he was offered a Ferrari works drive in 1953. That year he beat the great Fangio in a memorable French GP, and was fourth in the world championship – in his second season in single-seaters! He won one GP in 1954 which was followed by fruitless years with Vanwall and BRM (and part-time outings with Ferrari) before he rejoined Ferrari for the 1957–58

Honda RA272, 1965

The strain of driving a front-engined Ferrari shows in Mike Hawthorn's face in his world championship year. His goggles hide the bow tie for which he was famous

Robin Herd seems to be explaining to journalists that his concept of a six-wheeled GP car concentrates on using the 'extra pair' to provide extra traction, rather than the better aerodynamic penetration achieved by Tyrrell with four small wheels at the front. However, this March '2-4-0' never started in a Grand Prix

seasons. These brought him one GP victory, in France in 1958, the year he was also second five times and secured the world championship by a single point in the last race. He died in a road accident early in 1959, after he had retired.
World championship races: 45 starts, 127½ points, 3 wins: 1953 France; 1954 Spain; 1958 France. World champion: 1958.

Head, Patrick

A mechanical engineering graduate, Head came into racing with Lola in 1970–72. He joined Frank Williams in 1975, working on Hesketh and Wolf cars and the newly-independent team's March 761 before designing his first F1 car, the Williams FW06. This was a particularly neat 'conventional' Cosworth-powered car, but it appeared in 1978, the year of ground effects; Alan Jones' drives in the solo team car put Williams only ninth in the constructors' championship. For 1979–81 Head produced FW07–08s, which gained domination for Williams.

Typically, Head did not fully accept another new technique, carbon-fibre/Kevlar construction until he could control its manufacture with Williams' in-house facility. It was used in FW10 and FW11, which also used Honda engines, and were two more dominant Head cars.

Herd, Robin *1939–*

Herd came to motor racing from the Royal Aircraft Establishment at Farnborough as the result of an almost casual invitation to join the infant McLaren company. His first design for McLaren was the highly original M2B GP car in 1966, followed by the first of the extremely successful McLaren CanAm cars, as well as the team's first DFV-powered Grand Prix car. His originality was next shown in the four-wheel drive Cosworth GP car in 1969, which never raced, but then he had to be entirely practical as he set himself to designing the first March cars.

Some of his designs for Formula 1 in the 1970s were far from successful, and realistically March at times neglected the Grands Prix for more sensible lines of racing business. Herd became increasingly concerned with the business side of March. In the 1980s he was heading a large company that was enjoying great racing success in fields away from the Grands Prix, with Herd over-seeing design work on production sports cars, Indycars, F3000 cars and so on, as well as the high-tech and wind tunnel activities of the Comtec subsidiary. Herd was the only one of the four who founded March in 1969 still with the company when it was the first racing car manufacturer in the world to 'go public' in 1987.

Herrmann, Hans *1928–*

One of the first German drivers to emerge after the Second World War, Herrmann was an occasional Grand Prix driver, his most active F1 season being 1954 when he drove for Mercedes in five races and achieved his best-ever placing, third in the Swiss GP. His first GP was the 1953 German race, with a Veritas. He also drove Maseratis, a Cooper, a BRM (hence a very famous sequence of crash photographs from Avus, when his BRP-entered car flipped at

around 150 mph) and Porsches.
World championship races: 18 starts, 10 points.

Hesketh

Lord Alexander Hesketh's Grand Prix team had a short life, and to many outward appearances it was a merry one. Behind the glitter there was a serious team, but the high life attracted popular publicity and was counter-productive when sponsors were needed to keep the team racing.

Hesketh started his team with a Formula 3 car in 1972. A March 731 followed in which James Hunt scored 14 points in 1973, encouraging Hesketh to go ahead with the first Hesketh car, designed by Harvey Postlethwaite. He followed the lines of his March 731 design in the Hesketh 308B, which was notable for its clean aerodynamics. These were improved when twin hip radiators replaced the single nose radiator.

The 1974 record was good, with a victory in the non-championship Silverstone International Trophy, and 15 points for sixth place in the constructors' championship. 1975 was even better: 33 points and fourth place, including Hesketh's only championship race victory, in the Dutch GP. By that time the 308C was under

James Hunt in a Hesketh 308 – a pairing that caught the imagination of the press and the public

Honda RA272, 1965

development and some of the earlier cars were sold off to independent teams. The 308C was mechanically conventional but in its suspension Postlethwaite used Aeon rubber in compression as the springing medium for simplicity and to save weight. This arrangement was not developed to full raceworthiness that year, and in the 308C it was allied to an insufficiently rigid chassis.

With no backing forthcoming for 1976 Hes-

keth decided to pull out. Part of the team continued under team manager Anthony Horsley, to prepare and maintain DFV engines and run cars for hire. To this end the 308B was uprated to 'D' specification and run through 1976.

For 1977 Frank Dernie designed the 308E, and five were built for clients, and run to no great effect in that season or in 1978. Meanwhile, the two 308Cs had been sold to Walter

Below: Graham Hill on his way to the fourth of his five victories in the Monaco Grand Prix in a Lotus 49B in 1968.

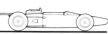
Honda RA272, 1965

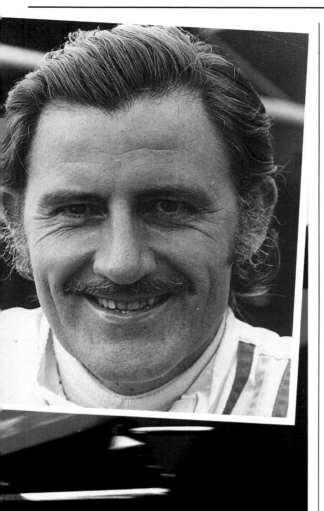

Wolf's new team, to become the first Wolf-Williams (FW05). Harvey Postlethwaite also joined Wolf, and the cars were revised to have conventional springing and strengthened chassis, for a fruitless 1976 season.
Constructors' championship: 1974 6th; 1975 4th.

Hewland Engineering

In 1957 Mike Hewland set up an engineering company and moved into motor sport engineering in 1958 when the UDT-Laystall team approached him for gearboxes for its F2 cars. A succession of Hewland 'boxes based on a VW case followed, beginning with Mk1 for F Junior in 1959. Since then Hewland gearboxes have been fitted to cars that have won countless championships, and became as basic to the 'British kit car' as Cosworth engines.

The HD of 1963 was the first F1 gearbox and the first not using bought-in components. In the early 3-litre years the DG came, to be followed in 1968 by the FG; and its FGA (1973) and FGB (1980) derivatives served through into the 1980s.

At times the only F1 teams not using Hewland gearboxes were Ferrari and Alfa Romeo, although this near-monopoly was challenged by the Weismann-MRD gearbox and more recently by Staffs Silent Gears. Some gearboxes that have masqueraded under team names have in fact been largely Hewlands.

Hill, Graham *1929–75*

Norman Graham Hill was admired for his courage and determination by a public far beyond the ranks of racing enthusiasts, and not simply for his widely-publicized recovery from a serious accident. That recovery was largely due to his tenacity and hard work, qualities he had used to get into motor racing, get to the top, and stay on top. He had talent, obviously, and he had a remarkably long career, starting in 176 Grands Prix, twice taking the world championship and winning at Indianapolis and Le Mans.

Hill drove four laps in a hired 500 cc Cooper-Norton at Brands Hatch in 1953, worked for Lotus as a mechanic, with some drives, and when Team Lotus entered Grand Prix racing in 1958 Hill became a Grand Prix driver.

His first world championship race was at Monaco, where he was enormously successful in later years, although in 1958 his Lotus 12 let him down. In 1960 he moved to BRM, where he stayed for seven seasons.

In 1961 he won his first points when he was third in the Dutch GP. In 1962 BRM's V-8-engined P57 was raceworthy and he won his first GP in it in the Netherlands. Subsequent victories at the Nürburgring, Monza and East

Left: Graham Hill, near the end of his illustrious driving career, when he was already concentrating on his new role as an entrant and looking towards becoming a constructor

London brought him his first world championship. In 1963 he scored the first of a hat trick of victories at Monaco and Watkins Glen – in 1963–65 those were the only GPs he won. He was runner-up in the championship in each of those seasons.

Hill returned to Lotus in 1967, to drive the new Cosworth-engined 49, which let him down five times when he was leading races. In 1968 he played a major role in keeping the team together after Jim Clark's fatal accident, doing so with victories in Spain, Monaco and Mexico, and a second drivers' championship. He began the 1969 season with a fifth victory at

The USA's first world champion, Philip Toll Hill Jr – Phil Hill

Monaco, his last Grand Prix victory. At the end of the season he crashed heavily at Watkins Glen, breaking his legs badly. Outsiders assumed his driving career had ended. However, he turned out to drive Rob Walker's Lotus for the South African GP despite having to be lifted in and out of the cockpit, and he drove it to finish sixth. When Walker withdrew at the end of the year Hill was expected to quit but he joined Brabham, to score his last F1 victory in the 1971 International Trophy and gain a couple of championship points in Austria. He doubled that score in 1972, when he also won his last single-seater victory at Monza in a car of his own F2 team. That became a Formula 1 team in 1973, using Shadow cars. In 1974 it ran Lolas with strong Hill influence, and he scored his last championship point, in Sweden. In 1975 the team redesignated its Lola T371s Hill GH1, which were followed by the Hill GH2. Graham failed to qualify for the 1975 Monaco GP, and coupled with the abilities of young Tony Brise, this brought on the decision to retire. In November he was killed with five members of his team in an aircraft accident.

World championship races: 176 starts, 289 points (270 net), 14 wins: 1962 Netherlands, Germany, Italy, South Africa; 1963 Monaco, USA; 1964 Monaco, USA; 1965 Monaco, USA; 1968 Spain, Monaco, Mexico; 1969 Monaco. **World champion:** *1962, 1968.*

Hill, Phil *1927–*

America's first world champion, and a driver with a particularly fine record in sports car racing, Phil drove his first Grand Prix in a Maserati at Reims in 1958, when he finished seventh. Late that year Ferrari ran him in the Italian and Moroccan GPs, and he was third in both races.

Four seasons with the Ferrari Grand Prix team followed. When he won the 1960 Italian GP he was the first American to win a Grand Prix since Jimmy Murphy in 1921, and the last driver to win one in a front-engined car.

In 1961 a Ferrari driver was almost bound to win the championship. The penultimate race was at Monza, where it seemed that the title would go to Hill's team-mate von Trips. The German was killed during the race, however, and the title was Hill's.

In 1962 the GP Ferraris were outclassed, and dissent split the team. Hill went with others to the ATS team, then he turned to Cooper for a last full GP season in 1964. He continued to race sports cars until 1967, then concentrated on classic car restoration, journalism and race commentaries.

World championship races: 48 starts, (once in an F2 category), 98 points (94 net), 3 wins: 1960 Italy; 1961 Belgium, Italy. **World champion:** *1961.*

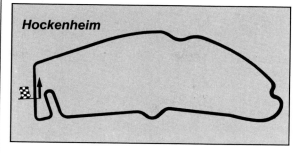

Hockenheim circuit

A circuit laid out in the flat woodlands near Heidelberg in the late 1930s was important to the recovery of German motor racing in the late 1940s and early 1950s. It comprised two near-straight stretches linked by a hairpin at one end and a long fast curve. In the early 1960s it was closed when an autobahn was built across part of it. Compensation paid for a modified track with a twisting section behind the pits, and in view of a huge amphitheatre of concrete grand-stands.

Beyond that, the circuit has a simple layout, and was seemingly made for slipstreaming until a chicane was built on each of the long straights. Following Patrick Depailler's fatal accident in 1980 a chicane was built in the challenging Ostkurve at the far end of the circuit from the pits.

The Hockenheimring was first used for a German GP in 1970, and was the GP venue in 1977–84 and 1986–88.

Lap distance: 4.223 miles/6.797 km. Lap record: 143.828 mph/231.462 km/h by Nigel Mansell in a Williams, 1987.

Hockenheim

Honda

The Japanese company entered Grand Prix racing in the 1960s with cars which enjoyed limited success, withdrew in 1968 and returned as an engine supplier in 1983.

The first GP Honda, in 1964, was the dumpy space-frame RA271, where efforts had been concentrated on the V-12 engine. This strongly echoed motor cycle practices, and while it was to become the most powerful engine of the 1.5-litre formula years, effective power was in a narrow rev range, which was to be a characteristic of Honda's F1 engines. In its second year up to 240 bhp at 11,000 rpm was claimed for it,

Honda arrived in the Grand Prix World in 1964 for an exploratory half season, returning in 1965 with a two-car team to contest a full programme. Their car was the RA272, which became an effective contender. Richie Ginther (in the second car) won the last Grand Prix of the 1.5-litre formula, in Mexico

Honda RA272, 1965

The Honda RA301 of 1968 was an overweight car despite the experience with its predecessor. Surtees did his best with it and ran with the leaders at some 'power circuits', although not here at Monaco where the transmission failed

and the safe upper rev limit was 14,000 rpm! It was mounted transversely in the chassis. Development led to the lighter monocoque RA272 in 1965, when experienced driver Richie Ginther twice placed a Honda sixth in European races, and won Honda's first Grand Prix victory, at Mexico City, the last race of the formula.

Honda decided to carry on in the first years of 3-litre Grands Prix, once again concentrating on their engines with too little attention paid to the chassis. The 90-degree V-12 (78 × 52.1 mm, 2,992 cc) produced perhaps 380 bhp in that first season — barely enough, as it was a big and heavy unit and was mounted in a fairly conventional monocoque car.

When this RA273 made its debut at the 1966 Italian GP, it weighed 1,543 lb/700 kg, some 40 per cent above the formula minimum. Ginther got the first car up to second place in that Italian

GP then crashed when a tyre failed. Later in the year he finished fourth in the Mexican GP.

John Surtees, widely experienced in the ways of Honda, was the team's driver-cum-technical-consultant in 1967–68, and he persuaded Honda to set up a base in England. Slightly lighter cars were built, but for a while Honda persisted in the view that real power (and noise!) would compensate for excess weight. That theory might have held good in 1966, but 1967 was the year that the elegant little Lotus 49 appeared.

In mid-season Honda agreed to a new chassis, to be built in England. Based on the Indianapolis Lola T190, it appeared for the Italian GP, when Surtees drove it to a surprise debut victory. For 1968 the V-12 was reworked as the RA301E, to produce well over 400 bhp with an effective rev limit of 10,500–11,000 rpm. The neater and 'lighter' RA301 to carry it turned out to be slightly heavier than its predecessor. During the year Surtees' best placing was a second in the French GP.

That was the race where Honda's revolutionary RA302 made its premature debut, after tests when Surtees pronounced it unready to race. It featured an air-cooled 380 bhp V-8 carried under a beam extended from the back of the rear bulkhead of the monocoque. When Schlesser drove it at Rouen this engine suddenly cut and he crashed and died as the magnesium skin of the monocoque blazed.

At the end of that season Honda withdrew, but came back to the European circuits in 1981, supplying engines to the Ralt F2 team, and then to Spirit. That team then brought the name Honda back into Formula 1, as it provided the vehicle for the RA163 turbocharged engine to be run in six Grands Prix in 1983. This engine was an 80-degree V-6, reputedly considerably over-square and with the narrow power band

almost traditional in Honda power units. It was available to the Williams team, which ran it in the last race of 1983, and it powered an FW09 to victory for the first time at Dallas in 1984.

In mid-1985 a revised 'E' specification engine was introduced, with the potential to produce over 1000 bhp in qualifying tune, and 800–850 bhp for a race.

Honda turbo engines remained exclusive to Williams to the end of 1986; in 1987 were also supplied to Lotus – between them Williams and Lotus won 11 championship races with the Honda V-6s. Williams used the power units particularly successfully, partly because of long experience, and many observers were puzzled when Honda ended the arrangement with Williams at the end of 1987.

Honda's preferred driver Nelson Piquet switched teams for 1988 to Lotus, which continued with the Honda engine. More significantly, McLaren also established a close liaison

A Honda 80-degree turbocharged V-6 in a Lotus 99T. The yellow tops of the turbo intakes stand proud of the bodywork, and the shaped undertray can be seen. This engine was powerful yet frugal, but on the debit side gained a reputation for excessive vibration

Honda RA272, 1965

Honda RA272, 1965

with Honda, and the MP4/4 powered by the Honda RA-168E commandingly won the season's opening races.

***Constructors' championship:** 1966 7th; 1967 4th; 1965 6th.*

Hulme, Denny *1936–*

Denny Hulme was the only one of a talented group of New Zealanders from the 1950s to win the world title.

His racing followed a local pattern: it started in reach-me-down cars (an MG and a Cooper), and then he followed Bruce McLaren as the New Zealand driver to Europe in 1959.

He raced in Formula Junior and had a one-off F1 drive in a Snetterton non-championship race. But generally he continued in Juniors, doggedly working in the service department of Jack Brabham's garage while racing for a successful breakthrough. His drives in the 1964 Brabham Juniors led to F2 with the team, and occasional non-championship F1 starts.

Hulme started in six world championship races with Brabham in 1965, and scored his first points with a fourth place in the French GP. That year he was fourth in the championship, and to Brabham's chagrin he won the title in 1967, having scored his first victories in the Monaco and German GPs – not the easiest pair.

Hulme also drove at Indianapolis, and in CanAm with the McLaren team, to which he moved for the rest of his Formula 1 career. He could drive hard, but did not do so habitually (especially if the conditions were bad) and in Europe seldom seemed to be highly rated as a driver – but he won eight championship races, many more than most fashionable drivers – and

Below: Hulme under great pressure on the second lap at Monaco in 1967. He is setting his Brabham up for the second part of the harbour-side chicane, with Bandini's Ferrari riding his gearbox in the cement dust, Stewart keeping his BRM (4) just a little off line to follow the pair through. Hulme went on to win the race. Towards its end Bandini crashed at this point and was fatally injured

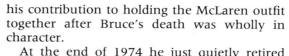

Honda RA272, 1965

his contribution to holding the McLaren outfit together after Bruce's death was wholly in character.

At the end of 1974 he just quietly retired from Formula 1 and returned to New Zealand. Then he started racing again, in saloons, and a dozen years after his 'retirement' a mellow Denny Hulme turned up at Silverstone and co-drove the winning car in the Tourist Trophy. ***World championship races:*** *112 starts 248 points, 8 wins: 1967 Monaco, Germany; 1968 Italy, Canada; 1969 Mexico; 1972 South Africa; 1973 Sweden; 1974 Argentina.* ***World champion:*** *1967.*

Left: Denis Clive Hulme, Denny 'the Bear' who was often underrated but was a worthy world champion in 1967

Hungarian Grand Prix

The first Hungarian GP was run on a park circuit in Budapest in 1936, and won by Nuvolari in an Alfa Romeo.

In the second Hungarian Grand Prix world championship racing crossed a major political boundary, into an eastern bloc country. Two hundred thousand spectators attended and the race was widely covered on East European television. The Hungarian government underwrote the race.

Bernie Ecclestone, representing FOCA, made the original approaches, and seemingly came close to a deal for a race in Moscow.

The 1986 race was a success and in the 1987 race, which Piquet won again, a Ferrari started from the front row of a grid for the first time for two years.

Winners (world championship GPs)

1986	N. Piquet	Williams-Honda
1987	N. Piquet	Williams Honda

Hungaroring

This is the first purpose-built Grand Prix circuit in an East European country, built in seven months in open country some 12 miles/19 km

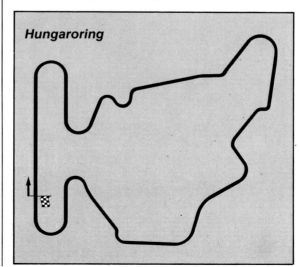

Hungaroring

Honda RA272, 1965

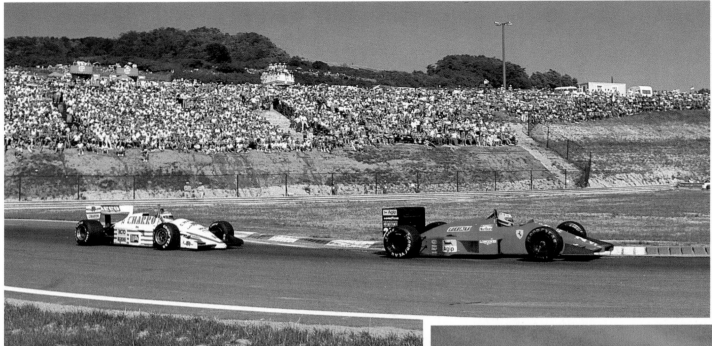

The Hungaroring brought Grand Prix racing into Eastern Europe. The first championship Hungarian GPs at this purpose-built circuit attracted large crowds and vast TV audiences. The hapless Pascal Favre in the sluggish AGS JH22 lapped by Alboreto (Ferrari) in the 1987 Hungarian Grand Prix

north-east of Budapest with a state loan. It was widely praised when the first world championship Hungarian GP was staged there in 1986.

The circuit designer made use of a valley and its generous 'natural' spectator areas, but arguably he incorporated too many bends which are not challenging and slow the circuit. There are 19 corners, a fairly long pits straight and two brief fast sections.

Lap distance: 2.495 miles/4.013 km. Lap record: 98.669 mph/158.794 km/h by Nelson Piquet in a Williams-Honda, 1986.

Hunt, James *1947–*

After a tempestuous early career — during his extraordinarily inconsistent F Ford and F3 days he seemed to accept the 'Hunt the Shunt' label, however much he might later weary of it — James Hunt matured as a forceful driver who thoroughly deserved his 1976 world title. Even that seemed to be resented by some of his detractors.

Hunt started racing a Mini, followed by a Formula Ford Alexis, before graduating to a two-year-old Brabham BT21 F3 car in 1969, then a March, a Lotus, a March, and a Dastle run by 'Bubbles' Horsley for Lord Hesketh.

That led to F2 in 1972, and for the 1973 Race of Champions an F1 Surtees was hired. Hunt was third, and the team's entry into Grand Prix racing with a March 731 followed. Suddenly Hunt was scoring points, and that year ended up with 14, six of them from a fighting second

Honda RA272, 1965

place in the US Grand Prix.

There were Hesketh cars in 1974–75, with a popular albeit shallow following, and Hunt's first Grand Prix victory caused more people to revise their opinions, as he beat Lauda in a straight fight at Zandvoort in 1975. As the main-line Hesketh team folded, James moved on to McLaren for three seasons.

In the first, he won the world championship from Niki Lauda, a title he defended stoutly in 1977, before the team slipped downhill in 1978. The invitation to join Walter Wolf's team in 1979 must have seemed timely, but once there his loathing of the rock-hard ground-effects cars led him to retire after seven races. He soon found a new outlet for his knowledge as a fluent TV commentator.

World championship races: 92 starts, 179 points, 10 wins: 1975 Netherlands; 1976 Spain, France, Germany, Netherlands, Canada, USA; 1977 Britain, USA (East), Japan. **World champion: 1976.**

Above: James Hunt (right) with John Watson during his championship season

Left: James Hunt in a McLaren M23, the outstanding all-round car he drove to win the championship

Honda RA272, 1965

HWM

The initial letters of Hersham and Walton Motors flit across Grand Prix history in the F2 world championship period.

The first HWM, in 1950, had an Alta engine, and that combination entered the GP arena in the F2 years of 1952–53. The engine was not very powerful, producing some 150 bhp in a heavily reworked form with Weslake heads in 1953 and, the chassis was run of the mill. Paul Frère placed an HWM fifth in the Belgian GP in 1952, Collins was sixth in the French GP and there were numerous lesser placings for the marque, but in 1953 Collins' eighth in the Netherlands was its best result.

One of the pair behind HWM, John Heath, was killed in a sports car accident in 1956, and George Abecassis (who had sometimes raced HMWs) gave up the racing side of the company.

Ickx, Jacky 1945–

One of the great sports car drivers – he shared the winning car in the Le Mans 24-hour race six times – Belgian Jacques-Bernard Ickx was a prominent Formula 1 driver in the late 1960s and early 1970s, and runner-up in the 1969 and 1970 championships.

He was 'spotted' by Ken Tyrrell and drove a Matra in Formula 3 and then in Formula 2 as number two to Jackie Stewart, winning the European Championship in 1967. Before he raced an F1 car he started in the F2 category of two German GPs and in 1967 qualified his Matra for the front row of the overall grid.

Late in 1967 he drove a Cooper-Maserati to sixth place in the Italian GP, which led to a Ferrari drive in 1968, and a first GP victory in the French race. In 1969 he had two championship race victories in Brabhams before returning to Ferrari for four years.

His early style mellowed, to the artistry perhaps best seen in his sports-car drives, and he was a consistent points scorer through to 1974. That was the first of his two seasons with Lotus, when he put in the odd memorable drive, especially in the wet, where he was a master. In the next three years he had drives with Williams and Ensign, then in 1979 he took Depailler's place in the Ligier team. Ickx did not like ground-effects cars, but he saw out the season before retiring from F1. He continued in sports cars, became a race administrator, involved in the rejuvenation of Spa and race director at Monaco, and a TV commentator.

World championship races: 16 starts (2 in an F2

class), 181 points, 8 wins: 1968 France; 1969 Germany, Canada; 1970 Austria, Canada, Mexico; 1971 Netherlands; 1972 Germany.*

Imola circuit

Originally built in 1950, this driver's circuit some 20 miles/32 km south-west of Bologna was substantially improved for its first Grand Prix in 1980. That 1980 Grand Prix at Imola was the Italian, but subsequent championship races there have been San Marino Grands Prix.

The Autodromo Dino Ferrari (after Enzo Ferrari's son) is in an attractive wooded setting. It has fast and slow corners, chicanes which have been criticized as they make it a power circuit, a steep plunge and corresponding climb. This variety means that it is demanding, with straights to put a premium on power to complement the corners which test brakes and call for good acceleration. Unlike some autodromes, it allows reasonable scope for overtaking.
Lap distance: 3.132 miles/5.04 km. Lap record: 127.151 mph/204.631 km/h by Nelson Piquet in a Williams, 1986.

Imola
1 Tamburello 2 Rettifilo (Villeneuve)
3 Tosa 4 Piratella
5 Acque Minerali 6 Variante Alfa
7 Rivazza 8 Variante Bassa

Indianapolis speedway

The 'Brickyard' has always looked simple with its four corners and two main straightaways, and in the 1950s the technique was decidedly to run in the groove. But drivers emphasize that all the turns are different, and all had to be driven even in those days when once a car was rolling it was effectively a one-gear track.

Indianapolis 500

The '500' was an oddity on the world championship calendar from 1950 until 1960 and any hopes that this might have brought together the then very different worlds of road and track racing were never fulfilled.

In its world championship decade Indianapolis was the realm of Offenhauser engines – cars with other power units placed in the top ten only three times during the period – and proprietary chassis by makers such as

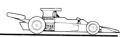

Kurtis, invariably bearing the name of their sponsor allied with 'Special'. Within a little-changing specification (tubular frame, rigid front axle, live rear axle, and so on) these roadsters became quite refined, and seemed admirably suited to their purpose.

Between 1950 and 1960 the 500 winning speeds increased very gradually, from 124.00 mph/199.51 km/h to 138.77 mph/ 223.28 km/h.

Winners (world championship races)

1950	Johnnie Parsons
1951	Lee Wallard
1952	Troy Ruttman
1953	Bill Vukovich
1954	Bill Bukovich
1955	Bob Sweikert
1956	Pat Flaherty
1957	Sam Hanks
1958	Jimmy Bryan
1959	Rodger Ward
1960	Jim Rathmann

Interlagos circuit

This Sao Paulo circuit was the venue for seven Brazilian GPs, losing the race to Jacarepagua and Rio in the 1980s. The circuit dates back to 1940 and the first Grand Prix to 1973.

It was appreciated as a driver's circuit, although the last GP was threatened by a boycott because of the deteriorating track surface. Its designer packed the track into a very small area but with different levels, so that one section seldom seemed to run alongside another. Remarkably few corners were actually slow, only two being hairpins, while there were several very fast curves leading onto straights. It was demanding for machinery as well as drivers.
Lap distance: 4.946 miles/7.96 km. Lap record: 119.568/192.421 km/h by René Arnoux in a Renault, 1980.

International Grand Prix Medical Service

This was the tangible outcome of a laudable effort to improve circuit medical facilities. Louis Stanley, usually associated with BRM's terminal period, put considerable work into bringing it into being in 1967, in effect as a fully-equipped mobile hospital to attend all major races and to be available to local doctors. It did attend many meetings, and perhaps its most useful purpose was in influencing local improvements. It was last reported to be functioning in one of the Middle East fields of conflict.

Ireland, Innes *1930–*

An extrovert driver, Ireland belonged in spirit to an earlier generation, and it was perhaps this factor in his make up that determined he would not enjoy a long run of Grand Prix successes.

Ireland joined Team Lotus in 1959, and was fourth in his first Grand Prix, in the Netherlands. In the same race in 1960 he was second in an 18, and with non-championship race wins as well showed that he could run with leading drivers. In 1961 he won the US Grand Prix, Lotus' first world championship victory, but there was no room for this Scot in Chapman's team in 1962.

He continued in the Grands Prix with independent teams – UDT-Laystall (Lotus), BRP (Lotus and BRM) and in 1965, Parnell (Lotus-BRMs). He retired after two late-1966 races to become a motor racing journalist, then to pursue other ventures before re-emerging as a journalist.
World championship races: 50 starts, 47 points, 1 win: 1961 USA.

Irving, Phil *1903–*

Australian designer, practical engineer and exemplary technical author, Irving was responsible for projects as varied as the classic Vincent big twin motorcycles and the development of Stan Jones' Maybach Special racing car in the late 1940s and 1950s, and with Frank Hallam he designed and supervised development of the Repco engines that powered Brabham cars to two world championships.

Iso-Marlboro

These were Frank Williams' second cars named after sponsors, the erstwhile Politoys FX3B being uprated for 1973 and followed by the John Clarke-designed IR01-IR04, retrospectively redesignated as the first cars in Williams' 'FW' sequence.

Italian Grand Prix

First run in 1921, the second national race for Grand Prix cars after the French event, this race traditionally closed the European season, and it often closed it on a high note. It still has a quality that makes it stand out among races of equal nominal importance, and it shares with the British GP the distinction of having been run in every championship season. All the world championship Italian GPs have been run at Monza, except the 1980 race at Imola, and four were run on the combined banked track and road circuit.

Its great races include Farina's drive in 1951 as he fought the Ferraris to the end, the fuel tank of his Alfa Romeo split and streaming fuel behind it through the closing laps as he drove it into third place.

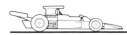

Iso IR, 1973

Above: The first lap of an Italian GP at Monza has often been a spine-tingling minute and a half, but in 1987 the first few hundred metres were remarkably straightforward, except for smoke betraying a moment of fierce braking among the mid-field runners. The two Williams cars lead Berger's Ferrari

Right: Innes Ireland in a Lotus 18 on the inside line, and Jo Bonnier in a BRM at Reims in 1960. Both teams had followed the Cooper lead and turned to rear-engined designs, and in the coming years both were very successful. In this French GP Ireland was seventh, while Bonnier retired

Vanwall won in 1957, when the grid was re-arranged from 3-2-3 to 4-3-4 so that there would be one Italian car on the front row. In 1960 the banked track was used, which led to a British boycott and a last victory for a front-engined Ferrari (and Phil Hill's first GP victory).

Jackie Stewart won his first GP in Italy in 1965 and Ludovico Scarfiotti won his only GP victory in the 1966 race, the last Italian GP win for an Italian driving a Ferrari.

There was a extraordinarily close finish in the 1971 race, when Peter Gethin won at the end of a great slip-streaming battle which had seven different leaders.

Through the early 1980s four teams each scored two victories, while Ferraris were in the top six from 1981.

Winners (world championship GPs)

Year	Driver	Car
1950	G. Farina	Alfa Romeo
1951	A. Ascari	Ferrari
1952	A. Ascari	Ferrari
1953	J.-M. Fangio	Maserati
1954	J.-M. Fangio	Mercedes-Benz
1955	J.-M. Fangio	Mercedes-Benz
1956	S. Moss	Maserati
1957	S. Moss	Vanwall
1958	C. A. S. Brooks	Vanwall
1959	S. Moss	Cooper-Climax
1960	P. Hill	Ferrari
1961	P. Hill	Ferrari
1962	G. Hill	BRM
1963	J. Clark	Lotus-Climax
1964	J. Surtees	Ferrari
1965	J. Stewart	BRM
1966	L. Scarfiotti	Ferrari
1967	J. Surtees	Honda
1968	D. Hulme	McLaren-Ford
1969	J. Stewart	Matra-Ford
1970	G. Regazzoni	Ferrari
1971	P. Gethin	BRM
1972	E. Fittipaldi	Lotus-Ford
1973	R. Peterson	Lotus-Ford
1974	R. Peterson	Lotus-Ford
1975	G. Regazzoni	Ferrari
1976	R. Peterson	March-Ford
1977	M. Andretti	Lotus-Ford
1978	N. Lauda	Brabham-Alfa Romeo
1979	J. Scheckter	Ferrari
1980	N. Piquet	Brabham-Ford
1981	A. Prost	Renault
1982	R. Arnoux	Renault
1983	N. Piquet	Brabham-BMW
1984	N. Lauda	McLaren-TAG
1985	A. Prost	McLaren-TAG
1986	N. Piquet	Williams-Honda
1987	N. Piquet	Williams-Honda

Jackie Ickx was runner up in the world championship with Ferrari in 1970 when he drove the striking 312B, which had its flat-12 engine hung beneath a beam projecting rearwards from the semi-monocoque main chassis

Jabouille, Jean-Pierre *1942–*

Frenchman Jabouille played a central role in Renault's Grand Prix programme, and won Renault's first world championship victory, in the 1979 French Grand Prix. He came to be respected for his self-taught and intuitive engineering skills.

He began racing in saloons in 1966, then

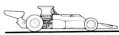

JPS Lotus 72, 1973

spent the rest of the decade in Formula 3. In the early 1970s he raced sports cars and in Formula 2, where in 1976 he won the European championship in an Elf, a car he designed.

Jabouille made his F1 race debut with a Tyrrell in the 1975 French GP, but his F1 career really started when he brought Renault RS01 to the grid at Silverstone in 1977. He did not score his first points until 1978, in the US Grand Prix (East). Jabouille had only one more points-scoring finish after his 1979 French victory when he won the 1980 Austrian GP, and late that year he injured a leg in a Canadian GP crash. He had already committed himself to Ligier for 1981, but after three races he had to retire from Grand Prix racing (although he competed in saloons).

World championship races: 49 starts, 21 points, 2 wins: 1979 France; 1980 Austria.

Jacarepagua circuit

The Autodromo Internacional do Rio de Janeiro was built on reclaimed marshland in the late 1970s and although it has a backdrop of steep-sided hills it is flat. It is the only championship circuit in the tropics, and heat and humidity makes extra demands on drivers.

It has the relief of a long straight, but otherwise features a number of long constant-radius corners. It tends to be bumpy (perhaps a reflection of its foundations?) but facilities are good. It staged its first Brazil GP, previously held at Interlagos in Sao Paulo, in 1978. It was renamed Autodromo Nelson Piquet after his third championship, in 1987.

Lap distance: 3.126 miles/5.031 km. Lap record: 120.305 mph/193.612 km/h by Nelson Piquet in a Williams, 1986.

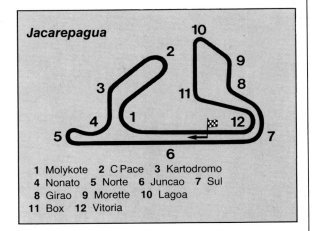

Jacarepagua

1 Molykote 2 C Pace 3 Kartodromo
4 Nonato 5 Norte 6 Juncao 7 Sul
8 Girao 9 Morette 10 Lagoa
11 Box 12 Vitoria

Jano, Vittorio *1891-1965*

An original Italian designer who built a great reputation in the 1920s and 1930s with some outstanding racing and sports cars, Jano was responsible for the Lancia D50 in the world championship period. This was a novel design in which he anticipated later practices by using the engine as a stressed chassis member. Its drivers had to get used to a car that did not carry a changing fuel load in its rear-most extremity, and was rather nervous on the tyres of the mid-1950s. When the D50s were handed over to Ferrari in 1955 Jano continued with them briefly, as a consultant to the Scuderia.

Japanese Grand Prix

The first world championship Japanese GP was the eleventh in a series that started in 1963, when a sports car race at Suzuka was won by Peter Warr, later Lotus team manager, driving a Lotus 23. The next five races were also for sports cars, in 1964 at Suzuka again, and then at Fuji. Then it was run as a Formula 2 race in 1971-75 (the winner in 1972 was John Surtees in one of his TS10s).

In 1976 the Japanese GP was the final round in the world championship, made intensely dramatic as bad weather lashed Fuji. Andretti scored his first GP victory in a Lotus, little noticed as Hunt had to finish third to take the title; he was fifth with three laps to go, third at the end of the last lap.

The Grand Prix was not a world championship event again until 1987, when Berger came out on top in a race at Suzuka that gained general approval.

Venues and winners (world championship GPs)

1976	Fuji	M. Andretti	Lotus-Ford
1977	Fuji	J. Hunt	McLaren-Ford
1987	Suzuka	G. Berger	Ferrari

Jarama circuit

This Spanish autodrome some 17 miles/27 km north of Madrid was first used for the Spanish GP in 1968, then was the alternate circuit to Montjuich until the mid-1970s when it became the event's permanent home until 1981.

A complex of tight corners between the end of the only straight and the fast right curve leading into it made it a slow circuit. Jarama was not popular, although its facilities were acceptable to the GP circus of the 1970s. It is still used for international championship events in other categories.

Lap distance: 2.058 miles/3.312 km. Lap record: 99.627 mph/160.329 km/h by Gilles Villeneuve in a Ferrari, 1979.

JBW

These were specials built by J. B. Naylor and F. Wilkinson on Cooper lines, entered with 2.5-litre Maserati engines in occasional 1959-60

JPS Lotus 72, 1973

GPs when they made no impression in Naylor's hands.

Jerez circuit

This modern Spanish autodrome, completed in 1986, is set within a bowl in the hills. It is virtually flat, and with only one straight where top gear is briefly justified and a succession of generally slow to medium-fast corners it is physically demanding, tailor-made for a driver to block passing attempts.
Lap distance: 2.621 miles/4.28 km. *Lap record:* 108.472 mph/174.566 km/h by Gerhard Berger in a Ferrari, 1987.

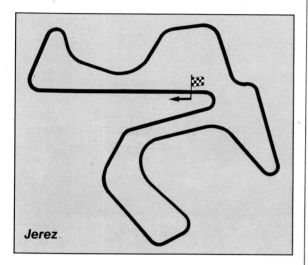

Jerez

Jim Clark Cup

To encourage Grand Prix entries with normal-ly-aspirated engines during a transitional period, the FIA Jim Clark Cup contest for drivers was introduced for 1987. It was clearly won by Tyrrell driver Jonathan Palmer (95 points). The Jim Clark Memorial, for a driver with outstanding all-round qualities, took its place in 1988.

Johansson, Stefan 1956–

This popular Swede has never achieved the results his talents seemed to promise. He raced karts, F Ford and F3, first contesting full seasons in the 1979–80 British championship, winning the title in 1980. He drove for Toleman and Spirit in Formula 2, briefly moved into F1 with the Spirit-Honda in 1983 but for 1984 had no established team, racing sports cars and F2 in Japan until Toleman recruited him to take Cecotto's place late in the summer. He scored his first points in the Italian GP.

A two-year contract with Toleman was waived early in 1985 when Johansson was urgently invited to take Arnoux' place in the Ferrari team. His spirit and flair compensated for the handling inadequacies of the F186, and he had good results. In a less-than-comfortable second year in the team Enzo Ferrari criticized his practice showings but he could tenaciously turn in good race performances.

In 1987 he drove for Ron Dennis, for whom he had once raced in Formula 3, and his good finishing record in McLarens included two second places, but never that elusive first win. In 1988 he joined Ligier.
World championship races (to end of 1987): 58 starts, 82 points.

Jones, Alan 1946–

The 1980 world champion was the son of Stan Jones, a leading Australian driver of the 1950s. He started competing in karts, then raced a Mini and a Cooper before venturing to Europe in 1970, very much to make his own way.

Alan Jones at the start of his comeback season with the ill-starred Beatrice team, still showing the determination that had taken him to the championship in 1980

JPS Lotus 72, 1973

Alan Jones in his championship season, driving the neat and compact Williams FW07 in the 1980 Dutch GP

1972 was his third F3 season, and he moved on to F Atlantic and F5000, where he drove a March 751 with a 3.4-litre Cosworth-developed Ford GA for John MacDonald and saw off the 5-litre runners twice in the second part of the 1975 season. By that time he had tried Formula 1, in four GPs with Harry Stiller's Hesketh 308 (three retirements, one finish) and four times with a Hill GH1, the last of these races, in Germany, also producing two world championship points.

He had regular drives with Team Surtees in 1976, and then succeeded Tom Pryce at Shadow. He won that team's only Grand Prix victory – and his first – in Austria, and moved to Williams for 1978.

That year he showed more than gritty tenacity, and whereas his 1977 Austrian victory was lucky, in 1978 he was unlucky not to win.

Williams had a ground-effects car in 1979, and Jones was strong and brave enough to exploit it fully. He made errors and had accidents, but consistent determination took him to four GP victories in the second half of the season, and third place in the championship. He won five races and the title in 1980. Jones did not like the kart-stiff suspension of the 1980 cars, but he defended his title hard. His teammate Carlos Reutemann did not help, nor did a mid-season change of tyres from Michelin to Goodyear, nor perhaps a season-long exchange

of vituperation with Nelson Piquet. At the season's end he dominated the Caesars Palace Grand Prix, then retired.

But he did not retire completely: he raced sports cars and in 1983 Arrows tempted him into an A6 twice. In 1985 a better-endowed team brought him out of F1 retirement again, and late that year he drove three 'development' races in the Hart-engined Beatrice Lola. That was a prelude to 1986, which proved to be a down-beat season, with only a fourth place in Austria and a sixth in Italy. Jones retired from Grand Prix racing, to continue in sports cars.
*World championship races: 116 starts, 199 points (206 gross), 12 wins: 1977 Austria; 1979 Germany, Austria, Netherlands, Canada; 1980 Argentina, France, Britain, Canada, US (East); 1981 US (West), Las Vegas. **World champion: 1980.***

Judd

Engine Developments was formed in 1970 by Jack Brabham and John Judd, a one-time Coventry Climax apprentice who was later employed by Brabham to work on his Repco engines. Engine Developments then became involved with DFVs, eventually with a DFV development programme for Williams.

In 1982 work started on Honda-based engines for Indycar racing, F3000 and Formula 1. The CV F1 engine, a 3.5-litre V-8 normally-

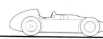

aspirated 600 bhp unit, uses a Honda block and other parts. Fifty were laid down for 1988, customers being March, Ligier and Williams, and the engine first ran circuit tests in a March chassis late in 1987.

Kauhsen

This was an abortive German attempt to break into Formula 1, with the WK (Willibald Kauhsen) ground effects car. Two appeared at two 1978 GP meetings, and failed to qualify. Kauhsen gave up, and some of the team's material was acquired by Merzario.

Klenk-Meteor

This Meteor was a 2-litre Veritas F2 car of 1953, adapted for F1 in 1954 when it made just one appearance in a championship race, Helfrich retiring from the German GP when its engine gave up.

Kojima

Matsuhisa Kojima built cars for Japanese national racing and F1 cars to run in the first world championship Japanese GPs, and when this event lapsed in 1978 the name disappeared from GP racing. One of the designers of the Maki, Masao Ono, was responsible for the Kojima KE007 of 1976, which was a Cosworth kit car with striking black bodywork. Masahino Hasemi placed it eleventh in the Japanese GP. For 1977 a pair of KE009s was built, and in the Japanese GP, Kazuyoshi Hoshino placed one eleventh.

Kurtis

World championship GP racing arrived in the USA in 1959, at Sebring, and the winner of that year's Indianapolis 500, Rodger Ward, elected to pit an Offenhauser-engined Kurtis midget against the European cars. It was outclassed, Ward qualified it last, and it retired after 22 laps of the 42-lap Grand Prix.

Kyalami circuit

Johannesburg has the best spectator catchment area in South Africa and its Kyalami circuit was an obvious venue for the South Africa Grand Prix. The first major single-seater race there was the 1961 Rand GP, won by Jim Clark in a Lotus, and the South African GP was run there from 1967 until it lapsed in 1985. For most of that time Kyalami was the highest circuit used, at 5,000 feet/1,520 metres above sea level.

The start-finish line was on a long undulating straight which ended at the demanding Crowthorne Corner. The track then dropped to a sweeping right, ran on to a flat-out gentle left and then a quick right leading into a slower section climbing from the Esses to Leeukop and the flat-out Kink, which is just a slight bend in the main straight.

Facilities were rated highly through to the early 1980s, when Kyalami fell short of higher international standards, and it was once a popular off-season test circuit. In 1987 part of the site was sold to a developer and work started on a new circuit.
Lap distance: 2.55 miles/4.1 km. *Lap record:* 134.715 mph/216.796 km/h by Keke Rosberg in a Williams, 1985.

Laffite, Jacques *1943–*

In a Formula 1 career that stretched from 1974 to 1986 Laffite drove for only two teams, Williams and Ligier. His early racing followed a conventional pattern – Formule Renault champion in 1972, French Formula 3 champion in 1973, third in the European F2 championship in 1974 and champion in 1975, both years with March-BMWs.

Laffite's initiation into Grand Prix racing was in Germany in 1974 with Frank Williams. He scored his first points in 1975, when he was second in the German GP. He spent the next seven seasons with Ligier; his first GP win was in a Ligier-Matra in Sweden in 1977, and his next two wins were with Ford-engined Ligiers in 1979.

He returned to Williams in 1983–84, when his best placings were two fourths. In 1985–86 he scored 16 and 14 points respectively in Renault-engined Ligiers, and in 1986 he added a second place (in Detroit) and a third (at Rio) to his tally.

At the start of his 176th Grand Prix, the 1986 British, Jacques Laffite was injured in another driver's accident, badly enough to end his Grand Prix career. A fresh race start meant that this French driver's record extends to only 175 Grands Prix, which fails to equal Graham Hill's total by one. That odd statistic had little meaning; the sad loss was of the presence of a laid-back man, who found fun in his sport yet was competitive.
World championship races: 175 starts, 228 points, 6 wins: 1977 Sweden; 1979 Argentina, Brazil; 1980 Germany; 1981 Austria, Canada.

An early test for the fascinating Lancia D50. The angled mounting of the engine can be seen and the outrigged sponsons containing the fuel tanks are obvious. A neat box of plugs for the now-forgotten ritual of changing from warm-up plugs sits ahead of the aero screen. Everybody, including driver Ascari, is wearing a tie – after all, the burly chap in the background is the boss, Gianni Lancia

Lamborghini

For more than a quarter of a century speculation that Italian supercar manufacturer Lamborghini would enter motor racing was no more than speculation. However, in 1987, following the Chrysler take over, a Lamborghini Grand Prix engine programme was initiated under ex-Ferrari designer Mauro Forghieri. March, Lola and Scuderia Italia committed to development programmes with this light and compact 80-degree V-12.

Lancia

Gianni Lancia took the company founded by his father in 1906 into a programme of Grand Prix racing for the opening seasons of the 2.5-litre formula in 1954. Vittorio Jano's design for the Lancia D50 F1 car was advanced by contemporary standards, when it appeared late in 1954. Its 90-degree V-8 (73.6 × 73.1 mm, 2489 cc) initially produced 260 bhp and it was used as a stressed member in the tubular frame.

The D50 was distinguished by outrigged panniers on each side, containing the fuel tanks. As well as improving the airflow between the wheels Jano aimed to keep weight distribution constant as fuel was used.

Ascari won two second-level races with D50s early in 1955, and was leading at Monaco before crashing into its famous harbour, the first racing driver to do so.

At the time, Lancia company fortunes were also crashing, mainly because of heavy expenditure on racing programmes. Fiat took over, and the Lancia Grand Prix team – its cars and all its equipment – was transferred to Ferrari, whose cars were then woefully uncompetitive.

The D50s slowly lost their individuality, for example as the engines were improved but lost their stress-bearing role and the panniers were merged into the bodies as conventional tail fuel tanks were used. As Ferraris, the cars won Grands Prix in 1956.

Lang, Hermann 1909–87

An ace German member of the Mercedes-Benz GP team in the late 1930s, Lang placed a Maserati fifth in the 1953 Swiss GP and as a

Lancia D50, 1955

Left: Niki Lauda

guest driver in a Mercedes W196 ran as high as second in the 1954 German GP before retiring. *World championship races: 2 starts, 2 points.*

Las Vegas circuit

Two Caesars Palace Grands Prix were run on this circuit, contrived, its critics emphasized, on a car park. Between the 3-foot/metre high barriers of interlocking portable concrete sections a sinuous track was built, with a series of tight turns, most to the left on this anti-clockwise circuit, and a 600-yard/550-metre straight. It was not as slow as pundits had predicted.
Lap distance: 2.26 miles/3.63 km. **Lap record:** *102.525 mph/164.994 km/h by Michele Alboreto in a Tyrrell, 1982.*

Lauda, Niki *1949–*

The most self-sufficient of all drivers, Niki Lauda took over from Jackie Stewart as the pace-setter, failing to gain the same hold with a public image until his quite extraordinary return to racing after a horrifying accident at the Nürburgring in 1976.

Below: Lauda forcing a 312T on during his fourth and last season with Ferrari, in 1977 when he was no longer quite at one with the team but gave of his best and was rewarded with his second world title

Niki Lauda in a
Brabham-Alfa BT46 in
1978

Opposite top: The
Ligier JS9 of 1978 was
a handsome and
substantial car, robust
and reliable but not a
winner in a season
dominated by ground
effects cars

Opposite bottom: The
Ligier JS31 of 1988
which Stefan
Johansson placed
ninth in its debut race,
in Brazil. The JS31 was
as original as its
predecessor had been
stolidly conventional.
Designer Tétu placed a
fuel tank ahead of the
Judd engine, and
another behind it, and
also offered drivers
power steering

Lauda competed in local Austrian events in a
VW and a Porsche, raced in Formula Vee in
1969, in an F3 McNamara in 1970 and raced a
Porsche in sports car events. He found backing
for F2 drives with March cars in 1971, and
hired a March for his first drive. He took the
same route in 1972, and in 1973 joined BRM,
scoring his first world championship point
when he was fifth in the Belgian GP.

That season led to a 1974 Ferrari contract.
That year he won his first Grand Prix, in Spain,
won again in the Netherlands and made errors
elsewhere. There were few errors in 1975,
when he won the championship. He defended
the title with determination in 1976, a season
of high drama, of protests and appeals, of that
fiery accident in Germany that came so near to
claiming his life. He fought back – his return to
racing within two months in the Italian GP was
astounding – but surrendered the title to James
Hunt when he dispassionately weighed up the
risks of racing hard in a saturated Japanese GP
and decided that life was more important. In

any case, he regained the championship in
1977, his last Ferrari year.

Lauda moved into a very different team in
1978, when he drove Brabham-Alfas, and a
second year with it proved most unrewarding.
He had other preoccupations, so made a very
brief acquaintance with the new Cosworth-
powered Brabham during practice for the
Canadian GP, then precipitately retired. He left
racing to concentrate on Lauda Air, but in the
early 1980s the airline business was in financial
difficulties and he had tax problems.

In 1981 Ron Dennis persuaded Lauda to join
the impressive new McLaren team, to a sporting comeback that succeeded. Lauda won with
the Cosworth-engined McLarens in 1982 and
with the TAG-powered cars in 1984, the year of
his third world championship. He retired at the
end of a disappointing 1985 season, when he
won only the Dutch GP. He led his last race, but
slithered haplessly out of that Australian Grand
Prix.

*World championship races: 171 starts, 420½
points, 25 wins: 1974 Spain, Netherlands; 1975
Monaco, Belgium, Sweden, France, USA; 1976
Brazil, South Africa, Belgium, Monaco, Britain;
1977 South Africa, Germany, Netherlands; 1978
Sweden, Italy; 1982 USA (West), Britain; 1984
South Africa, France, Britain, Austria, Italy; 1985
Netherlands. World champion: 1975, 1977, 1984.*

Lancia D50, 1955

LDS

L. D. Serrurier built single seaters for South African national racing, and two Alfa Romeo-engined cars ran in the 1962–63 South African GPs, Serrurier placing one eleventh in the 1963 race.

Lec

The name of the Bognor-based refrigeration company was carried into GP racing by this neat low-budget Cosworth-powered car designed by Mike Pilbeam. It was built for David Purley, son of Lec's owner, who drove it to finish in two 1977 GPs, then crashed with exceptional violence in the British GP practice.

Le Mans Bugatti circuit

The first of all French Grands Prix was run over an immense 64.12-mile/103.18 km circuit to the east of Le Mans in 1906; the 1967 race was run on an inadequate track which used the pits straight and a bend from the circuit so well-known for the 24-hour race, plus a linking stretch with undemanding constant-radius bends. Jack Brabham won that 1967 GP in one of his own cars.
Lap distance: 2.65 miles/4.26 km. Lap record: 102.29 mph/164.624 km/h by Graham Hill in a Lotus, 1967.

Ligier

Guy Ligier is a self-made millionaire in the heavy construction industry, a one-time French rugby international who also contested a dozen Grands Prix, most of them in a bulky Cooper-Maserati, and scored a championship point in the 1967 German Grand Prix. He stepped down to Formula 2 in 1968, then retired from active racing when his friend and business partner Jo Schlesser was killed (Ligier cars were later to have a 'JS' designation for Schlesser).

In the late 1960s Ligier embarked on a sports car programme, with a GT car and in 1971 the JS2 and JS3 sports-racing cars, both designed by Michel Tétu. In 1975 the Ligier team, managed by former Matra designer cum team manager Gérard Ducarouge, was second in the Le Mans 24-hour race. Its principal sponsor SEITA, the Gitanes cigarettes firm, was keen to move into Formula 1, and that became feasible as Gitanes had also backed the Matra programme, defunct but with a legacy that included a V-12 engine.

The JS5 F1 car which made its race debut in the 1976 Brazilian GP echoed Matras. Once its enormous engine air box had disappeared it had handsome sweeping lines, and it enabled the one-car Ligier team to find its feet.

Jacques Laffite continued as the sole driver. In 1977–78 the JS7 was a winner. Laffite drove it to victory in the Swedish Grand Prix but it was increasingly outclassed in 1978, as Matra engine development slowed, and the JS9 offered no great advances. So the JS11 ground-effects car was designed for Cosworth DFV power. It was another immensely strong car using the engine as a stressed member, and with wide side pods to maximize ground-effects airflow. It was instantly competitive: Laffite won the first two GPs of 1979 in it and team-mate Patrick Depailler won the Spanish GP.

In 1980 the team had revised JS11s and the JS15; Laffite and Pironi each won a race, and Ligier was second to Williams on the constructors' championship.

Ligier brought Talbot into the Grands Prix in 1981 which meant that the DFV engine, with its Ford associations, had to go. A Matra V-12 **was** used, nominally as a stand-in power unit until a Talbot turbo engine was developed. The old V-12 revised to produce more than 500 bhp at 12,500 rpm (later a little more at 13,000 rpm) powered the JS17. Ligier was flat-footed by Brabham's hydro-pneumatic suspension system, but later in the year caught up and Laffite won two championship races.

JS17s and the less handsome JS19 carried on with Matra V-12s in 1981, still with Talbot prominently displayed. Ducarouge had left, and the JS19 was set back when its rearward bodywork (reckoned to contribute 30 per cent of the downforce) was declared illegal.

There was more bodywork trouble in 1982, and the team slumped. The Talbot connection ended with the year, and Ligier went back to the DFV engine. Initially this was used in adapted JS19s, then in JS21s, driven by Boesel and Jarier, neither of the calibre of Ligier's earlier drivers; no points were scored in 1983.

In 1984 Ligier was distracted by an Indycar project, when the team might have applied more effort to developing their JS23. This was powered by the Renault turbo engine, but it did not live up to its promise and de Cesaris and Hesnault were let down too often.

Then Gérard Larrousse was dismissed by Renault and joined Ligier, bringing Michel Tétu back with him in time to have some influence on the JS25 design, and develop it in 1985. Laffite also returned and scored reliably; his team-mates were the unpredictable de Cesaris, replaced for the last few races by Streiff.

Ligier had three new JS27s ready for the opening of the 1986 season, still with Renault engines, thanks to French government subsidy. Laffite and Arnoux scored well from the first race, but then there was a setback as Laffite crashed heavily at Brands Hatch. Alliot took his place while Arnoux' results became patchy.

That was the pattern for 1987, as Ligier slumped again. The team started the year with Alfa Romeo turbo engines, but the Italian company backed out of its contract following ill-judged criticism by Arnoux. The JS29s were hastily adapted as JS29Cs to accept the Megatron S4 (née BMW) four-cylinder engines, and the Ligier team was out of contention again.

Early 1988 saw the innovative – almost idiosyncratic – JS31, powered by the Judd V-8, which designer Michel Tétu mounted amidships with one fuel tank low down ahead of it and a second tank between the engine and the gearbox. It was a very low car, with the unusual option of power steering. Development posed problems.

Constructors' championship: *1976 5th; 1977 8th; 1978 4th; 1979 3rd; 1980 2nd; 1981 4th; 1982 8th; 1985 6th; 1986 5th.*

Lola

In the late 1950s the development of Lola and Lotus seemed parallel; Eric Broadley and Colin Chapman both started building competitions cars for their own use in British racing and both progressed to racing much more sophisticated cars. Chapman was the first of the two very original designers to go into Formula 1 and he was dedicated to it, whereas Broadley followed the more commercial path of building cars for customers, so Lola's F1 history is spasmodic.

The first F1 Lola was the Mk 4 in 1962, built for the short-lived Bowmaker team and also run by Parnell in 1963. It was a Climax-engined space-frame design, initially with four-cylinder engines, later with V-8s. In 1962 John Surtees drove it to victory in a non-championship race and scored 19 points in Grands Prix.

The next F1 cars, the T130 in 1967 and the T180 in 1968, were developed for Honda engines at Surtees' instigation. F1 work lapsed again until 1973–74, when the T370 was developed from an F5000 design for Graham Hill's team. It was a big Cosworth-engined car, very conspicuous with its wide track and high airbox, but never very successful.

The Beatrice Lola-Hart THL-1 which ran in three races late in 1985 was a state-of-the-art F1 design by Neil Oatley and John Baldwin, utilizing a carbon-fibre monocoque, and actually built away from the Lola plant by FORCE. When the THL-2 was ready in 1986 the customer deal had fallen apart, and the cars were run until the end of the year as Haas-Lolas.

For 1987 Ralph Bellamy designed the LC87 for the little Larrousse/Calmels team to run in the normally-aspirated category. It was a compact, clean car which served the team well, and led to the Lola liaison being extended through 1988 with the LC88.

Constructors' championship: 1962 4th; 1986 8th; 1987 9th.

Lombardi, Lella *1943–*

Lella Lombardi has the distinction of being the first and only woman to score in the world championship, in the shortened 1975 Spanish GP. That was in her only full season, when with a March she showed as much ability as other back-of-the-grid drivers in the same year. After a couple of races in 1976 the Italian slipped out of the Grand Prix circus, back to sports car and touring car racing.

World championship races: 12 starts, ½ point.

Long Beach circuit

The concept of this track was enterprising, and significant for racing as it showed how a circuit could be created in an urban area and meet the modern requirements for spectacle and safety. Local travel agent and racing enthusiast Chris Pook persuaded the local authorities to endorse his proposals for a circuit. This was contrived with concrete barriers, fences, sand-filled oil drums to retain barriers, old tyres to absorb the energy of errant cars, and some modifications to existing roads (these remained bumpy or rough in places).

The lap started on a short straight, with three right-angle turns soon after the start, a left bend into a reverse direction hairpin, then the long curve-straight-curve of Shoreline Drive. This

The first Grand Prix Lola, the Coventry Climax-engined space-framed car of 1962, driven by John Surtees

Above: The Lola LC87 was neat and conventional, an ideal car for the new Larrousse-Camels team to find its feet in 1987

Below: The Lotus 72 was another of Chapman's outstanding innovative cars, handsome in the original Gold Leaf or later JPS colours. This 72 is driven by Emerson Fittipaldi in his first full GP season, 1971

ended in another hairpin, and then a series of corners linked by short straights led back to the start-finish line.

A successful F5000 'test race' in 1975, won by Brian Redman in a Lola T332, was followed by eight world championship Grands Prix but eventually the financial demands of a world championship GP became too great and after 1983 a CART race took its place.

Lap distance: 2.02 miles/3.251 km. Lap record: 91.094 mph/146.328 km/h by Nelson Piquet in a Brabham, 1980.

Lotus

Lotus is the only team to approach Ferrari's record of race victories and the Italian marque has been active since 1950, whereas Lotus entered the GP field – hesitantly – eight years later. Lotus' periods of successes and failures tended to coincide with Colin Chapman's innovations being outstandingly successful, or flops.

Lotus was born in a boom period for road racing in Britain, and the 12 was its first single-seater, intended for Formula 2 but run in F1 guise with 1,960 cc or 2,208 cc Coventry Climax FPF engines, and first raced in a GP at Monaco in 1958. Chapman's first Grand Prix Lotus as such, the 1958 16, again had its Coventry Climax engine mounted ahead of the driver.

The rear-engined 18 arrived in 1960 and the more important 21 in 1961. That year Rob Walker's independent 18 was driven to two championship victories by Stirling Moss, while Innes Ireland scored the first victory for a Team Lotus car, with a 21 in the USA. These were space frame designs and were followed in 1962 by the sleek 24. This had a low frontal area, achieved by seating the driver in a semi-reclining position and the new Coventry Climax FWMV V-8, and it seemed to promise development potential. But to the chagrin of independent entrants who chose to run it, Chapman made it obsolete within months of its first race.

At the 1962 Dutch Grand Prix Jim Clark drove the Lotus 25 in its debut race, finishing ninth, and a month later he won the Belgian GP in a 25. This handsome little car shared the lines of the 24, but instead of a space frame it was built around a monocoque, and it introduced a new era in racing car construction. The basis of the 25's monocoque was the pair of side pontoons, linked by the floor and bulkheads. This stiff structure meant that softer suspension could be used with attendant road-holding

Lancia D50, 1955

Left: The Lotus 78 was the first full ground effects car, in 1977.

The monocoque was very slim, its side pods broad and flat-topped. Angled water radiators at the front of the pods on each side exhausted air at the top (the nose radiator was the oil cooler). There was a fuel tank behind each water radiator, with the main tank on the centre line.

The underside of each side pod between front and rear wheels swept up towards the back, to form the 'inverted aerofoil' vital to ground effects.

Below: Lotus cars wore new colours in 1987, used Honda engines, and from the first race in Brazil the 99Ts ran with a sophisticated active suspension system (here driven by Senna)

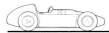

Right: Graham Hill giving the Lotus 16 its Grand Prix debut, at Reims in 1958. The 12 was the first Lotus to run in Grands Prix, but the 16 'mini-Vanwall' was a much more sophisticated car, packaging the essential components (including the driver!) as tightly as possible with a front-engined layout

Below: Jim Clark in a Lotus 33 on his way to his third consecutive Dutch GP victory, heading Graham Hill in a BRM in 1965. The 33 was to all intents and purposes a derivative of the landmark 25

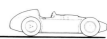

advantages, and higher cornering speeds. The 25 and its 1964 successor, the 33, made Lotus the most significant marque of the 1.5-litre formula years.

The team started the period of the next formula with 'stretched' Climax engines in 33s, or the weighty and complex BRM H-16 engine in the 43 – Lotus took the only championship race won with this power unit, at Watkins Glen in 1966. These were interim cars, for Lotus was about to move into another golden period, with the 49 and the DFV engine.

Chapman had brought Keith Duckworth of Cosworth and Walter Hayes of Ford together, to discuss his need for a Grand Prix engine. Remarkably quickly, and for a remarkably small investment, Ford backed the design and development of the DFV engine, exclusive to Lotus for its first season.

The DFV-powered Lotus 49 was an integrated design, with the cross-section of its monocoque determined by the dimensions of the compact V-8. That was bolted directly to the rear bulkhead, and served as a load-bearing chassis member, with the gearbox and rear suspension attached to it. The overall car was elegant, and its design timeless. Most of the changes during its four years in the front line were superficial.

A replacement for the 49 was needed as the 1960s ended. In common with other constructors, Lotus essayed a four-wheel drive car (the 63) and in 1971 ran an F1 version of the Indianapolis gas-turbine-powered 56, the 56B. However, the main-line successor to the 49 was the 72. Chapman sought an advantage as most other teams used DFV engines, and came up with this sophisticated version of his 'wedge' theme. The car had torsion bar suspension, with inboard brakes – suspension loads were light, and ride was soft and the wheels were isolated from heat generated by the brakes, so very soft compound tyres with better grip could be used. The suspension was modified several times (importantly, to suit a change to Goodyear tyres from Firestones) and aerodynamic appendages were altered during the five years the 72 served. This was at least a season beyond its time as the 76 failed.

In 1976 the 77 was used to try combinations of track, wheelbase and suspension elements, in some of which it led to the 78. This gave Team Lotus drivers an enormous advantage, for it was the first ground-effects car in single-seater racing. Refined as the 79 in 1978, it became a quite outstanding car, in appearance, performance and achievement: Andretti and Peterson drove 79s to eight wins that year.

The Lotus 80 was intended to take ground effects aerodynamics a stage further, but instead it introduced the term 'porpoise' to racing, to describe the behaviour induced by its

aerodynamics. The faults seemed beyond correction, and an answer was sought in the 86, the 'dual-chassis' car, which was never allowed to race by the authorities. The 87 was another stopgap in 1981, and the 87B in 1982. The true successor was the 91, a straightforward derivative of the 87. Elio de Angelis drove one to Lotus' first Grand Prix victory since 1978 when he won the 1982 Austrian race. It was Lotus' 72nd Grand Prix win and 48th victory of the 3-litre Formula. Colin Chapman died during the following winter.

Team Lotus continued, Peter Warr running it as it had been for more than a decade as a Formula 1 constructor – apart from an Indycar that was never raced, other activities had been

Lotus 100T shows the 'needle-nose' approach adopted by most designers in 1988, when a new safety regulation required drivers' feet to be behind the centre line of the front wheels. In its first races the 100T was disappointingly 'off the pace'

Lancia D50, 1955

set aside. The Renault turbo-engined 93T turned out to be a cumbersome car and never looked a winner. Gérard Decarouge joined the team in the early summer of 1983 and for the British GP in mid-July the competitive 94T had been designed and built. For 1985 Ayrton Senna drove Lotus, and Team cars won again.

Long-standing sponsorship by Players, which had been broken only occasionally since 1968, finally ended in 1986, and in the following year the Lotus 99Ts were running in bright Camel colours. Moreover, the cars ran throughout the season with 'active' suspension, a system developed by Lotus Engineering and tested before Chapman died. This was not perfect − there were just too many variables − but Senna drove an 'active' car to win two Grands Prix. At a little cost in power − maybe 10 bhp − and 20 kg in weight, the system gave optimum ride height, and therefore handling, throughout a race, as the fuel load changed. Although the team abandoned the system for 1988, it was appropriate that Lotus should have been in the technical forefront again − Chapman would have approved.

The sleek needle-nosed 100T for 1988 appeared with 'passive' suspension while a simplified active-ride system was developed.

Constructors' championship: 1958 6th; 1959 4th; 1960 2nd; 1961 2nd; 1962 2nd; 1963 1st; 1964 3rd; 1965 1st; 1966 5th; 1967 2nd; 1968 1st; 1969 3rd; 1970 1st; 1971 5th; 1972 1st; 1973 1st; 1974 4th; 1975 7th; 1976 4th; 1977 2nd; 1978 1st; 1979 4th; 1980 5th; 1981 7th; 1982 6th; 1983 7th; 1984 3rd; 1985 3rd; 1986 3rd; 1987 3rd.

Lyncar

Martin Slater built four F Atlantic cars and a Cosworth-engined hill-climb car before undertaking an F1 car for McLaren's DFV engine builder John Nicholson.

The F1 Lyncar was a neat little narrow track machine, with a Cosworth DFV engine and Hewland gearbox. Its only GP start was in the 1975 British race, where Nicholson placed it 17th. He then abandoned car racing, while the Lyncar was run in a British national series.

Mader

Henri Mader Racing Components is a Swiss engine development and preparation company which took on the 'upright' BMW engines (as Megatrons) and as normally-aspirated engines came back in 1987 also handled Cosworth engines for three lesser teams.

McLaren, Bruce *1937–70*

This stocky New Zealander was the youngest driver ever to win a world championship race, the 1959 US Grand Prix when he was 22, and he also established the highly successful team that still bears his name.

His entry to motor sport was through building and competing with an Austin-based special. In 1956 and 1957 he ran ex-Brabham Coopers, and won the first New Zealand Driver to Europe award, for 1958.

That year he started in Formula 2 and in his first race on mainland Europe he won the F2

division of the German GP. That led to a Cooper F1 drive through 1959, and at the end of that season to his first GP victory.

He continued as number two to Brabham, and took Jack's place when the Australian left to form his own team. During that period McLaren's only championship victory was at Monaco in 1962. In the following year he formed Bruce McLaren Motor Racing to campaign Coopers in the Tasman series, and then moved towards becoming a constructor with the Zerex Special sports-racing car.

McLaren left Cooper to drive his first sports and F1 cars. These were beset by engine prob-lems, but he persevered and in the 1968 Belgian GP drove a McLaren to victory. In June 1970 he was running a CanAm car through routine tests at Goodwood when he crashed and was killed.

World championship races: *101 starts, (2 in F2 categories), 198½ points (190½ net), 4 wins: 1959 USA; 1960 Argentina; 1962 Monaco; 1968 Belgium.*

McLaren

Bruce McLaren brought his team into Grand Prix racing in 1966 and fittingly he scored its

Bruce McLaren in his M2B at Monaco. The M2B was an adventurous design with a racing career that was anything but distinguished. Its novel Mallite construction was not at fault, but its linered-down Ford Indy V-8 produced inadequate power. The M2A, incidentally, was a single-seat test vehicle, used for early aerofoil experiments by Robin Herd

Mercedes-Benz W.196, 1955

Bruce McLaren cranking his M7A through Druids hairpin at Brands Hatch during the 1968 British GP, when his choice of rain tyres proved to be a mistake

Herd designed the workmanlike M7A, then he left and the cars were built under the supervision of Gordon Coppuck. The M7A won first time out, in the non-championship Race of Champions, Bruce won the Belgian Grand Prix and his team-mate Denny Hulme won the Italian and Canadian races. The cars were still used by the team in 1969, when there was only one victory, by Hulme in Mexico. A distraction that year was a four-wheel car, the M9A designed by Jo Marquart; it was raced once, Derek Bell failing to finish in the British GP.

The next main-line F1 car was the M14, an evolutionary car that was not a winner, competent though it was, while the M14D which had an Alfa Romeo V-8 made little impression. Ralph Bellamy designed the M19, which outwardly combined 'Coke-bottle' flanks with a flat-topped nose, and had troublesome rising-rate suspension. It was never an outstanding car, but was a fairly reliable points-scoring machine which served on to 1973.

It was followed by one of the great McLarens, the M23. In this Coppuck followed his Indianapolis car wedge theme, using the suspension from the M19. The engine was of course the Cosworth DFV, and the gearbox a Hewland FG400. Its monocoque was integral with the side pods, an unusual arrangement to increase impact protection, and the cockpit was narrow, as the surround rising from the flat-topped hull showed. It was a handsome car, in the colours of Yardley or Marlboro, which largely supplanted Yardley in 1974 (that year the cars were raced in both colours) and remains McLaren's main backer to this day.

The M23 was a front-line car for four seasons. Emerson Fittipaldi drove it to win the drivers' title in 1974 and to be runner-up in the 1975 championship. In the highly dramatic 1976 season McLaren's new recruit James Hunt snatched the drivers' title from Niki Lauda in the final race. The works team ran M23s in 1977 while the M26 was developed. M23s were also run for a Canadian driver, Villeneuve, who made quite an impression at Silverstone, and for F2 ace Bruno Giacomelli in the Italian GP as well as by independents. In 1978 a young Brazilian F3 star, Nelson Piquet, drove his second GP in an M23, had two more drives in it, and placed it ninth in the Italian GP. That ended the remarkable career of the McLaren M23.

Its 1976 successor, the M26, was another Coppuck design, with a honeycomb chassis but otherwise a straightforward evolutionary car. Nevertheless, its development took time, as handling shortcomings had to be ironed out. Hunt won three GPs with the M26 in 1977, and it was brought out again in 1978, when it was outclassed by ground-effects cars.

The bulky M28, the M29, the M29C in 1980

first world championship victory, in the Belgian GP two years later. The first F1 McLaren was the 1966 M2B designed by Robin Herd. This had a novel stressed skin hull formed of a 'sandwich' material of two sheets of aluminium bonded to balsa wood, which was light and bulky but exceptionally rigid. Two unsatisfactory engines were replaced by the BRM V-8, in an adapted F2 M4B which McLaren placed fourth at Monaco in 1967. Late that year the BRM V-12 became available and powered the M5A, which was a conventional light-alloy monocoque car. In its first races this was competitive but the V-12 obviously did not match the new Ford-Cosworth V-8, so as that engine became available for 1968 McLaren became a customer.

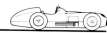

Yardley Mac, in this case an M19C driven by Denny Hulme in the 1972 French GP, shows off its Coke-bottle lines

and the M30 saw McLaren in decline. The company had changed considerably. In the 1970s it had built highly successful series of CanAm and USAC cars at the modest Colnbrook plant, but at the end of that decade McLaren, like other constructors, abandoned distractions from the Grand Prix programme.

Teddy Mayer agreed to a merger with Ron Dennis' successful Project Four Formula 2 team late in 1980 – a shotgun marriage, really, with Marlboro fingers on triggers! Coppuck left, opening the way for John Barnard to become chief engineer. Very soon manager Teddy Mayer left too. Barnard had joined Project Four from Chaparral, encouraged by the knowledge that Dennis intended to enter Formula 1. He designed the MP4, a magnificent car. It was the

first car to use carbon-fibre monocoque construction, which made for a very stiff chassis, even for the very slim monocoques required in ground-effects cars, and one that was crash-resistant (in 1981 the team had the ideal driver to field-test that quality, Andrea de Cesaris). The first moulded monocoques were produced for McLaren by the US Hercules Corporation, and were costly (at $150,000).

The rest of the MP4 was conventional, with Cosworth engine and Hewland gearbox. John Watson drove one to win the 1981 British GP, the first championship victory for McLaren since 1977. In 1982 he was joined by Niki Lauda; both drivers won two GPs in slightly revised MP4s.

For 1983 the design had to be revised in 'flat-

The first DFV-engined McLaren, the M7 of 1968, running with a little out-rigged fuel tank between the wheels that was reminiscent of the Lancia D50, apparently to balance handling. The M7B had side tanks integral with the main hull, with the same objective. In 1968 the M7s won three Grands Prix. Before McLaren became a sponsored team the cars were run in orange livery

bottom' form to meet the new regulations, and while another fundamental change was developed to raceworthiness these MP4/1Cs served until the summer, the last race for the Cosworth-powered cars being at Zandvoort.

Dennis and Barnard could have bought in a turbo engine, but wanted exclusivity. They eventually commissioned a turbo V-6 from Porsche with financial backing from Techniques d'Avant Garde (TAG). Porsche sometimes found Barnard's requirements hard to accept and there were problems with a major component supplier, Bosch. But in the summer of 1983 the McLaren-TAG was raced, in an interim form.

As such it gave little indication of its potential. The MP4/2 was ready for the opening race of 1984, when Prost drove it to a first victory. That season the French driver won six more races, while Lauda won five and with a better finishing record took the drivers' title.

Revised for 1985, the car had the cumbersome title 'Marlboro-McLaren MP4/2B TAG Turbo'. Interestingly McLaren was to publish a fuel consumption figure for it (67.5 litres/100 km, or 4.2 mpg). There were problems with brakes, but seemingly remarkably few resulting from the change from Michelin to Goodyear tyres.

For 1986 there seemed to be little change, and most of the work on the MP4/2Cs was in the late-1980s essentials such as overhauling the electronic engine management system. But there were fuel consumption problems for part of the season, drivers Prost and Rosberg had

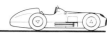

Left: The Marlboro-McLaren MP4 was a quite remarkable car, a total design with no afterthoughts visible in either of its first guises, with Cosworth DFV engines in the back in 1981 and from the summer of 1983 onwards with TAG turbo engines

Below: The brand-new MP4/4 on its way to a debut victory in Brazil in 1988, in the hands of Alain Prost – an outstanding achievement as the Honda engine was new to the team and there had been little time for shake-down running. The entrant was Honda Marlboro McLaren, hinting at a changed order of McLaren allegiances, as well as the very large budget behind this team

very different styles and requirements, and during the season Barnard left, for Ferrari. Nevertheless, Prost was supreme, clinching the championship in the final race of the year.

In the 1986–87 off season Porsche and Bosch worked to improve the fuel consumption and power output of the V-6, although through 1987 its development was to lag. Steve Nichols laid out the MP4/3, in which the first fundamental redesign since 1984 aimed at producing more downforce, and Gordon Murray joined on the design side.

Prost as ever was superbly professional, and although the McLarens were generally outrun by Honda-engined cars he won three Grands Prix; his team-mate for the year, Stefan Johansson, was perhaps unlucky not to score his first victory. He then had to make way for another driver, in part due to the replacement of the TAG engine with the Honda turbo V-6 for 1988, when the team drivers were Prost and Senna. By the end of 1987 the MP4s had won 31 Grands Prix, 25 with TAG engines, and the Barnard design that had revived McLaren had served for a remarkably long span.

The team – now Honda Marlboro McLaren – maintained its success rate as the 1988 season opened and the brand-new and little-tested MP4/4 was driven to a first-race victory by Prost; later he drove one to score McLaren's 50th Grand Prix victory, at Monaco.

Constructors' championship: 1966 7th; 1967 8th; 1968 2nd; 1969 4th; 1970 4th; 1971 6th; 1972 3rd; 1973 3rd; 1974 1st; 1975 3rd; 1976 2nd; 1977 3rd; 1978 8th; 1979 7th; 1980 7th; 1981 6th; 1982 2nd; 1983 5th; 1984 1st; 1985 1st; 1986 2nd; 1987 2nd.

Maki

This attempt to break into Formula 1 with a Japanese 'Cosworth kit car' seemed misguided from its debut in the 1974 British GP to its quiet demise in 1975. Designers Mimura and Ono laid out the F101 around an aluminium alloy monocoque and conventional suspension, although the execution gave rise to pit-lane misgivings.

Howden Ganley failed to qualify the F101 for the 1974 British GP, and was injured when 'something broke' and it crashed heavily in practice for the German GP. Neither Fuchida nor Trimmer could qualify the F101-02 to start in a championship race in 1975 (although Trimmer did place it 13th in the non-championship Swiss GP) and the promised 1976 successor and the Maki engine failed to materialize.

Mansell, Nigel 1954–

Determination is Mansell's outstanding quality: it has kept him in racing when lesser men would have given up and made him habitually drive flat out when the few drivers who have an infinitesimal extra degree of talent might just ease off. And it has brought him success, not the championship yet, but a rare six Grands Prix wins in a single season in 1987.

After success in F Ford in 1976–77 Mansell struggled through a first F3 season, and continued in F3 until 1981. That year he had a Lotus test contract which included three GP drives, first in Austria, when he suffered petrol burns as fuel slopped about his Lotus 81B cockpit.

In 1982 he was number two in the Lotus team, and scored his first points with a third place in the Belgian GP. He remained with Lotus until the end of 1984, although after Colin Chapman's death he became increasingly demoralized.

He joined Williams in 1985, and towards the end of that year made the great breakthrough when he won the European Grand Prix at Brands Hatch, and then won the South African race. Beating his seemingly more talented team-mate Nelson Piquet strained relationships. Mansell flirted with Ferrari, and paid a price.

He was a fast and strong driver in 1986–87, when he drove the supreme Williams-Honda to five and six Grand Prix victories. Yet he was a disappointed and disgruntled driver, as his championship chances evaporated after he had slammed into a Japanese tyre wall during practice for the penultimate 1987 Grand Prix.

World championship races (to end of 1987): 104 starts, 200 points, 13 wins: 1985 Europe, South Africa; 1986 Belgium, Canada, France, Britain, Portugal; 1987 San Marino, France, Britain, Austria, Spain, Mexico.

March

March was set up in 1969 to build cars for the established formulas by a British quartet whose initials form the company name – Max Mosley, Alan Rees, Graham Croaker and Robin Herd. Of these, only Herd remained with the company in the 1980s, when it had become the world's largest racing car producer, with well over 1,000 cars sold, and was the first racing car manufacturer to go public, in 1987.

The first March was a Formula 3 car, the 693. A Grand Prix car design was set in train for 1970, and it came at a most opportune time: Ken Tyrrell needed a chassis, STP backed a works team and another car for Andretti, and Colin Crabbe ran a car for Peterson. That amounted to an order book, and the 701 had to be a simple Cosworth-engined car, if it was to be designed, built and proved. It was utterly conventional, and it was heavy, but interestingly it had inverted aerofoil side pods alongside the 'bath tub' monocoque. The whole thing

Nigel Mansell early in 1988 — before he cleaned his upper lip!

became credible when Jackie Stewart put a Tyrrell March on pole for the marque's first Grand Prix, and won the second GP of 1970.

The 711 had rounded lines based on Frank Costin's aerodynamic advice with a nose aerofoil on a single pylon. The aerodynamics let it down, and bodywork parts tended to be left off, especially around the engine.

A derivative proved ineffectual in 1972 and was superseded by the 721G, which was developed from the 1971 F2 car — it was 'designed' and built in nine days! Variations were tried through the year to try to overcome handling shortcomings. There were no victories, or prospects of any.

There had also been diversions, such as the 71X, with Alfa engine and Alfa gearbox between engine and final drive in an echo of the Italian company's sports-racing car layouts. The German Eifelland team put some outlandish bodywork on a 721 and called it an Eifelland.

After that season March F1 cars derived from their successful F2 models, generally run for second-string drivers. The 751, which was driven to the marque's second GP victory in Austria in 1975, was a slim, narrow-track car, with obvious straight-line speed potential, with which Vittorio Brambilla led races and then won in Austria in 1975. Peterson returned to March in 1976, to a team run on a minimal budget like Brambilla in 1976 leading races and once, in Italy, winning one. The 2-4-0 six-wheeled car built that year was never raced.

In 1977 the team ran 761B and 771 cars, with a very poor record — 22 starts, nine DNQs, six finishes, no points. March F1 interests were sold. In 1981 the name was back in F1, March building the 811 and 821 for the RAM team, whose drivers struggled to qualify them. RAM-built cars in 1983 were sometimes referred to as March-RAM.

March returned in 1987, with a single-car team in the normally-aspirated category of the Grands Prix. Designed by Gordon Coppuck, this was a typically economic car, Cosworth DFZ-powered and the first really new F1 March for

The decisive moment of the 1987 British Grand Prix when Nigel Mansell slashed past his team-mate in the closing laps at Silverstone. Mansell won most races that year, but Piquet won the championship

ten years. Driven by Ivan Capelli, it made an excellent impression and ensured that this March return would not be short-lived.

Under Adrian Newey the design team laid out the distinctive Judd-powered 881 for 1988, a small neat car with a heavy emphasis on aerodynamic aspects. The team's drivers were Capolli and Gugelmin. March also undertook a test chassis for the Lamborghini V-12 engine.
Constructors' championship: *1970 3rd; 1971 3rd; 1972 6th; 1973 5th; 1974 9th; 1975 8th; 1976 7th.*

Martini

Tico Martini's Automobiles Martini started building cars in 1963, initially for the Magny Cours school. These were followed by Formule Renault cars, the first F3 Martinis in 1969, and by the F2 cars that gave Laffite and Arnoux the European championship in 1976 and 1977.

A move to Formula 1 must have seemed logical, with some sponsorship as an inducement and René Arnoux available to drive. So the Martini Mk 23 took shape for 1978, as a conventional slim Cosworth-engined car not unlike a Williams FW06. Arnoux qualified it to start in four races, and twice placed it ninth. But the company's scanty resources were being squandered and in the nick of time Martini pulled out of Formula 1.

Maserati

The Maserati brothers had sold their company to the Orsi family before the world championships were instituted and the Italians only involvement was in the 4CLT/48 derivative of their 4CLT. Independent efforts were made to uprate this as the Maserati-Milan in 1949 and then in 1950 Scuderia Platé developed an F2

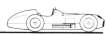

Left: The new Leyton House team's normally-aspirated March 871 driven by Ivan Capelli in the 1987 Spanish GP. 1987 was a season of learning for the team

Below: The first Grand Prix March, the 701, driven by Mario Andretti in his first Grand Prix in Europe, in the 1970 Spanish race when he finished third, lapped by winner Jackie Stewart in another 701. Designed and built quickly, the 701 was therefore essentially simple and straightforward

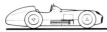

Mercedes-Benz W.196, 1955

version as a stop gap, with no success.

For the Formula 2 championship seasons Maserati built the A6G CM and SG on a sports car base, but the challenge to Ferrari did not succeed until the last race of 1953, when Fangio drove an A6G SG to win the Italian GP.

By that time work on the one outstanding Formula 1 Maserati was well advanced. In this, the 250F, designer Gioacchino Colombo followed the pattern of the straight-six engine used in the 2-litre cars (84 × 75 mm, 2493 cc), in a more advanced multi-tubular frame, using coil spring ifs and a de Dion rear axle with a combined four-speed gearbox and final drive (transaxle). The overall lines of the car were timeless, and during four years in the front line the power output was increased from some 240 bhp to 270 bhp.

The 250F was driven to a debut victory by Fangio in the 1954 Argentine GP, but 250Fs did not win championship races again until 1956,

when Stirling Moss won at Monaco and Monza. Fangio returned to Maserati in 1957, to drive 250Fs to four championship victories.

Throughout the period the 250F had also been the mainstay of the Grands Prix, and especially the non-championship races that were still run all over Europe — it was an ideal private entrant's car, simple, straightforward and available. Including two cars that were in some respects conversions of 1953 cars, 32 250Fs were built, and no fewer than 12 appeared on one race grid. Among them were some lightweight cars and two with a V-12 engine.

This really came too late, for Maserati had to withdraw from racing. A 3-litre version of the V-12 was developed for Cooper to use in Formula 1 cars in 1966–68, successfully as this new formula got under way hesitantly, although they were outclassed by 1968.
Constructors' championship: 1958 5th.

A Maserati 250F driven by Alberto Ascari in the 1954 French GP, when he was 'on loan' to race for Italy while the Lancia team to which he was contracted built the D50 F1 cars. The 250F was a front-rank car for four seasons

Mass, Jochen *1946–*

A German who was more successful in top-flight sports car racing than in Grands Prix, Mass started racing in the VW-based categories before moving on to F3 and F2, scoring his first notable success in the 1972 Eifelrennen in a March, then finishing runner-up in the 1973 F2 championship with Team Surtees.

That year he had his first F1 drive with Surtees in the British GP, and he contested a full season with the team in 1974. However, he did not score his first points until 1975, when he drove a McLaren into third place in Brazil. He won his only GP with McLaren, in Spain that year, and continued with the team for two more seasons.

His 1978 season with ATS produced nothing, and little came out of 1979–80 seasons with Arrows. His last GP season was 1982, with a RAM March; he was involved in two very bad accidents, at Zolder and Paul Ricard, and at the end of the year left Grands Prix racing.
World championship races: 105 starts, 71 points, 1 win: 1975 Spain.

Matra

Matra — Mecanique-Aviation-Traction — is primarily a French aerospace company which found itself involved in high-performance car manufacture almost by accident and had substantial government support for its GP programme.

As a creditor Matra acquired Automobiles René Bonnet and created a Matra Sports division under Jean-Luc Lagardère to continue production of the Bonnet Djet road car. In 1965 a Matra F3 car appeared, with a monocoque chassis built to very high standards, and at the all-important French GP at Reims Beltoise scored a most timely victory. Significantly, one of these Matras was adapted for tests as an F2 car by the Tyrrell team.

A Tyrrell-run Matra F2 team was the direct outcome, and that pointed towards a Matra GP team. A chassis and a 3-litre V-12 were laid down, and meanwhile Tyrrell had backing, a driver and an order accepted for the DFV engines that were to be available for 1968. Tyrrell needed a chassis, Matra needed an alternative to their complete car, as a safeguard. The upshot was two Matra teams in 1968.

An interim MS9 was used by Tyrrell for early-season races, before the DFV-powered MS10 was completed. It used the side pontoons as fuel tanks without internal bag tanks (this meant that bulkheads could be used to give extra rigidity, and that all joints had to be sealed — flaking sealant blocking a fuel system was to cost at least one race).

Jackie Stewart gained Matra's first GP victory in the 1968 Netherlands GP, later scored a superb victory at the Nürburgring, and also won at Watkins Glen. The 1968 MS11 with Matra's V-12 was less successful, with Beltoise' second place in the Netherlands the only good result. The V-12 (79.7 × 50 mm, 2,992 cc) was rated at 400 bhp in 1968, compared with the DFV's 410 bhp, and in decibel output has seldom been equalled.

For 1969 the MS80 was designed by Bernard Boyer, who concentrated on a central position for the fuel load, giving rise to the 'Coke-bottle' planform and the car's distinctive appearance. In such aerodynamic respects as 'wings' and fences to control airflow the car was exemplary. Jackie Stewart won six Grands Prix and the world championship in it, an excellent record for a constructor in only its second year. Yet Matra severed the Tyrrell link, mainly as it became involved with Simca (a Chrysler subsidiary) and a Ford engine could not be tolerated. Moreover, Matra would not build a new car for Tyrrell to regulations which required bag fuel tanks.

Matra MS10, during its debut race at Monaco. The V-12 looked very complex and untidy compared with the compact and neat DFV which was setting the standards in 1968

Jean-Pierre Beltoise locks a brake on the left front of the substantial MS120B during practice at Monaco in 1971

For 1970 Matra was back with another distinctive car, this time angular rather than portly. This MS120 was powered by Matra's V-12, for which some 435 bhp was claimed. The team persevered until the end of 1972 but despite the drivers' efforts – and Chris Amon in particular deserved success – there were no GP victories. The splendid Matra Le Mans

record rather overshadowed that, at least in French eyes, so the Grand Prix programme was closed down. The last car variant was the more rounded, wide-nosed MS120D.

However, there was an eternal search through the 1970s for F1 engine alternatives to the Ford-Cosworth DFV. There was a tentative Matra-engined Shadow project in 1975, but a French team, Ligier, was naturally preferred. Ligier made good use of it, winning the 1977 Swedish GP, but then turned to the DFV again.

In 1981 Matra revised the V-12 for Ligier, to produce more than 500 bhp. Laffite won the Austrian and Canadian GPs with Matra-engined JS17s, and the team was encouraged to continue with the V-12 through 1982. There were no victories, and at the end of the year the Matra V-12 was replaced by the DFV engine again and Matra disappeared from the circuits. *Constructors' championship: 1968 3rd; 1969 1st; 1970 6th; 1971 7th; 1972 8th.*

Mays, Raymond *1899–1980*

A prominent figure in British racing between the world wars, Raymond Mays and designer Peter Berthon conceived the original BRM and carried the project through in the face of enormous difficulties, many of their own making as the V-16 concept was far from realistic.

Matra MS10 on the grid for the 1968 Spanish GP at Jarama, when Jean-Pierre Beltoise drove it into fifth and last place, after two pit stops (and only 13 cars started in this race!). However, Beltoise did set the fastest lap in it

Mercedes-Benz

The German company's reputation for advanced racing car technology and invincibility on the circuits survives more than three decades after it last fielded a Grand Prix team although it was never fully justified in the mid-1950s.

In 1951 three of Mercedes' 1939 cars were sent to run in two *formule libre* races in Argentina as the company felt its way back into the sport (they were beaten by Ferraris in both events), then in 1954 it returned to the Grands Prix with the W196.

Oddly, this had a straight-eight engine, which was notable for its fuel injection and desmodromic (positively-operated) valve gear, hailed as a breakthrough at the time but not featured on later main-line racing engines. This was rated at up to 290 bhp. The car had a tubular space frame with independent suspension front and rear, the latter by low-pivot swing axles, and the brakes were mounted inboard – one feature that was to re-appear. An initial streamlined body was soon discarded for all but the high-speed tracks.

In 1954 Mercedes' success depended largely on the talents of Juan-Manuel Fangio, who had another top-class driver, Stirling Moss, as a team-mate in 1955. The W196s were run in twelve world championship GPs, winning nine, more a reflection of their competitors' inadequacies than their qualities.

Merzario

Arturo Merzario had a more successful career in sports-racing cars than in GP cars (he started in 56 GPs). In 1978 he became a constructor, with the Merzario A1 which proved as ineffectual as it appeared substantial. It was of course a Cosworth kit car, and so were the A2s which followed it. Gianpaolo Dallara helped Simon Hadfield and Merzario with the layout of the second edition of this model, and in his use of the Kauhsen material bought when that team folded, but this failed to change the little Italian team's fortunes.

Mexican Grand Prix

A Mexican GP became well established on the championship calendar in the 1960s, when eight races were run following a 'proving' event in 1962 that was won by Jim Clark/Trevor Taylor, and Clark drove a Lotus 25 to win the first championship race in 1963. The most notable race during this period was in 1965, with Honda's first GP victory (and the only one for a car with a transverse 12-cylinder engine).

Undisciplined spectators swarming over the fences and barriers in 1970 led to the race being halted and to the Grand Prix being abandoned until 1986. Ickx had led Regazzoni in a Ferrari 1-2 in that 1970 race, in which Stewart retired at half-distance after damaging suspension and steering when he hit a dog, and Jack Brabham

Mercedes' W196 of 1954, the threat the Italian teams feared in the mid-1950s. Initially it was run with full-width bodywork, but that was not ideal and it was normally seen in this open-wheel form. And, yes, the cockpit did offer something approaching armchair conditions, by the standards of its rivals, let alone later F1 cars

Mercedes-Benz W.196, 1955

retired from third place in his last Grand Prix when his engine blew.

Winners (world championship GPs)

1963	J. Clark	Lotus-Climax
1964	D. Gurney	Brabham-Climax
1965	R. Ginther	Honda
1966	J. Surtees	Cooper-Maserati
1967	J. Clark	Lotus-Ford
1968	G. Hill	Lotus-Ford
1969	D. Hulme	McLaren-Ford
1970	J. Ickx	Ferrari
1986	G. Berger	Benetton-BMW
1987	N. Mansell	Williams-Honda
1988	A. Prost	McLaren-Honda

Mexico City circuit

Originally named after local driver Ricardo Rodriguez, who was killed in practice for the first Mexican GP, and later Autodromo Hermanos Rodriguez after both racing brothers, this circuit within the Magdalena Mixhuca park and sports complex has changed little since that 1962 race.

The altitude of 7500 feet/2.286 metres above sea level and high temperatures have always posed problems for race engineers, especially for teams with normally-aspirated engines, which in the case of a DFV could suffer a 'loss' of some 100 bhp. Turbo teams tended to use larger turbochargers, and fit larger radiators and intakes.

The long straight after the start/finish line originally ended in a fast right, but for 1986 a slower right-left-right sequence was put in to lead into the second straight. A hairpin at the end of that was abandoned in favour of three corners as adequate run-off space could not be provided. A series of bends led to a spectacular banked 180-degree curve leading onto the pits straight.

Apart from crowd restraints, a lot of work was put into the circuit facilities for the 1986 revival, but the track itself was criticized for being bumpy, and it remained so in 1987.
*Lap distance: 2.747 miles/4.421 km. **Lap record:** 124.98 mph/201.093 km/h by Nelson Piquet in a Williams, 1987.*

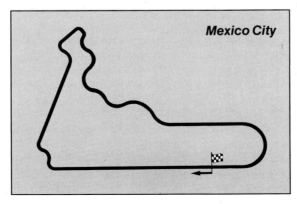

Mexico City

Minardi

In the 1980s small teams seemed to appear as frequently in Italy as they had in Britain in the preceding decades, among them Minardi. Giancarlo Minardi worked logically through the single-seater categories until he commissioned a Formula 2 car design from Giacomo Caliri's Fly Studio for 1980. The F1 Minardi M185 which was unveiled in 1984 was another sound Caliri design. A DFV engine was used while the Motori Moderni V-6 was completed.

In 1985 the Minardi was classified as a finisher – a lowly finisher – in three races while a dozen starts ended in accidents, incidents or retirements. A two-car team in 1986 ran cars revised in detail (M185B). Andrea de Cesaris kept a presence in F1, by recording 14 retirements, one DNQ and one eighth place. Alessandro Nannini often matched the more experienced driver's pace, and except that his finish was a 14th, he also matched his race record!

The 1987 M186 was evolutionary, with a reputation for good handling, but lacking reliability and competitive power and drivers Nannini and Adrian Campos scored no points with it. For 1988 Minardi continued with Spanish drivers Campos and Luis Sala, and the Cosworth DFZ-powered, Caliri-designed M188.

Modena, Stefano 1963–

An Italian from Modena, home of Ferrari, Modena spent almost a decade racing karts, catching the attention of the racing car world with his victory in the 1986 Monaco F3 race and an excellent F3000 season in 1987, when he won the championship in a March run by Mike Earle. His GP debut was in the Australian race that year, when he showed flair in his first drive in a turbo car (a Brabham in that team's last race). For 1988 he joined the new Euro Brun team.

Monaco circuit

This was devised by Anthony Noghès for the first Monaco GP in 1929, and apart from a realignment of the famous chicane it was little changed until 1973.

When the first championship race was run on it, in 1950, the pits were under trees separating the Boulevarde Albert Premier from the Quai of the same name; the start-finish line and pit counters were usually on the former road, and nowadays the start-finish invariably is (occasionally it used to be on the Quai).

From the usual start line, however, the first corner is the Ste Dévote right hander, once a testing corner with an adverse camber on the exit line, slowed with a chicane, but still sees early-race incidents.

Mercedes-Benz W.196, 1955

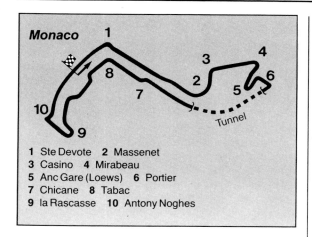

Monaco

1 Ste Devote 2 Massenet
3 Casino 4 Mirabeau
5 Anc Gare (Loews) 6 Portier
7 Chicane 8 Tabac
9 la Rascasse 10 Antony Noghes

A climb to the Massenet left hander leading to Casino Square follows, then the circuit dips down a stretch to Mirabeau, to the hairpin of the old station, on down to the right under a bridge to Portier. This right hander leads to the famous tunnel under Loews Hotel (where a kitchen fire in 1981 delayed the start because the tunnel was awash).

Out of the tunnel there is a short curving stretch down to the chicane, which has been changed several times, then another burst alongside the harbour to the Tabac. This left led to a long curve towards the gasworks hairpin, along the old Quai that is now a pits lane, for the circuit-row runs to near right angles round a swimming pool – left-right-right-left – and then to a series of very tight bends (La Rascasse) before it rejoins the start-finish straight.

Fangio set a lap record at 68.69 mph/ 110.17 kmh in 1955, and before the 1973 modifications Stewart left the record at 85.59 mph/137.71 kmh in 1971. The changes extended the lap to 2.058 miles/3.312 km (Alboreto lapped this version at 89.654 mph/ 144.284 kmh in 1985), while minor modifications made it 2.068 miles/3.328 km in 1986.
Lap distance: 2.068 miles/3.328 km. Lap record: 85.975 mph/138.335 kmh by Prost in a McLaren, 1986.

Monaco Grand Prix

This is far and away the most widely known championship race, despite its shortcomings for modern racing and the proposition that it has been obsolete for two decades. The racing world cannot ignore it, and it is a fashionable magnet.

Prestige associated with the race is high, as disputes in 1984 emphasized. There was a dispute about TV rights, and FISA decided on disciplinary action after race director Jacky Ickx stopped the race after 31 laps, in heavy rain and when it appeared that Alain Prost was about to lose the lead to Ayrton Senna. In the aftermath Ickx initiated a slander action against FISA

president Balestre, while towards the end of the year the wider dispute became a state matter, as Monaco's Prince Rainier approached President Mitterand of France about the FISA threat to strike the Monte Carlo Rally and the Grand Prix from the 1985 calendar. Both were run.

The first championship race, in 1950, was remarkable for Fangio's avoidance of the multicar accident at Tabac which eliminated nine cars. In the next, in 1955, Ascari's car made a spectacular dive into the harbour in a Lancia (a feat repeated by Paul Hawkins in 1965).

Jack Brabham won his first Grand Prix at Monaco in 1959, and Stirling Moss' third victory, in 1961, was a classic as he defeated the superior Ferraris in Rob Walker's Lotus 18.

Graham Hill started on a hat-trick run in 1963, and at the end of the 1960s won two more races at Monaco.

The end of the 1982 race was chaotic: in the last two laps it was led by Prost, Patrese, Pironi, de Cesaris and finally again by Patrese, who had restarted his stalled engine after a push 'to a place of safety' had set his Brabham rolling.

Winners (world championship GPs)

Year	Driver	Car
1950	J.-M. Fangio	Alfa Romeo
1955	M. Trintignant	Ferrari
1956	S. Moss	Maserati
1957	J.-M. Fangio	Maserati
1958	M. Trintignant	Cooper-Climax
1959	J. Brabham	Cooper-Climax
1960	S. Moss	Lotus-Climax
1961	S. Moss	Lotus-Climax
1962	B. McLaren	Cooper-Climax
1963	G. Hill	BRM
1964	G. Hill	BRM
1965	G. Hill	BRM
1967	D. Hulme	Brabham-Repco
1968	G. Hill	Lotus-Ford
1969	G. Hill	Lotus-Ford
1970	J. Rindt	Lotus-Ford
1971	J. Stewart	Tyrrell-Ford
1972	J.-P. Beltoise	BRM
1973	J. Stewart	Tyrrell-Ford
1974	R. Peterson	Lotus-Ford
1975	N. Lauda	Ferrari
1976	N. Lauda	Ferrari
1977	J. Scheckter	Wolf-Ford
1978	P. Depailler	Tyrrell-Ford
1979	J. Scheckter	Ferrari
1980	C. Reutemann	Williams-Ford
1981	G. Villeneuve	Ferrari
1982	R. Patrese	Brabham-Ford
1983	K. Rosberg	Williams-Ford
1984	A. Prost	McLaren-TAG
1985	A. Prost	McLaren-TAG
1986	A. Prost	McLaren-TAG
1987	A. Senna	Lotus-Honda
1988	A. Prost	McLaren-Honda

Monsanto circuit

A traditional circuit of public roads, Monsanto was the venue for only one championship

Mercedes-Benz W.196, 1955

Above: Sparks fly as Nigel Mansell's Williams bottoms at the exit from the Monaco tunnel in 1986

Right: 1986 Monaco GP winner Alain Prost in a McLaren leads Alboreto (Ferrari), Boutsen (Arrows), Rosberg (McLaren) and Johannson (Ferrari) into the Tabac corner by the harbour. The chicane, which has been another feature of the circuit in varying forms through the history of the race, is in the background

Opposite: At the 1987 Monaco Grand Prix a group led by a Williams, a Lotus, another Williams, a Ferrari and a McLaren round the Ancien Gare, for many years the Station hairpin. The railway went underground (a road was built on its old track bed) and a hotel was built on the site of the station. But the line of the circuit at this point has remained unchanged since 1929

Portuguese GP, in 1959. Roughly triangular, its longest straight ran along a motorway with the start-finish line on a shorter straight and the winding link leg using the access roads of a park. That sole GP was eventful: Graham and Phil Hill collided and Brabham had a rare accident. Moss easily won the race.
Lap distance: 3.38 miles/5.44 km. Lap record: 97.3 mph/156.55 km/h by Stirling Moss in a Vanwall, 1959.

Montreal circuit

The most permanent home for the Canadian Grand Prix was the Circuit Gilles Villeneuve on the Ile Notre Dame, an island that was the site of Expo '67. The inaugural Grand Prix in 1978 was won by local hero Gilles Villeneuve, after whom the circuit was later named.

It is a tight track, narrow in places, which has led to problems with slow cars at most GP meetings. The pits straight is short – indeed, there is no straight of any length on the whole lap – and it is followed by a series of fast swerves leading to a hairpin which introduces the return leg. This comprises a series of varying bends and short straights leading to another hairpin, where the track turns back towards the start-finish line.

The circuit gained a reputation for being hard on cars and drivers. Some drivers have admitted that they found it difficult to achieve a rhythm and some dislike the circuit.
Lap distance: 2.74 miles/4.41 km. Lap record: 115.455 mph/185.808 km/h by Nelson Piquet in a Williams, 1986.

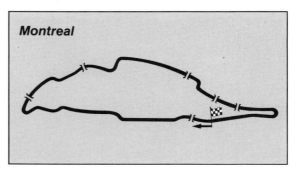

Montreal

Mont Tremblant circuit

Also known as St Jovite, or Mont Tremblant-St Jovite, this appeared to be a French-Canadian alternative venue for the Canadian GP, and the race was run there in 1968 and 1970. It is some 90 miles/150 km north of Montreal, in attractive wooded and hilly country, and is narrow and bumpy, to aggravate its twisting and turning layout.
Lap distance: 2.65 miles/4.36 km. Lap record: 103.47 mph/166.48 km/h by Clay Regazzoni in a Ferrari, 1970.

Monza circuit

There has been an autodrome in the one-time royal park north-east of Milan since 1922, and a new road circuit was built in 1948, and a banked track in 1955. Like their forerunners these could be combined, and the 1955, 1956, 1960 and 1961 Italian GPs were run on this road cum track circuit.

In 1955 the road circuit was modified, in

Mercedes-Benz W.196, 1955

Monza

1 Rettifilo Tribune   2 Curva Grande
3 Curva della Roggia   4 Curva di Lesmo
5 Curva del Serraglio   6 Variante Ascari
7 Curva Sud   8 Curva Parabolica

1972 chicane work produced a 25-metre extension, and in 1976 it was further modified to its present length. Chicanes altered Monza's characteristics of long straights and fast curves, which had led to dramatic slip-streaming races.

The first chicane was built towards the end of the start-finish straight, past the point where the old banked track turned off, to slow cars into the Curva Grande, which used to be taken at dauntingly high speeds. The next was made before the two testing Lesmo curves. The circuit then dropped under the track to Vialone, where a well thought-out chicane was added into the corner (and known as the Variante Ascari, for it was here that the great Italian driver of the 1950s died). Before the chicane was built Pescardo set the GP lap record at 153.49 mph/ 247.016 km/h in 1971.

The Rettifilo Centro straight leading to the final curves is one of the most familiar Monza images, with its walls of spectators and the backdrop of Alpine foothills. The final curve is actually two, Curva Sud and Curva Parabolica, where drivers were once inclined to slingshot out in a dash for the line.

A narrow pits road and barely adequate pits and paddock facilities somehow survived the hyper-critical FISA and FOCA elements until 1987, when improvements were demanded.

Monza has staged great racing, and has also claimed the lives of great drivers in the world championship era – Alberto Ascari, Wolfgang von Trips when he was champion-elect in 1961, Jochen Rindt in 1970 and Ronnie Peterson just after the start in 1978.
Lap distance: 3.6 miles/5.8 km. Lap record: 149.484 mph/240.564 km/h by Ayrton Senna in a Lotus, 1987.

Moroccan Grand Prix

A race with this title was run in the early 1930s then it lapsed until 1957 when a non-championship Formula 1 GP was run on the Ain-Diab circuit.

The only Moroccan world championship event was of great current interest as it decided the 1958 championship – Stirling Moss won, but by finishing second in a Ferrari Mike Hawthorn took the title. The race was over-shadowed by Vanwall driver Stuart Lewis-Evans' fatal accident.
Venue and winner
1958   Ain-Diab   S. Moss   Vanwall

Mosport circuit

Set in rolling country near Lake Ontario some 60 miles/95 km east of Toronto, Mosport staged eight of the first ten world championship Canadian Grands Prix.

The lap included one long and slightly curving 'straight', two really slow corners and several fast bends, including a sweeping right leading back to the short start-finish straight.
Lap distance: 2.46 miles/3.96 km. Lap record: 120.549 mph/194.343 km/h by Mario Andretti in a Lotus, 1977.

Moss, Stirling *1929–*

There is still magic in the name, for Stirling Moss was in many ways the first of the super-

star generation, the first British Grand Prix driver to become a household name and the sport's uncrowned champion.

Son of a racing driver, Moss started single-seater racing with a 500 cc F3 Cooper in Britain. In 1949 he made his mark on the continent when he drove a Cooper-JAP in an F2 race at Garda. He showed the versatility that was to set him apart as he competed in a wide variety of cars.

His first world championship race was in the 1951 Swiss GP in an HWM, when he was eighth. He had GP drives in the lost-cause ERA G-type, with Connaughts, and with a Cooper-Alta. To a degree, patriotism had influenced his choices of car, but for 1954 he was persuaded to prove his potential with a Maserati 250F.

At last he scored world championship points, with a third place in the Belgian GP, and Mercedes signed him for 1955 as number two to Fangio. The Argentinian did not challenge Moss as he led a crushing team victory in the British Grand Prix.

Moss led the Maserati team in 1956, driving flawlessly but to only two championship victories. He chose to drive Vanwalls in 1957 and he took over Brooks' car at Aintree to score the marque's first championship race victory. In 1958 he won four GPs, and for the fourth successive year he was runner-up in the championship; for the next three years he finished third in the table. Some of his contracts restricted his choice of cars, and he became notorious for his mechanical tinkering, often to no good end.

One of his greatest victories was in Argentina in 1958, the first in the world championship for a rear-engined car, Rob Walker's Cooper. He drove for Walker again in 1959, and also in a British Racing Partnership BRM. In 1960 he scored two victories in Walker's Lotus, and also had his first major accident, at Spa. In 1961 he provided the serious opposition to Ferrari, beating the much more powerful Italian cars at Monaco and the Nürburgring – the two circuits where skill was far and away the greatest asset.

His Formula 1 career ended at Goodwood early the following year, when his Lotus 18-21 inexplicably crashed into a bank on the outside of a bend, and he was critically injured. He eventually came back to racing, but in saloons and then in an historic sports car, 'for fun'.

Stirling Moss during one of his great races, pursuing Ginther in a 'shark nose' Ferrari through Casino Square at Monaco in 1961. He won the race in Rob Walker's theoretically outclassed Lotus 18

Mercedes-Benz W.196, 1955

Masters, sometime team-mates, sometime rivals: Stirling Moss with Juan-Manuel Fangio

The broad start/finish area at Monza in 1958, with Ferraris (Dino 246s) centre stage, being pushed against the race direction to their grid positions, while the British teams almost seem to be skulking along with their green Lotus and Coopers further away from the vociferous Ferrari supporters! There is no signalling wall in front of the pits, but in most other details there has been little change since, largely because the circuit lived in unhappy partnership with park and tree conservationists

Moss is still restlessly active, often around motoring affairs where his personal appearances are valued.

World championship races: 66 starts, 186½ points (185½ net), 16 wins: 1955 Britain; 1956 Monaco, Italy; 1957 Britain, Pescara, Italy; 1958 Argentina, Netherlands, Portugal, Morocco; 1959 Portugal, Italy; 1960 Monaco, USA; 1961 Monaco, Germany.

Motori Moderni

Carlo Chiti sometimes appeared a man out of his time with the Alfa Romeo and Euroracing teams in the 1980s, but his traditional Italian enthusiasm for motor racing was indisputable. So when he was fired in 1984 it came as no surprise to find him involved in another racing enterprise, in partnership with Piero Mancini in Motor Moderni, formed to build racing engines.

A Motori Moderni Formula 1 turbo engine was ready for racing in the 1985 season, when the little Minardi team used it for all but the first two races. It was a 90-degree V-6 (80 × 49.7 mm, 1498.9 cc) with a claimed

power output of 720 bhp at 11,3000 prm.

In 1986 Motori Moderni engines were also supplied to AGS, but in 1987 Minardi was again the sole client. The engine was still unreliable, and still did not deliver competitive power. At the end of the season Motori Moderni withdrew from Formula 1, but early in 1988 announced a collaboration with Subaru to develop a normally-aspirated F1 engine.

Murray, Gordon 1947–

An enthusiast with a background in engineering draughtsmanship who turned designer, Gordon Murray spent his professional motor racing career with Motor Racing Developments, 1969–87, and laid out cars that were trend-setters, or controversial, often elegant and successful.

His first design was a one-off sports car for his own use in his native South Africa (he later became a British citizen). In 1969 he moved to England, and worked as a draughtsman at MRD on the detail of cars such as the BT33 and BT34. When Tauranac left he continued under Ralph Bellamy, then took his place, and started work on a replacement for the BT37.

This produced the BT42, which was neat and simple, small with its short wheelbase and narrow track, aerodynamically efficient with good penetration and well-balanced with its fuel load carried low in its distinctive triangular-section chassis. In the BT44 the design was refined, and these cars established Murray as a top-flight designer.

All his skills were called on to provide mounts for the Alfa Romeo engines used in the BT45 and its successors. These were not notably successful, but during this period Murray essayed two original designs. The sharp-nosed BT46 with its surface radiators (in fact heat exchangers) along the flanks did not work; the BT46B 'fan car' worked only too well, but was allowed to race only once.

Late in 1979 the BT49 marked Brabham's return to Cosworth DFV power, and to Murray's crisp lines – aesthetically, this car and its successors were the most pleasing of the period. Murray's lines could be followed through the team's ups and downs, through the years to 1987 when Brabham used BMW engines. For 1987 Murray moved on to McLaren.

Musso, Luigi 1924–58

An aristocratic Roman, Musso was the last front-rank driver of an Italian generation. He started racing in sports cars in 1950, graduating to a first Grand Prix drive at Monza in 1953 and scoring his first championship points with a fine second placing with a Maserati in the 1954 Spanish GP – only his third championship race.

Mercedes-Benz W.196, 1955

In 1955 he contested the full championship series for the first time, racing 250Fs in the Maserati team. He switched to Ferrari for the next three seasons, occasionally driving a Maserati in regional GPs and sports Ferraris. His only GP victory was in a shared drive with Fangio in the 1956 Argentine race.

In 1957–58 he won secondary events, and was twice second in a championship race in each year. After the death of Castellotti he was encouraged to uphold Italian honour, which may have made him drive beyond himself in the French GP of 1958. He crashed fatally in a curve that was full-throttle only for the masters. Ferrari was reported to have said 'I have lost the only Italian driver who mattered'.

World championship races: 24 starts, 44 points, 1 win: 1956 Argentina.

Nakajima, Saturo *1953–*

The first Japanese driver to score points in the world championship, Nakajima raced karts when he was a teenager, turned to cars in 1976 and competed in various national categories. His first races outside Japan were in Australian saloon car events. In single-seaters he won the Japanese F2 title five times. He ventured into British F3 racing in 1978 and European F2 in 1982. Beyond that, he undertook Williams-Honda test driving in Japan, competed at Le Mans, and raced F3000 in 1986.

So Lotus took on an experienced driver as number two to Senna, and he scored his first point in the second race of 1987, at San Marino, and later in the year was fourth at Silverstone.

World championship races (to end of 1987): 16 starts, 7 points.

Nannini, Alessandro *1959–*

Highly rated as a stylist, the Italian 'Sandro' Nannini was unable to achieve matching results in the machinery he drove for his first two GP seasons, in 1986–87.

Nannini started racing in the Fiat Abarth category, winning the championship in 1981, drove F2 Minardis in 1982–84, had F3 outings in 1983 and also drove for Lancia in endurance races.

In 1986–87 he drove Minardis in the Grands Prix, starting 15 times and finishing just once (14th in Mexico) in 1986. After an equally futile season in 1987 he joined the Benetton-Ford team for 1988.

World championship races (to end of 1987): 31 starts.

Netherlands Grand Prix

The first Grands Prix at Zandvoort were non-championship races in 1950–51, both won by Louis Rosier in a Talbot. The first championship races run in 1952–53 went to the all-conquering combination of Alberto Ascari in a Ferrari 500. Two British milestones, when Stirling Moss in a Vanwall beat two BRMs in 1958, and when Jo Bonnier won BRM's first Grand Prix in the following year, were passed there.

In the 1.5-litre years the race went to form but the 1961 race was the first, and so far only, world championship race in which all the starters ran through non-stop to finish. Graham Hill won his first GP at Zandvoort in 1962, Jim Clark scored a hat-trick in the following years and then won first time out with the Cosworth-powered Lotus 49 in 1967, Niki Lauda won for Ferrari in 1974 but narrowly lost in 1975 as James Hunt won Hesketh's only *grande épreuve*.

The Zandvoort circuit has made for good racing; accidents at the end of the main straight were sometimes spectacular, and elsewhere sadly cost the lives of Courage and Williamson. Financial problems have dogged the race, and account for gaps in its history.

Winners (world championship GPs)

1952	A. Ascari	Ferrari
1953	A. Ascari	Ferrari
1955	J.-M. Fangio	Mercedes-Benz
1958	S. Moss	Vanwall
1959	J. Bonnier	BRM
1960	J. Brabham	Cooper-Climax
1961	W. von Trips	Ferrari
1962	G. Hill	BRM
1963	J. Clark	Lotus-Climax
1964	J. Clark	Lotus-Climax
1965	J. Clark	Lotus-Climax
1966	J. Brabham	Brabham-Repco
1967	J. Clark	Lotus-Ford
1968	J. Stewart	Matra-Ford
1969	J. Stewart	Matra-Ford
1970	J. Rindt	Lotus-Ford
1971	J. Ickx	Ferrari
1973	J. Stewart	Tyrrell-Ford
1974	N. Lauda	Ferrari
1975	J. Hunt	Hesketh-Ford
1976	J. Hunt	McLaren-Ford
1977	N. Lauda	Ferrari
1978	M. Andretti	Lotus-Ford
1979	A. Jones	Williams-Ford
1980	N. Piquet	Brabham-Ford
1981	A. Prost	Renault
1982	D. Pironi	Ferrari
1983	R. Arnoux	Ferrari
1984	A. Prost	McLaren-TAG
1985	N. Lauda	McLaren-TAG

Nilsson, Gunnar *1948–78*

A late start was no impediment to this ambitious and likable Swede who proved that in a

motor racing personality these qualities can live together. He drove Vee and Super Vee cars in 1973, moved to F3 in 1974, and started winning F3 and F Atlantic races – his first-ever victory was in an F3 race that year, and he ended the season as British F3 champion with a Lotus F1 contract for 1976!

He proved an ideal number two at this stage and quite capable of winning. His first points were scored in his third Grand Prix, the Spanish, when he finished third. All the promise seemed to be confirmed in the first half of 1977, when he won the Belgian Grand Prix. But a third placing in the British race was his last points-scoring finish. Before he died of cancer in 1978 he worked for the disease's treatment campaign that came to bear his name, that was to be energetically pursued by his friends, and supported by his many admirers.

World championship races: 31 starts, 31 points, 1 win: 1977 Belgium.

Nivelles-Baulers circuit

This little respected venue for two Belgian GPs was between the villages of Nivelles and Baulers some 18 miles/30 km south of Brussels; a club circuit was opened in 1971 and the full GP circuit in 1972. It was a typical 'autodrome facility', well equipped and with good run-off areas and safety provision. A variety of corners was a challenge when setting up cars, but not to drivers in racing conditions.

Lap distance: 2.314 miles/3.723 km. Lap record: 116.819 mph/187.962 km/h by Denny Hulme in a McLaren, 1974.

Nunn, Morris

Mo Nunn doggedly kept an F1 team going for a decade, sometimes as Ensign, sometimes under other names. His team grew out of a successful F3 car business, when he built a few cars for sale and ran a team. One of his F3 drivers, Rikki von Opel, financed the first GP Ensign for 1973, then moved on. Nunn battled on until the last Ensigns were absorbed into Yip's Theodore team in 1983. At the end of that year Nunn turned away from F1, to CART racing.

Nürburgring

Traditionalists lament the passing of the grand Nürburgring in the Eifel forest, some 45 miles/

Gunnar Nilsson (left) with Ronnie Peterson, Sweden's greatest drivers, and two of the good guys of the Grands Prix

Morris Nunn, Ensign N 176, 1976

Graham Hill's Lotus 49B with all four wheels clear of the road at the Nürburgring during the 1969 German Grand Prix

56 km from Cologne, the longest circuit regularly used for world championship races – only the once-used Pescara circuit was longer – and all-round the most demanding.

It dates from 1925 and the *Nordschleife*, which effectively became the GP circuit, had 4 km of proper straight (and until 1970 that had significant humps as it ran between hedges). The rest was a succession of varied corners, climbs and descents, and there were points, most notably the *Flugplatz*, where GP cars jumped, wheels clear of the track like latter-day rally cars. The F1 lap record for this 14.17-mile/22.77-km circuit was 119.979 mph/192.79 km/h, set by Regazzoni in 1975.

This circuit staged much racing drama – Fangio beating Collins and Hawthorn in 1957 after a masterful tactical pit stop, Phil Hill's lap in under nine minutes in 1961 and Moss's stupendous victory in that race, the race-long battle between Graham Hill, John Surtees and Dan Gurney under the dripping trees in 1962, Jackie Stewart's phenomenal drive in fog, rain and sleet in 1968 and Lauda's fiery accident in 1976.

The circuit was 'reconstructed' in the interests of safety in 1970, but it was never going to be a suitable arena for performances by the modern GP circus so a new autodrome was built. This has superb facilities, several short straights which hardly qualify to be so described and a selection of generally undemanding bends.
Lap distance: 2.822 miles/4.542 km. **Lap record:** *148.948 mph/239.701 km/h by Niki Lauda in a McLaren, 1985.*

Oldest driver

The oldest drivers to start in championship GPs were Louis Chiron, who was 55 when he drove

in the 1955 Monaco GP, Philippe Etancelin, 55 when he drove in the 1952 French GP, and Luigi Fagioli, 53 when he drove in the 1951 French GP.

The oldest drivers to win championship GPs were Luigi Fagioli, who was 53 when he shared his Alfa Romeo with Fangio in the 1951 French GP; Giuseppe Farina, 46 when he won the 1953 German GP and Juan-Manuel Fangio 46 when he won the 1957 German GP.

Oliver, Jackie *1942–*

Oliver's greatest racing successes were in sports cars, including a win at Le Mans; the Briton never quite reached the same heights in Formula 1. He almost anticipated the age of sponsorship when he ran a Formula 2 Lotus in the colours of the Herts and Essex Aero Club, which paid some racing bills.

That was in 1968, and when Jim Clark died Oliver was brought into the Lotus F1 team, in the first year that its cars ran in a sponsor's colours. He scored his first point in the Belgian GP, moved to BRM at the wrong time, had only four GP drives (with McLaren and BRM) in 1971–72 while he raced sports cars, and NASCAR stockers, then moved back into Formula 1 with Don Nichols.

He drove for only one full season with the Shadow team before becoming an executive on the commercial side, and he was very much a Constructors' Association man.

He was one of the Shadow managers who set up Arrows, and with Rees and Wass continued with Arrows as managing director.
World championship races: 50 starts, 13 points.

Oporto circuit

This was a street circuit in the old tradition, with varying road surfaces including cobbles, with tram tracks, kerbs, walls and street furniture 'protected' by straw bales. Main streets and side streets were used to make up its relatively long and fairly fast lap. It was first used in 1950 and was the venue for the world championship Portuguese Grands Prix in 1958 and 1960.
Lap distance: 4.603 miles/7.407 km. **Lap record:** *112.309 mph/180.744 km/h by John Surtees in a Lotus, 1960.*

Osca

Two of the Maserati brothers, Ernesto and Bindo, sold the Maserati company to the Orsi family in 1947, then set up OSCA Maserati (soon to be just Osca) to build small sports cars. The company also produced a 4.5-litre V-12 which could be used to uprate 4CLT/48 Maseratis, but this combination was uncompetitive. A complete 4.5-litre car was no better

Osella FA1H, 1987

– driven by Franco Rol in the 1951 Italian GP its best lap was 14 seconds slower than Farina's fastest race lap.

For the 1952–53 Formula 2 Osca built two straight-six cars, which were run in five championship races, and made no impact. Osca was last recorded in Grand Prix archives when de Tomaso offered an Osca engine option in his 1.5-litre F1 cars in 1961.

Osella

In 1974 the Italian Vincenzo 'Enzo' Osella entered the single-seater world with Formula 2 cars, against a background of building and racing successful sports cars since he had taken over from Abarth in 1971.

The first GP Osella, the 1980 FA1, was an overweight and unwieldy Cosworth-powered ground-effects car designed by Osella and Giorgio Stirano. Eddie Cheever failed to qualify it for its first GPs, but he helped to develop some competitiveness into it.

In the lighter 1981 FA1B Beppe Gabbiani, the regular driver, dismally failed to make his mark with 12 DNQ, 3 DNF, and three paying drivers got nowhere with it. Jarier joined the team and with his experience finished in the last four races with FA1C, a smaller, lighter and stiffer car, developed by Giorgio Valentini. Jarier scored Osella's first points with it, at Imola.

FA1D was raced in the first races of 1983, in flat-bottom form and still with Cosworth power, while the FA1E was completed. The first

was in effect a conversion, the definitive FA1E being a Southgate design, and the advantages of Alfa Romeo V-12 engines were questionable: Fabi and Ghinzani managed only three race finishes between them.

Osella joined the turbo ranks in 1984 with FA1F and the Alfa 890T V-8. The car was modelled on the Alfa Romeo 183T (indeed, the first FA1F used an Alfa 183T monocoque). Drivers Ghinzani and Gartner each scored a fifth place, both rather fortunately. The FA1F served on into another season, until its successor was completed.

The FA1G was a little lighter, and aerodynamically perhaps a little more efficient. Giueseppe Petrotta designed it, and was also responsible for FA1G and FA1H for 1986–87, with rather dated chassis and the Alfa V-8s no more powerful and just as thirsty. Ghinzani was back for 1986, trying bravely but finishing just once. Danner left after six races, Canadian Alan Berg brought sponsorship, and recorded three finishes, but Alex Caffi failed to qualify at his one appearance. He was the only driver in the solitary FA1H in 1987; Nicola Larini succeeded him in 1988, when the FA1L was rejected by the scrutineers at its first appearance.

Osterreichring

Unlike most modern autodrome circuits the Osterreichring in the Styrian hills is a challenging circuit on a grand scale.

It is very fast, through fast corners rather than long straights. From the start-finish line

Alain Prost leads Nigel Mansell at the Osterreichring in 1986. The scenic backdrop of the circuit is unsurpassed, and was one of many reasons why purists were unhappy as the Austrian GP was dropped from the 1988 championship calendar

Osella FA1H, 1987

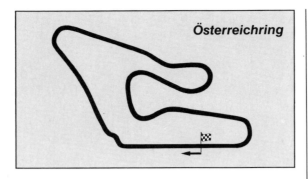

Österreichring

the circuit climbs to the Hella-Licht corner which has been preceded by a chicane since Donohue's fatal crash in 1975, then runs down to a long right-hander. This leads into a gently curving section, with a little kink just before the fast downhill Bosch-Kurve right turns the track through almost 180 degrees to a pair of fast left corners. It climbs to the Rindt-Kurve, with a fast exit onto the pits straight.

The straight was the scene of two multiple accidents at the start(s) of the 1987 Austrian GP, and FISA officials required it to be widened. This could not be guaranteed to be completed by the summer of 1988, so the Austrian GP was dropped from the 1988 calendar. Then a shorter cirtuit was prepared.
Lap distance: 3.69 *miles/5.94 km.* **Lap record:** *150.505 mph/242.207 km/h by Nigel Mansell in a Williams, 1987.*

Pace, Carlos *1944–77*

A successful driver in his native Brazil before he moved to Europe in 1969, Pace seemed to be on the point of breaking through to real success when he was killed in a light aircraft crash.

He had raced in Formula 3 and 2, then spent a season in Frank Williams' Politoys March 711 in 1972 (scoring his first point in Spain), before driving for Surtees through 1973 and part of the 1974 season. He moved to Brabham in mid-1974, and in the following year won his only Grand Prix, driving a Brabham BT44B to beat Emerson Fittipaldi in a straight fight on their home circuit of Interlagos.

That year was Pace's best for championship points, for the long grind of trying to make something of the Alfa-engined Brabham followed. In this 'Moco' Pace turned out to be a good development driver, diplomatically good for this particular Anglo-Italian relationship, and greatly appreciated by team boss Bernie Ecclestone.
World championship races: 72 starts, 58 points, 1 win: 1975 Brazil.

Palmer, Jonathan *1956–*

As a medical student Jonathan Palmer started racing with a Marcos sports car in 1976, moving on to F Ford in 1978, then to dominate the British F3 championship in 1981. That caught the attention of F1 teams, and the British driver tested with Lotus, Williams and McLaren. Surprisingly, he was not asked to join an F1 team, so he went with Tauranac's Ralt-Hondas into Formula 2 in 1982, and with the same team in 1983 he clearly took the title. He also drove in a Grand Prix for the first time, finishing 13th in the European GP at Brands Hatch. In his first full F1 seasons he failed to qualify a RAM-Hart only once in 1984, his best placing in 14 starts being eighth in Brazil. Two seasons with Zakspeed followed, working with a new team to make its new machinery effective – 23 starts in 1985–86 produced 9 finishes.

In 1987 he switched to Tyrrell, scored his first world championship points when he was fifth at Monaco, ended the season with five more points and was clear winner of the Jim Clark Cup with 95 points.
World championship races (to end of 1987): 55 starts, 7 points.

Parnell, Reg *1911–64*

A leading figure in post-1945 British racing, Reg Parnell started competing at Donington in the 1930s and started racing more seriously with a Maserati 4CL after the war, gaining the respect of Continental teams. One outcome was that he was the only British driver to race an

Penske PC4, 1976

Alfa Romeo 158, placing it third in the 1950 British GP. He grappled with the problems of the original V-16 BRM, raced less frequently as the 1950s passed and retired in 1957 to become Aston Martin's team manager. He then ran the Bowmaker-Yeoman F1 team, which became the Reg Parnell Racing Team and was taken over by his son on his death.
World championship races: 6 starts, 9 points.

Parnell, Tim *1932–*

A bluff genial man who fits the role of Derbyshire farmer perfectly, Tim Parnell raced sports cars and F2 in the late 1950s, then F Junior in 1960. He drove occasionally in GPs in a Lotus in 1961, when his best placing was tenth in the Italian GP, then was out of racing for almost two years while he recovered from an accident at Brands Hatch.

He came back to drive very few races but successfully take up team management, first with his father's team, running Amon and Hailwood and later promising newcomers including Courage and Attwood. He ran the BRM Tasman teams for a few seasons, with drivers of the calibre of Hill and Stewart, then in 1969 took on the BRM F1 team, which had its last good seasons in 1971–72. Parnell left in 1974 and became a circuit manager for a few years.

Parnelli

Velco Miletich and USAC driver Rufus Parnelli Jones were successful American partners in racing, and when Jones retired from race driv-ing at the end of 1969 they obtained Firestone backing for a team enterprise. They contracted a number of Lotus luminaries, including designer Maurice Phillippe, and Mario Andretti drove for them in USAC track events and F5000. In 1975 a base was set up not far from the Lotus factory in Norfolk.

The first three Parnelli cars were built for USAC racing, and the VPJ4 did not arrive until 1974, to make its racing debut in the North American events that year. It was a neat car, very much on Lotus 72 lines, and ran through 1975. However, the team principals seemed to have little interest in races outside North America, Firestone's withdrawal was a setback, and development work was negligible. Andretti drove it to score just five points in 1975, but gave it another go in 1976.

A revised car was prepared, with coil springs in place of torsion bars in the suspension, but it started only twice (Andretti scoring a point with it in South Africa) and the Vel's Parnelli Jones team gave up Formula 1.

Patrese, Riccardo *1954–*

One of the durable drivers of modern racing, the Italian Patrese is one of few who have started in more than 150 Grands Prix. His first season in Formula 1 was controversial, for his fellow drivers tended to blame him for collisions early in races, to the extent that he was excluded from the US Grand Prix.

Patrese was a kart champion in 1974, then European and Italian F3 champion in 1976, and shared fourth place in the 1977 F2 champion-

The sleek Parnelli VPJ4 showed strong resemblances to the Lotus 72 in its overall wedge shape and radiators flanking the engine. Like that car, it also had inboard brakes and torsion bar suspension. Mario Andretti gave it an encouraging debut by finishing seventh in the 1974 Canadian GP

Penske PC4, 1976

Riccardo Patrese driving the gold Arrows A1 that was built in a great hurry to replace the banned FA1 in the summer of 1978. Patrese drove Arrows from 1978 until 1981. He once had a reputation as a ruthless driver, but he matured to become the Grand Prix driver with most race starts

ship with Giacomelli. That year he also drove for Shadow, starting his GP career at Monaco and scoring his first world championship point in Japan at the end of the season.

He spent the next four seasons with Arrows. He sensationally led the team's second-ever race for 30 laps, in South Africa, and finished second in Sweden in 1978, but in 1979 and 1980 he slipped back, as did Arrows.

He left for Brabham in 1982, which should perhaps have been the season when Patrese came good. He won his first Grand Prix, a quite extraordinary victory at Monaco after he had spun to a standstill on the penultimate lap but restarted. That was his best year for championship points. He had another victory in the following year, but generally the results did not come.

For 1984–85 he went to Gianpaolo Pavanello's Euroracing Alfa Romeo team. He scored just eight points in 1984, and none in 1985, so it was back to Brabham in 1986, when the lowline BT55 was a problem car. In 1987 matters were a little better, notably with a surprise third place in Mexico, then for the last race of the year he was released to drive for his 1988 team, Williams.

World championship races (to end of 1987): 160 starts, 81 points, 2 wins: 1982 Monaco; 1983 South Africa.

Paul Ricard circuit

Built by drinks magnate Paul Ricard on arid land near le Castellet, its alternative name, some 12 miles/20 km inland from Bandol, this autodrome became one of the more permanent venues of the French GP in its long history,

even before a formal agreement to that end came into effect in the mid-1980s.

It is nearly flat and has excellent facilities. Its principal characteristic was the very long Mistral straight, ending in the testing Signes corner and a sequence of bends. The 3.61-mile/5.81 km lap was reduced in 1986 because of shortcomings shown up by Elio de Angelis' fatal accident there during tests.

Lap distance: 2.369 miles/3.813 km. Lap record: 122.81 mph/197.603 km/h by Nelson Piquet in a Williams, 1987.

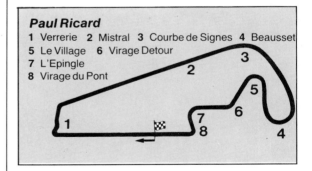

Paul Ricard
1 Verrerie 2 Mistral 3 Courbe de Signes 4 Beausset
5 Le Village 6 Virage Detour
7 L'Epingle
8 Virage du Pont

Pearce

London motor trader J. A. Pearce laid out an F1 car to follow the Ferrari-engined Cooper he ran in 1966, with the Ferrari V-12 in his first spaceframe car, with mundane bodywork which made it look bulky, while two more cars were built for the Martin V-8. All three were destroyed in a fire at Silverstone.

Penske

American Roger Penske made his name in sports car racing before becoming a patron,

running cars in several US classes but generally with the emphasis on sports cars and usually with Mark Donohue as driver. After they won the 1972 CanAm championship their thoughts turned to Formula 1.

The Penske PC1 was designed by ex-Brabham man Geoff Ferris and built in New Zealand driver-constructor Graham McRae's old shops at Poole in Dorset. It was a handsome conventional wedge car powered by the Cosworth DFV.

The PC1 was first raced in the 1974 Canadian GP, Donohue's eleventh place seeming to promise well for the first full season. That promise was not fulfilled, although Donohue did score Penske's first points with a fifth place in the Swedish GP. Penske bought a March 751 for direct comparison, and this was to lead to the PC3. Sadly, this made its debut in John Watson's hands in the US Grand Prix, for Donohue had crashed fatally in the March before the Austrian GP.

Watson drove the PC3 to a fifth place in South Africa, then it was succeeded by the sleek PC4 in mid season. This was a front-running car – Watson was third in the French GP before being disqualified, fourth in the British GP, and then first in Austria. That proved to be the high point for the team, as Penske had decided to abandon the GPs for US track racing and at the end of the season the PC4s were sold to the ATS team.

Pescara Grand Prix

Between the world wars this was one of the principal European regional races, as the Coppa Acerbo often attracting leading teams – the first race, in 1924, was won by Enzo Ferrari driving an Alfa Romeo. In 1957 it had world championship status and was run over 18 laps of the 16-mile/25.84 km circuit of public roads outside the southern Italian city.

Winner (world championship GP)
1957   Coppa Acerbo   S. Moss   Vanwall.

Peterson, Ronnie 1944–78

A real racer, with an exuberant style and a car control that spectators could really appreciate, coupled with an attractive out-going personality, 'Super Swede' would have made a great world champion. But he only made runner-up, in his second championship season, 1971, and his last, 1978.

From kart racing he graduated into F3 in 1969, and in 1970 was driving in Formula 2 for the new March team; he won the F2 championship in 1971. Meanwhile he had started on his Grand Prix career, with Colin Crabbe's Antique Automobiles' March 701. In 1971 he

Ronnie Peterson in a Lotus 78 at Kyalami. He returned to Lotus in 1978 to drive the 78 and 79 'wing cars'

A Penske PC3 and a six-wheeled Tyrrell P34 in 1976, driven by John Watson and Patrick Depailler respectively

Penske PC4, 1976

drove a works March 711, scored his first points, at Monaco, was four times second, and was second to Jackie Stewart in the championship. But the 1972 March was a failure, and despite his happy relationship with the team, Peterson moved to Lotus for 1973.

That season he won four GPs, the first in France, and had three more wins in 1974. He was not a great development driver, and could do nothing with the Lotus 77, so Chapman released him to return to March in 1976 to drive the uncomplicated 761. He won a Grand Prix in it, too: something few drivers achieved in a March!

The Tyrrell six-wheeler was in its overweight period of decline when Peterson drove it in 1977, and hardly rewarding. He was back with Lotus in 1978, most loyally backing up Andretti and picking up two victories.

He died the day after crashing at the Italian Grand Prix.

World championship races: *123 starts, 206 points, 10 wins: 1973 France, Austria, Italy, USA; 1974 Monaco, France, Italy; 1976 Italy; 1978 South Africa, Austria.*

Phillippe, Maurice 1932–

Another respected designer who came to racing cars from aviation, Phillippe took his first steps towards motor sport with his one-off sports-racing special in the mid-1950s. That led him to Ford as a project engineer, and in 1965 to Team Lotus.

There he was involved until 1971 in a wide range of cars, including the BRM H-16-engined 43, the gas turbine 56, the classic 49 and the 72. The concept of these cars was usually acknowledged to be Chapman's, and his designers were credited with the execution – but the stunning 72 was announced by GLTL as '. . . primarily the work of Maurice Phillippe, the chief designer for Team Lotus . . .'

However, he never designed anything quite as original as the 72 again. When his Lotus contract expired in 1971 he went to the Vel's Parnelli Jones team to work on three USAC cars and design the VPJ-4 Formula 1 car, on Lotus 72 lines.

He joined Tyrrell as Gardner left in 1977, and has remained there ever since, enjoying support in the late 1970s from Karl Kempf and in the late 1980s from Brian Lisles.

Piquet, Nelson 1952–

The three-times world champion started racing karts and saloons in his native Brazil then spent a season in European F3 in 1977. He won the Euro title in 1978, driving a Ralt to win 13 races in the BP series and clearly beat Warwick to the then more important British title.

That year he also made his GP debut in an Ensign in the German GP, and then had three drives in a McLaren M23 run by BS Fabrications and one in an Alfa-engined Brabham BT48. That led him to the Brabham team, to a single points-scoring finish (fourth in the Netherlands in 1979) with an Alfa-engined car and to a string of successes as Brabham reverted to Cosworth engines. Piquet's first victory was at Long Beach in 1980, and two more wins that year took him to second place in the championship. Three wins, a second place and three thirds gained him the world title in 1981.

His patience in breaking in the Brabham-BMW in 1982 was eventually rewarded with a win in Canada, and with a second championship in 1983. He had two more years with Brabham, and three more GP victories, then left for Williams.

There he found he was not the absolute centre of attention. His team-mate Nigel Mansell challenged him and beat him on occasions. He won four GPs in 1986, three in 1987 and his

Nelson Piquet inspires conflicting reactions among the fans and his fellow drivers, but in 1988 he started a new season as reigning champion for the third time

third Championship in 1987. Then he moved on to Lotus for 1988.

World championship races (to end of 1987): 141 starts, 381 points (378 net), 20 wins: 1980 USA (West), Netherlands, Italy; 1981 Argentina, San Marino, Germany; 1982 Canada; 1983 Brazil, Italy, Europe; 1984 Canada, USA (East); 1985 France; 1986 Brazil, Germany, Hungary, Italy; 1987 Germany, Hungary, Italy. **World champion:** *1981, 1983, 1987.*

Pironi, Didier *1952–87*

This self-contained, self-confident man was born in Paris, although his father was Italian. He therefore fitted well into 'Latin' teams, although his F1 career began with Tyrrell.

From the French national categories Pironi moved naturally on to Formula 3, and won the Monaco Junior GP in 1977. His flair caught Tyrrell's eye, and he drove for him through two seasons, scoring his first championship points in the second race of 1978, in Brazil. His first Grand Prix victory was in Belgium in 1980 with a Ligier.

In 1981 Pironi drove the Ferrari 126C, and continued with the team in its less agricultural cars in 1982. He was teamed with Villeneuve, and by all accounts the two drivers were friendly until the San Marino GP, when Pironi ignored the team plan and 'stole' the race on the last lap.

Pironi won in the Netherlands and was piling up points, seemingly favourite to take the championship, when in heavy spray during practice at Hockenheim he crashed. After a long

series of operations to his legs was able to drive an F1 car again. But he only tested, and turned his competitive talents to power boat racing, only to die in a crash in 1987.

World championship races: 70 starts, 101 points, 3 wins: 1980 Belgium; 1982 San Marino, Netherlands.

Politoys

The Italian model company sponsored the first Williams car, designed by Len Bailey and designated Politoys FX3. It started in the 1972 British GP but crashed after seven laps. The FX3B in the following year took on the name Iso-Marlboro.

Porsche

This German company's excellent racing reputation was largely earned by innumerable sports-car successes and the Porsche-designed and developed TAG P01 turbocharged Formula 1 engine used by McLaren 1984–87.

Single-seater derivatives of the RSK sports-racing cars appeared at the end of the 1.5-litre Formula 2, leading directly to GP cars in 1961.

In the following season Porsche seemed poised to make a real challenge, with the new flat-eight-engined Type 804. Built almost entirely in-house, it had a low and wide body, a six-speed gearbox and an air-cooled engine producing 180 bhp. That power was adequate by 1961 standards, but not in 1962 when the BRM and Coventry Climax V-8s were race-worthy. So results were disappointing — just

Porsche's sole world championship race victory was scored by Dan Gurney in the 1962 French GP, driving this 804. It had an air-cooled flat-eight engine, and generally was outclassed, so Porsche withdrew from the Grands Prix to concentrate on the less competitive field of sports car racing for many years. The German company returned, very successfully, as McLaren's engine supplier, 1983–87

Penske PC4, 1976

Nelson Piquet at Monaco in a Williams FW11B during his third championship-winning season, 1987

one championship race victory, scored by Dan Gurney in a race of attrition in France – and at the end of the season the Porsche management abandoned their GP programme.

They returned as a contracted engine supplier to McLaren, with a V-6 labelled TAG (Techniques d'Avant Garde) to proclaim backing from the Ojjeh family's concern. The water-cooled KKK-turbocharged engine, designed by

Hans Mezger, was first shown early in 1983, when the McLaren MP4 for which it was intended was already running (with Cosworth engines). Later that year it appeared in the MP4/1E and by 1984 was fully raceworthy. It powered Niki Lauda to the world championship in 1984 and Alain Prost to the title in 1985–86; Porsche officially withdrew at the end of 1987, when the TAG engine had won 26 races.

The TAG turbocharged V-6 in a McLaren MP4/3 in 1987, the final season this engine was used and a disappointing one for both partners. The FISA pop-off valves, which restricted turbo boost to four bar in 1987, are above the rear of the engine (behind the modest 'made by Porsche' label)

Penske PC4, 1976

Portuguese Grand Prix

The first Portuguese GPs were sports cars races, but in the last three years of the 2.5-litre formula championship events were run at Oporto and Monsanto. The Grand Prix then lapsed until 1984, when it was revived at the Estoril autodrome. In the first GP, at Oporto in 1958, Stirling Moss drove a tour de force race in the wet and the 1985 race provided a drive to equal it as Senna exploited his reflexes and ability on a streaming wet track to score his first championship win. Nigel Mansell was dominant in 1986, and in the 1987 race Alain Prost at his professional best scored a record-breaking 28th victory.

Venues and winners (world championship GPs)

1958	Oporto	S. Moss	Vanwall
1959	Monsanto	S. Moss	Cooper-Climax
1960	Oporto	J. Brabham	Cooper-Climax
1984	Estoril	A. Prost	McLaren-TAG
1985	Estoril	A. Senna	Lotus-Renault
1986	Estoril	N. Mansell	Williams-Honda
1987	Estoril	A. Prost	McLaren-TAG

Postlethwaite, Harvey

A designer with aerodynamics specialization in his background, Dr Harvey Postlethwaite came to the fore as he left March to develop the Hesketh team's 731, then design the Hesketh cars until the team effort was drastically reduced. As elements of it passed to Wolf, he went with them, to design that team's successful cars and its later WR7-9, which became the basis of the 1980 Fittipaldis. Postlethwaite designed their F8 successors for 1981.

After that he joined Ferrari, to be jointly credited with Forghieri with the chassis of the turbo 126Cs. His real role with the Italian team, however, was to drag it into the 1980s age of aerodynamics, and in that he succeeded as his subtle work on the F187 transformed that car into a race winner.

Prost, Alain 1955–

Prost was the outstanding driver of the 1980s, by almost any yardstick. In 1987 he set a new record when he won a 28th Grand Prix, more than Jackie Stewart's 27, Jim Clark and Niki Lauda's 25 and Fangio's 24.

Prost started his racing with karts, in 1975 won the 'Volant Elf' championship, took the French *formule Renault* championship in the following year, the European *formule Renault* championship in 1977, the French F3 title in 1978 and the European F3 title in 1979. He moved straight from F3 to F1, with McLaren in

Alain Prost in one of the TAG-engined McLaren MP4s, looking into a corner, holding the front wheels on full lock, at Monaco in 1987

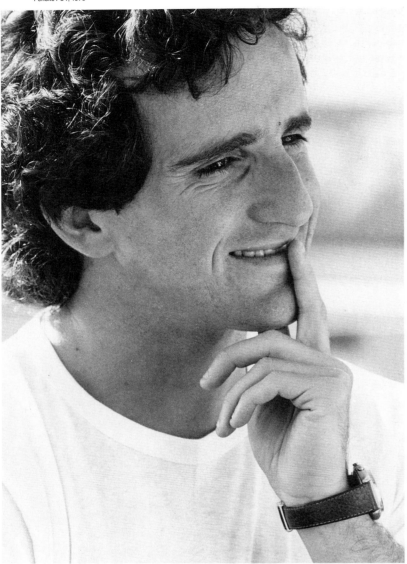

Penske PC4, 1976

Alain Prost, the most professional driver of the modern era, winner of more world championship Grands Prix than any other driver

Defending the title was no easy task, and in 1986 the outcome had to wait until a dramatic final race in Adelaide, when race leader Nigel Mansell retired and Prost won the race and the championship, the first driver since Jack Brabham in 1959–60 to win the title in successive years.

In 1987 the McLaren was outclassed by Honda-powered cars, there were reliability problems and Prost even made odd driving errors. But he won three races, in Portugal he won that historic 28th Grand Prix and in the next race took his points total past 400. His 30th GP victory, at Monaco in 1988, also saw him set a points record.

World championship races (to end of 1987): 121 starts, 404½ points 401½ (net) 28 wins: 1981 France, Netherlands, Italy; 1982 South Africa, Brazil; 1983 France, Belgium, Britain, Austria; 1984 Brazil, San Marino, Monaco, Germany, Netherlands, Europe, Portugal; 1985 Brazil, Monaco, Britain, Austria, Italy; 1986 San Marino, Monaco, Austria, Australia; 1987 Brazil, Belgium, Portugal. **World champion: 1985, 1986.**

Pryce, Tom *1949–77*

A Welshman whose talent in Grand Prix racing was widely recognized but denied maturity by an early death, Tom Pryce worked as a mechanic while he learned race craft in F Ford before moving up to Formula 3 and Formula 2. After a promising outing in the one-off Token in the 1974 Belgian GP Pryce joined Shadow, won the 1975 Race of Champions, briefly led the British GP that year, was third in Austria and fourth in Germany. He was killed during the 1977 South African GP.

World championship races: 42 starts, 19 points.

Purley, David *1945–85*

Purley's approach was summed up by his pleasure at the hazards of racing an F3 car on Belgium's Chimay circuit of public roads, where he won in the early 1970s, and his dislike of some of the FOCA barons. This British driver is remembered for his bravery in stopping during the 1973 Dutch GP to make a vain attempt to save Roger Williamson from his burning car, and for his accident during pre-qualifying for the 1978 British GP when it was estimated that his Lec stopped from 110 mph in 18 inches. When he had recovered from his appalling injuries Purley drove Lec CRP2 at Goodwood, satisfied himself by putting in competitive times, and made a fleeting comeback in 1979, driving Lec CRP2 and then a Shadow DN9B in three Aurora AFX races in Britain. He retired and took up aerobatic flying, and was killed when he crashed into the sea in 1985.

World championship races: 7 starts.

1980, not a particularly good move, as the team was in the doldrums. In 11 races with the team Prost scored just five points, the first in his first world championship race, the Argentine GP.

A move to the French Renault team seemed natural for this French driver, and in the three years he drove for it he won nine GPs, the first in the 1981 French GP. At mid-season the French grasp on the 1983 championships seemed total but the season ended acrimoniously, with a bureaucratic post-mortem and some incisive comments on team management by committee.

Prost returned to a very different McLaren team from the one he had left at the end of 1980, and one which was equipped with the superb MP4. Prost and fellow McLaren International driver Niki Lauda won 12 of the 1984 season's 15 races, the Austrian piling up points to take the title while Prost equalled Jim Clark's record of seven GP wins in a season. In 1985 he won five Grands Prix, and the title.

RAM Racing

Mick Raph and John Macdonald, partners in London motor trade activities from the early 1960s, ran Alan Jones in the RAM Racing March 75A in the 1975 ShellSport F5000 series with great success and were encouraged to run a pair of Brabham BT44s in 1976, only to be brought down to earth by F1 realities.

In 1981 RAM brought March back into the Grands Prix with the 811. This had a weak chassis, and despite the attentions of Robin Herd and Gordon Coppuck it was never competitive – indeed, qualifying remained a problem for drivers Daly and Salazar.

March 821s were run in 1982, handicapped by a tyre switch, and for 1983 RAM built its own Cosworth-engined cars to a design by Dave Kelly, initially retaining the name March in the designation of RAM 01. These cars seldom qualified, but 1984 looked brighter, with sponsorship for two cars, to be driven by Alliot and Palmer. Hart 415T turbos were used in converted 1983 cars while Kelly's new 02 design was built. But 27 starts produced only nine finishes, the best being Palmer's eighth place in Brazil.

For 1985 Gustav Brunner designed the Hart-powered RAM 03, up to the minute, small and neat, but with shortcomings, such as inadequate cooling to be attended to as the season went on, and the cars recorded only three finishes from 21 starts.

Early in 1986 a 1985 car, with Australian backing, was tested at Rio by Mike Thackwell, who was nominated to drive a single RAM in Grands Prix. The tests went badly, the backers withdrew, and a new RAM design by Brunner never took shape.

Rebaque, Hector 1956–

Mexican Hector Rebaque was eventually accepted as a competent driver, after an uncertain entry into Formula 1 when he qualified a Hesketh only once in six attempts in 1977. In the following year he ran Lotus 78s to score his first championship point in the German GP.

He continued with a Lotus 79 in 1979, when he also essayed the Rebaque HR100 which followed Lotus 79 lines closely and was built at the Penske plant under the supervision of Geoff Ferris. Rebaque failed to qualify his Rebaque twice, started once (in Canada, where he retired) and then abandoned the project.

He turned up with the Brabham team in the summer of 1980, acquitted himself well, and

did better in 1981 when he drove Brabhams hard and was placed fourth in three GPs. At the end of that season he disappeared from the Grand Prix scene.

World championship races: 41 starts, 13 points.

Regazzoni, Gianclaudio 1940–

Clay Regazzoni had the bearing of a tough Italian driver of the old school, although he was Swiss, and he made his way in racing very much by his own efforts, sometimes roughly, never consistently.

Regazzoni started competing in minor events, then had three seasons in F3 from 1964. He drove Tecno F2 cars in 1968, and gained the marque's first F2 win in 1970 (in the intervening year he drove Ferrari's uncompetitive F2 cars). His F1 debut was with Ferrari in 1970, when he was fourth in his first race (in the Netherlands) and at the end of the year he drove a Ferrari to win the Italian GP.

In the next two seasons with the Italian marque he had no more victories, 1973 with BRM brought little, then it was back to Ferrari for three years and a GP win every season.

Ensign in 1977 and Shadow in 1978 seemed to suggest a career in gentle decline, but there was one more good F1 year for Clay. He spent 1979 with Frank Williams' team, and he won its first Grand Prix, at Silverstone.

He was back with Ensign in 1980. At Long Beach he crashed heavily, and was left partly paralysed.

World championship races: 132 starts, 212 points, 5 wins: 1970 Italy; 1974 Germany; 1975 Italy; 1976 USA (West); 1979 Britain.

Reims circuit

This was one of the classic circuits of Europe, albeit in a manner of Grand Prix ages that seem long past. Devised in 1925, it was roughly triangular. It was used for 11 world championship French GPs between 1950 and 1966; when the energetic secretary-general of the controlling AC de Champagne, Raymond 'Toto' Roche, died the circuit just faded.

In 1950 it still followed the pre-war line through the village of Gueux, but in 1953 this was by-passed, the new road following a very fast right curve and then climbing gently through another sweep to the near-hairpin of Muizon. Here it joined the Soissons-Reims road, running straight down through the corn fields to another near-hairpin at Thillois, once an everyday name in racing. The original lap length was 4.85 miles/7.815 km, in 1953 it was 5.18 miles/8.347 km, then the hairpins were eased to give its final length.

The last Grand Prix to be run on the circuit through Gueux, in 1951, was the longest-ever

The long straight past the pits at Reims, with the field on the second lap of the 1959 GP d'Europe led by Tony Brooks in a Ferrari from Stirling Moss in a BRP-entered BRM. This is now one of the lost circuits of Europe, its facilities quietly mouldering

world championship GP (374 miles/601.8 km).

Reims was fast, through the 1950s seemingly in competition with Belgium's Spa for the pointless title of 'the fastest circuit in Europe'. In some respects it was also deceptively simple – for example, the bend by-passing Gueux was 'flat' for only the top-flight drivers.

Lap distance: 5.16 miles/8.301 km. Lap record: 141.44 mph/227.618 km/h by Lorenzo Bandini in a Ferrari, 1966.

Renault

A Renault won the first French Grand Prix ever run, in 1906, but two years later the French company withdrew from GP racing. It came back in the 1970s, and initiated a line of development that revolutionized Formula 1 racing. The Regie enjoyed much success but failed to win the championships that would have brought world-wide prestige to justify an

Clay Regazzoni swinging a 312B3 into Portier, the corner before the entrance to the tunnel at Monaco, in 1974. He was a favourite among enthusiasts as an old-fashioned hard-trying driver, and while he may be recalled most often as the first driver to win a Grand Prix in a Williams car his best years were with Ferrari

enormous investment in new technology.

The Renault GP team of the 1970s had its origins in Alpine and Gordini. In 1972 Renault started on a sports car programme built around a 2-litre V-6. Jean Terramorsie, competitions director, initiated a turbocharged version of this engine, which emerged as the CHS in 1975, the year Renault decided to embark on a Formula 1 programme. Meanwhile the 2-litre engine had dominated F2 in 1976–77 and the objective of a Le Mans victory was at last achieved in 1978.

A single-seater *Laboratoire* built by Alpine for development purposes in 1976 led to the RS01 which made its race debut in the 1977 British Grand Prix. Development had not been rapid because of a preoccupation with Le Mans, and a work-split between the Alpine plant at Dieppe and the Renault-Gordini plant at Viry-Chatillon

Renault's RS01 when it first ran in public, during the test days for the 1977 British GP, before the race in which it was to make its first start. It brought a new sound into the pit lanes as Renault introduced turbocharged engines to the Grands Prix

A Renault RE60B at Paul Ricard, driven by Patrick Tambay. By 1985 the French team was in decline, ironically when its cars were most handsome

had not helped; Gérard Larrousse, who took Terramorsie's place in 1976, brought them together as Renault Sport, at Viry.

RS01 was designed by André de Cortanze around an aluminium monocoque with conventional suspension, and the car ran on Michelin tyres, for Renault had brought another French giant into GP racing. All that, however, was overshadowed by the turbocharged engine. This derived from the CH series of 90-degree V-6s designed by Francois Castaing, and the F1 engine (designated EF1) was developed by Bernard Dudot. Its bore and stroke of 86 × 42.8 mm gave a capacity of 1492 cc, and with the single Garrett turbo first fitted it was rated at a modest 500 bhp at 11,000 rpm, which seemed to bear out Renault contentions that the equivalency factor between normally-aspirated and turbo engines of 2:1 was harsh!

The single RS01 was entered in five GPs in 1977, failing to qualify to start in the Canadian race and failing to finish in the others. Development continued through 1978 to overcome throttle lag and overheating which caused loss of power, and the car showed its potential. Jabouille usually had no problems in qualifying it; in the US Grand Prix he scored Renault's first championship points when he finished fourth.

Michel Tétu had joined Renault to design the RS10, which had more elegant lines, and a very large rear aerofoil – the engine, with twin KKK turbochargers in 1979 as well as other improvements such as water intercoolers, produced some 520 bhp and could pull this wing without losing straight-line speed superiority. Reliability was still elusive, but a breakthrough came in the French Grand Prix at Dijon when Jabouille and Arnoux finished first and third. Nobody in racing doubted that the era of the turbo had arrived.

With the RE20-25 Renault entered 1980 as a leading championship contender. The designation acknowledged the team's principal sponsor, Renault Elf replacing Renault Sport, and at the same time Tétu took over technical direction from Castaing. The car had a three-quarter monocoque, with the EFI V-6 acting as a load-bearing member at the rear. Through the year there were too many niggling failures, particularly with valve springs and brakes, so the cars finished only 12 times from 27 starts – Arnoux won two GPs, and Jabouille one.

The 1980 cars were updated for the opening of the 1981 season while the RE30 was completed. This was lighter, the engine was developed to give 540 bhp at 11,500 rpm and,

as important, low-inertia KKK turbochargers made for better throttle response, while Renault's own Type 30 gearbox superseded the Hewland units. A new team driver, Alain Prost, won three GPs. But that year Ferrari also had turbo cars, and they won races in their first season.

With Prost's late-1981 successes and the revised RE30B Renault entered 1982 with high hopes. The car was by this time a little conservative and although Renault's own new electro-mechanical fuel injection gave more power, their injection pump was a major source of trouble. Prost won two GPs, Arnoux two.

Tétu designed the flat-bottom RE40 with a carbon-fibre composite chassis and a revised rear suspension for 1983. Bernard Dudot developed the engine to give 650 bhp at 12,000 rpm, using larger turbochargers and with water injection that did not completely cure turbo overheating – indeed, inconsistency here cost the team dear. Prost won four GPs, but Nelson Piquet in a Brabham-BMW became the first driver to win the championship with turbocharged cars. The post-mortem at Renault was bitter, and almost unbelievably Prost was the scapegoat. He was fired and went to McLaren, where he won championships.

For 1984 new drivers Patrick Tambay and Derek Warwick were equipped with the RE50, smaller and lighter, with pullrod suspension and an alloy-block version of the engine with twin Garrett AiResearch turbochargers which gave 750 bhp. But the chassis was suspect, especially around the front suspension pick-up points, fuel consumption problems meant cars ran out of fuel during some races and team morale was low. Renault did not win a single GP. Larrousse left, and took Tétu to Ligier with him, so that the only man left of the original top team was engine development engineer Dudot. Quality control engineer Gérard Toth was appointed Renault sport director.

Renault was no longer a front-line contender – customers, especially Lotus, which started using the Renault turbo engine in 1983 were making better use of it – but there was a last GP Renault. The RE60 started life overweight, but it did have the EF4 engine rated at 760 bhp or the new EF15 producing 810 bhp, up to 1,000 bhp with qualifying turbo boost.

Renault did not win a race with the RE60, or the slightly lighter RE60B, and in the summer of 1985 announced that the team was to be withdrawn. Its disappearance was mourned at one level because the team personnel were in the main a friendly bunch, at another because Grand Prix racing could only benefit from the presence of a major manufacturer. But the very fact that it was a department of a large company had been at the root of many problems.

The engine had been made available to other teams through the Mecachrome preparation company, which continued to supply Ligier and Tyrrell, while Lotus became a favoured customer and was supplied with the latest engines direct. Engine development continued, and in 1986 the fuel-efficient EF15B with compressed air valve operation was introduced, and when limitations imposed by valve springs were removed the maximum rpm of the engine was substantially increased, to 12,500 rpm with 13,000 rpm possible. Engines were built for other teams for two seasons after Renault's withdrawal from active participation, but only Lotus won races with them, to add to the 18 won by the Renault team.

After months of rumours, Renault confirmed an intention to return to F1 racing, supplying the RS1 V-10 engine to the Williams team for 1989.

Constructors' championship: *1979 6th; 1980 4th; 1981 3rd; 1982 3rd; 1983 2nd; 1984 5th; 1985 7th.*

Repco

In the early 1960s the Australian Repco (Replacement Parts) company prepared and maintained the Coventry Climax engines used in 2.5-litre Tasman Series cars and Phil Irving

Above: An RE25 driven by Rene Arnoux at Zandvoort in 1980 (he took pole position for the Dutch GP, and finished second). Jones follows in a Williams FW07B

Right: Renault's number two driver Eddie Cheever at Silverstone in 1983, a good year for Renault, when RE40s were run for most of the season and the team was second in the constructors' championship, shaded by Ferrari. Alain Prost scored Renault's four victories (and was second in the drivers' championship). Cheever was sixth in the championship with a second place in Canada, his best finish

Renault RE 50, 1984

and Frank Hallam headed the modest design team on a replacement Type 620. This V-8 ran for the first time early in 1965, whereupon a 3-litre version was initiated for Brabham.

This was an unprepossessing racing engine based on the Oldsmobile F85 light alloy production engine – hence unfinished blocks cost a mere £11! The sohc V-8 was available for the first season of 3-litre Grands Prix in 1966, and although the 620 produced less than 300 bhp as the European season opened, slightly more as it ended, it produced usable power over a wide revs range. That year the Repco-Brabhams won four championship GPs.

A refined 330 bhp version, the centre-exhaust 740, was adequate in 1967, but in 1968 the more sophisticated twin-ohc V-8 was a failure.

Repco continued their racing involvement in Australia with constructors such as Matich until the mid-1970s when it withdrew from racing. Its association with Jack Brabham continued until he retired in 1970.

Reutemann, Carlos 1942–

Reutemann started racing saloons in Argentina, and from 1965 drove in local Formula 2 races. In 1970 the Automovil Club Argentino and YPF backed him for a season in European Formula 2; he found his feet in Brabhams that year and drove them with verve in 1971.

A move to the Brabham F1 team was logical, and Reutemann quite sensationally qualified a BT34 for pole position in his first drive for the team, in Argentina. He stayed with Brabham for five years, scoring his first world champion-

ship points with a fourth place in Canada in 1972 and driving a BT44 to his first Grand Prix victory in South Africa in 1974.

The Alfa-engined Brabhams in 1976 brought little joy and Reutemann moved to Ferrari, where he was overshadowed by Niki Lauda in 1977, but when the Austrian moved to Brabham he led the team and won four GPs in 1978. In the 1979 season with Lotus he had good early-season performances, then no scores at all in the last eight races – the 79 was still competitive in the early races and the 80 which followed it was hopeless.

He spent his last two seasons with Williams, one of the strong GP teams of the early 1980s. Reutemann won three Grands Prix in 1980 and was championship runner-up in 1981. That was the year 'Lole' Reutemann seemed to be running away with the title, and although he went to the last race with a points lead, he seemed not to fight for the title. He retired, hesitated and came out to race for Williams in the first events of 1982, finishing second in South Africa before retiring for good. He competed in odd rallies in the mid-1980s, which seemed a strange waste of an outstanding racing talent.

One remarkable record stands to Reutemann: in Belgium in 1980 he started on a run of 15 consecutive finishes in the top six, when he scored 81 points, an average of 5.4 points per race.

World championship races: *146 starts, 310 points, 12 wins: 1974 South Africa, Austria, USA; 1975 Germany; 1977 Brazil; 1978 Brazil, USA (West), Britain, USA (East); 1980 Monaco; 1981 Brazil, Belgium.*

Carlos Reutemann in 1981, his last full season, when he went to the last race seemingly poised to take the championship with the very effective Williams FW07C. But at Las Vegas he 'lost' the title by one point

Renault RE 50, 1984

Revson, Peter *1939–74*

Although he was by no means the playboy newspapers liked to portray, Revson had no career or real need of one when he started racing sports cars in Hawaii before moving on to Formula Junior in 1963. The young American tried to break into Formula 1 in 1964, finishing last in a Lotus-BRM in the German and Italian GPs, then dropped back to F2 and F3 in Europe before spending the rest of the 1960s in the USA, racing sports cars, TransAm and USAC cars, occasionally driving sports cars outside North America.

A one-off GP with Tyrrell in the 1971 US race brought Revson back into Formula 1, and very early retirement from that event did not deter him as he accepted a full McLaren drive in 1972–73, as number two to Denny Hulme. He scored his first points with a third place in South Africa in 1972 and in 1973 won the British GP with a well-judged drive and then was declared winner of a confused Canadian GP.

Unhappy with internal feuds at McLaren, Revson joined UOP Shadow for 1974, but was killed while testing at Kyalami in South Africa.
World championship races: 30 starts, 61 points, 2 wins: 1973 Britain, Canada.

Jochen Rindt with the trophy for his first Grand Prix victory, in the 1969 US race. A year later he was the sport's first posthumous champion, with five more GP victories to his credit. To his right on the podium stands Piers Courage, an excellent second in Williams' Brabham

Rial

In 1987 the unpredictable Gunther Schmid, whose ATS team had an odd GP career 1978–84, commissioned Gustav Brunner to design a Cosworth-powered F1 car to carry the name of his Rial wheels company into the GPs in 1988. This ARC1 proved to be a typically neat, conventional car. The driver for the German team was Andrea de Cesaris, fully able to match the patron in unpredictability.

Rindt, Jochen *1942–70*

Rindt was motor racing's first posthumous world champion, for he had amassed 45 points as the European part of the 1970 season reached its climax at Monza, where he was killed in a practice accident, and no other driver scored as many points.

Rindt made his name very suddenly, in two F2 races run one holiday weekend in England in 1964. In the American GP that year he had his first championship drive, a one-off outing in a Brabham. In 1965 he was in the Cooper team, and scored points for the first time in the German GP. In 1966 he did well with Cooper-Maseratis, then not very well with them in 1967. He moved to Brabham, at the wrong time as the Repco engines were unreliable in 1968, then joined Lotus.

Rindt did not always see eye to eye with Chapman, but he continued to drive forcefully, and at the end of the year scored an overdue Grand Prix victory, in the USA. He led the team in 1970, hurling an old 49 round the streets of Monaco to a dramatic victory, and once the 72 was raceworthy he used it to the full, reeling off four more victories before his death.
*World championship races: 60 starts, 109 points (107 net), 6 wins: 1969 USA; 1970 Monaco, Netherlands, France, Britain, Germany. **World Champion: 1970.***

Riverside circuit

In the uncertain early period of the US Grand Prix the 1960 race was run at this venue, then a busy circuit some 60 miles/95 km east of Los Angeles. Several variations were possible, all sharing a wriggling stretch against a backdrop of low hills from the start and a long straight on the return leg. The only GP at Riverside was the last of the seven-year 2.5-litre formula.
*Lap distance: 3.28 miles/5.28 km. **F1 lap record:** 100.9 mph/162.35 km/h by Brabham in a Cooper, 1960.*

Rodriguez, Pedro *1940–71*

Pedro was the older of two racing brothers, whose performances in local Mexican events

Renault RE 50, 1984

gained them drives with the North American Racing Team (NART) in sports car events. Ricardo was the first Mexican driver to score world championship points, four in five races with Ferrari in 1961–62, before he was killed in a Lotus during practice for the non-championship 1962 Mexican GP.

Pedro had odd GP drives in North American races in 1963–65, and scored his first point when he placed a Ferrari sixth in Mexico in 1964. He joined Cooper for a full season in 1967, and that year won the South African GP. In 1968 he joined BRM, and did well to score 18 championship points in their uncompetitive cars. Fortunes slumped with BRM and Ferrari in 1969, but picked up when he returned to BRM in 1970, and won the Belgian GP at a shattering 149.94 mph/241.31 km/h.

He also raced sports cars with great success, and is still recalled for his spectacular drives in JWA team Porsche 917s. He died when he crashed in an insignificant German sports car race in July 1971.

World championship races: 55 starts, 71 points, 2 wins: 1967 South Africa; 1970 Belgium.

Rosberg, Keke *1948–*

Self-assured and a professional through and through, Rosberg was very much a driver of the commercial and promotional age of Grand Prix racing, and he did not fit the popular image of a Finnish driver so well as the many rally aces from that country.

Rosberg raced karts until 1972, then in F Vee and F Super Vee until 1975. He spent two years with Fred Opert's shoestring teams in F Atlantic, F Pacific and Formula 2, travelling the world and showing the raw car control that was to mark him out in a F1 car when a smooth style was supposed to be all-important.

His first F1 drives were in 1978, at the pauper end of grids. But Rosberg announced his arrival by keeping a Theodore on the sodden road to win the Silverstone International Trophy. He had five races with ATS, and three with Wolf at the end of 1978. He joined Wolf permanently when James Hunt abruptly gave up in the early summer of 1979. Wolf withdrew and Rosberg found himself with Fittipaldi in 1980–81, in a team strapped for cash. Rosberg could not qualify for seven races in 1981, but did score his first points, in Argentina in 1980.

Four fruitful seasons with Williams followed. He took Alan Jones' place at short notice, won the last-ever Swiss GP at Dijon and won the 1982 championship. He did so not just by collecting points, for he drove competitively to win races.

He won four more Grands Prix with Williams and then moved on, for a last season in 1986 with McLaren. The car just did not suit his style

and he retired at the end of a relatively subdued season.

World championship races: 114 starts, 159½ points, 5 wins: 1982 Switzerland; 1983 Monaco; 1984 US (Dallas); 1985 US (Detroit), Australia.
World champion: 1982.

Rouen circuit

The Grand Prix circuit of public roads in the forest of Les Essarts staged its first races in 1950 and was used for France's world championship event in 1952, 1957, 1962, 1964 and 1968. The valley setting was attractive for spectators and challenging for drivers, particularly a sequence of bends running down to a cobbled hairpin. These had to be driven hard and bravely for a good lap time, and this led to many accidents. Jo Schlesser's fatal crash in a novel Honda in the 1968 Grand Prix marked the end of Formula 1 racing at Rouen. Autoroute construction cut the circuit to 3.44 miles/5.54 km in 1972, and this truncated version remained in use for minor events until 1987.

Lap distance: 4.06 miles/6.542 km. Lap record: 111.288 mph/197.096 km/h by Pedro Rodriguez in a BRM, 1968.

Keke Rosberg was a totally committed natural driver who eventually battled through to the world championship

Shadow DN8, 1977

Jochen Rindt in his championship year, 1970, on his way to his fourth win of the season (and his third in succession), at Brands Hatch. His Lotus 72 is being pursued by Jack Brabham in a BT33 — Jack took the lead with 11 laps to go, then ran out of fuel and as he coasted to the flag Jochen swept past to win

San Marino Grand Prix

The 1980 Italian Grand Prix was successfully run at Imola, but returned to Monza for 1981. The Imola organizers decided to run a Grand Prix there in the name of nearby San Marino, and thwarted opposition by giving the proceeds to a disaster fund. That established the principle that two championship races would be run in Italy.

The San Marino Grands Prix have seen excellent racing, and one near-farce, in 1985 when the hard-driving leaders ran out of fuel in the closing laps, the driver who took the flag (Prost) was disqualified, the man declared the winner was in a car made uncompetitive by useless brakes and the car declared to be second coasted to stop with its front wheels on one side of the line, its rear wheels not crossing the line.

Winners (world championship GPs)

1981	N. Piquet	Brabham-Ford
1982	D. Pironi	Ferrari
1983	P. Tambay	Ferrari
1984	A. Prost	McLaren-TAG
1985	E. de Angelis	Lotus-Renault
1986	A. Prost	McLaren-TAG
1987	N. Mansell	Williams-Honda
1988	A. Senna	McLaren-Honda

Scarab

Lance Reventlow brought together a group of talented people in his Scarab projects – Warren Olson, Chuck Daigh, Troutman and Barnes – and they produced a handful of sports-racing cars that were very successful in US West Coast racing. This sparked Formula 1 ambitions, and rather too slowly for the pace of change in F1 at the time, an original design for their American contender took shape: a front-engined car, intended for the 1959 season. It had a space frame, all-independent suspension by wishbones and coil springs and an original four-cylinder engine with desmodromic valve gear. Development of this slowed the programme and by the time the handsome cars reached the circuits in 1960 they were obsolete. Reventlow and Daigh failed to qualify for the first two GPs they attempted, Daigh retired from the car's only European GP (at Spa) and placed tenth in the only other GP appearance at Watkins Glen. Reventlow sensibly retired from the GP scene.

Scarfiotti, Ludovico *1933–68*

An Italian gentleman driver, 'Ludo' Scarfiotti was extraordinarily versatile, and successful in single-seaters, sports cars in endurance racing, and in the European Mountain Championship in its heyday. He died on one of the hill climbs, during practice at Rossfeld when his ultra-light Porsche left the road.

Shadow DN8, 1977

In single seaters he had raced a little in F Junior, and after a string of success in Ferrari sports cars had his first GP drive in the Netherlands in 1963, when he scored a point. Next time out he crashed in practice, and he did not race an F1 car again until the 1964 Italian GP. His next recall was for two races in 1966, and he won the second of them – an Italian, he drove a Ferrari to victory in the Italian GP. In the following year he parted company with Ferrari, then had an Eagle drive and three races in Coopers in 1968, when he twice placed a BRM-engined car fourth.

World championship races: 10 starts, 17 points, 1 win: 1966 Italy.

Scheckter, Jody 1950–

The only outstanding Grand Prix driver to come from South Africa, Scheckter gained a reputation for hard driving and hard work, won the world championship, and retired.

He started racing in saloons in 1968, won a driver to Europe award with his F Ford performances in 1970 and startled British observers with his aggressive approach in 1971, when he won eight F3 races. In 1972 McLaren gave him his first F1 race, in the US Grand Prix, and five more GP drives in 1973. That year he led the French GP, and seemed to be attempting to win the British GP on the first lap when he lost control and triggered an enormous accident at Silverstone.

For the next three seasons he had the calming benefit of driving for Ken Tyrrell, scoring his first points in the Spanish GP and his first victories in Sweden and Britain. He won his home GP in 1975, then scored the only win for

the six-wheeled Tyrrell P34 in Sweden in 1976.

Scheckter was the new Wolf team's driver in 1977. He won its first GP, the GP at Monaco where he and Walter Wolf lived and the GP in Canada, Wolf's adopted country. There was less joy for Wolf and Scheckter in 1978, and to the surprise of many Scheckter joined Ferrari for 1979.

That move brought him three GP victories, including the Italian, and he won the championship. Then he honoured his contract through a last and very lean season before retiring. He was involved in motor cycle race organization in South Africa, then drifted away from the sport.

World championship races: 112 starts, 255 points, 10 wins: 1974 Sweden, Britain; 1975 South Africa; 1976 Sweden; 1977 Argentina, Monaco, Canada; 1979 Belgium, Monaco, Italy. **World champion: 1979.**

Jody Scheckter, impetuous and impulsive through much of his racing career, eventually a convincing champion

Jody Scheckter driving a Ferrari 312T-5 carrying the racing number 1 to signify that it is driven by the reigning world champion. Scheckter's 1980 season with this car was dreadful, as the ill-handling 312T-5 was never competitive

Scirocco

American Hugh Powell backed this team in 1963, and the construction of its pair of simple F1 cars with space frames that had been laid out by Paul Emery, with BRM engines. The first GP for Scirocco was the 1963 French race, and in subsequent GPs in Europe two cars were entered, for Tony Settember and Ian Burgess: Settember finished second to Brabham in the non-championship Austrian GP that year. One car, re-engined with a Climax V-8, appeared on the GP fringes in 1964.

Sebring circuit

A one-time bomber training airfield in central Florida, Sebring first staged sports car racing in 1950 and was the venue of the first US GP, in 1959. It was naturally flat, and also featureless with an angular plan that reflected the use of runways.
Lap distance: 5.2 miles/8.3 km. Lap record: 101.13 mph/162.72 km/h by Maurice Trintignant in a Cooper, 1959.

Senna, Ayrton 1960–

A rare, and in his early days arguably precocious, talent was displayed by this young Brazilian kartist in F Ford in 1981, in F Ford 2000 in 1982 and in Formula 3 in 1983, when he finished first in ten successive races on his way to winning the British championship. Late that year he had invitations from leading F1 teams, at least to test cars; he joined Toleman for 1984, and scored a point in his second Grand Prix, in South Africa. He would also have won the Monaco Grand Prix if it had been allowed to run for its scheduled length. Lotus prised him away from Toleman for 1985, when he took pole position with the Lotus 97Ts seven times, and drove a masterful race in the wet to

Ayrton Senna

win his first Grand Prix in Portugal. He scored two more victories in 1986.

In 1987 he had Honda power in his Lotus 99T, and was firmly committed to Lotus' computer-controlled 'active suspension' system – he used it from the start of the year, won races with a car which was not quite the equal of the year's dominant Williams and was very critical of its chassis. Already he was looking for a team to carry him towards his championship destiny in 1988 and he joined McLaren, to win his second race with the MP4/4.
World championship races (to end of 1987): 62 starts, 163 points, 6 wins: 1985 Portugal, Belgium; 1986 Spain, US (Detroit); 1987 Monaco, US (Detroit).

Serenissima

The modified Ford Indy engine Bruce McLaren tried in his first F1 car was disappointing, so he turned briefly to a Serenissima V-8. This was a sports car unit designed by ex-Alfa, ex-Ferrari engineer Alberto Massimino, and unusual in its 70-degree included angle. In other respects it was a straightforward V-8, for which Serenissima claimed 310 bhp at 9,700 rpm. That was

optimistic by at least 40 bhp, but Bruce won the first point for his marque, when he drove the M2B that had been modified for this engine into sixth place in the 1966 British GP.

Shadow

The smart black cars seemed to hold bright promise for this newcomer to Formula 1 in 1973. Don Nicholls' British-based F1 operation was backed by Universal Oil Products (in those early days, Shadow was sometimes prefixed by AVS – Advanced Vehicle Systems – or UOP). Personnel involved included designer Tony Southgate, Jack Oliver and Alan Rees.

The Shadow DN1 was a Cosworth-engined car, with chisel nose and nipped-in waist, which proved a little delicate. Nevertheless, George Follmer placed one of them sixth in the team's first Grand Prix, in South Africa in 1973.

A DN1 was bought by Graham Hill for his new team, but as far as Shadow was concerned it was superseded by the DN3 in 1974. This car showed that Southgate had come to terms with the Cosworth DFV (the DN1 had been his first design for the V-8), but there was an early setback when Peter Revson was killed in a test

accident in South Africa. The other 1974 works driver, Jean-Pierre Jarier, carried on with Brian Redman as a team-mate, then Bertil Roos, then Tom Pryce. The pairing of Jarier and Pryce settled, and continued into 1975 with the DN5. This really was a competitive car, its performance undermined by incidents and failures, but Pryce won the Race of Champions in it.

Almost as an aside during 1975, a DN7 with the Matra V-12 was raced twice by Jarier, to two retirements; Matra then chose to work with one team only, Ligier.

Another chapter ended as UOP withdrew, and another as Southgate left. Dave Wass took over completion of the DN8 design. Shortage of funds meant that just one DN8 was completed, late, and meanwhile Jarier and Pryce raced DN5Bs. Pryce died in an accident in a DN8.

Alan Jones took his place, while the ineffectual Renzo Zorzi's seat in the other Shadow was usually filled by Patrese in his first F1 season. Southgate returned to develop the DN8, and with Jones' forceful driving coupled with a little luck things looked up. The Australian won a Grand Prix for Shadow, in Austria.

At the end of the season Oliver and Rees, together with designers Southgate and Wass,

The black Shadow of Don Nicholls' team's first season driven by George Follmer at Monza in 1973. The team experienced many problems with the DN1 as it settled into Formula 1, despite the accumulated experience of personnel including Oliver, Rees and Southgate

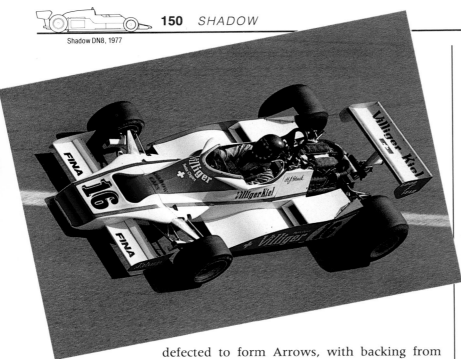

Shadow DN9 was the last effective car to carry the name, although it was by no means outstanding – Hans Stuck scored points with it only once in 1978, to set against ten retirements. Uprated to B specification, it had to serve on in 1979, and its DN11 successor was a failure in 1980

defected to form Arrows, with backing from Shadow's erstwhile sponsor Ambrosio. Legal action prevented Arrows racing a largely Shadows-derived car, but that did not help the team in 1978.

The principal drivers in 1978 were Regazzoni and Stuck, who managed few finishes and only six points between them. In 1979 Elio de Angelis in DN9Bs scored only three points and Lammers none. The 1980 DN11, designed by Gentry and Morris, recorded only one start and one finish in ten attempts, so it was superseded by the DN12. The first of these was completed as Teddy Yip acquired the fading team, which he used as the basis of his Theodore equipe.
Constructors' championship: 1973 8th; 1974 8th; 1975 6th; 1976 8th; 1977 7th.

Shannon

A one-off special appeared for one Grand Prix, the 1966 British race, in which it retired when its fuel tank split on the second lap. It could have been interesting, as one of its creators, Paul Emery, had acquired the unraced Coventry Climax FPE V-8s from the mid-1950s, and one was installed in the Shannon.

Siffert, Jo *1936–71*

Josef 'Seppi' Siffert was a very forceful driver, however mild he might have seemed away from a car; to enthusiast spectators his racing qualities were perhaps displayed best in his drives in such brutally powerful sports-racing machines as Porsche 917s, while to F1 colleagues he was sometimes a competitor to be challenged warily.

This Swiss driver's racing career started in F Junior in 1960. He was soon winning races, and in 1962 he had his first F1 drives in a Filipinetti Lotus. In 1963 this team ran him in a Lotus-BRM, and he scored his first point in the French GP. He ran a BRM-engined Brabham in 1964 and in 1965 as a member of Rob Walker's team, where he stayed until the end of the 1960s, with a Cooper-Maserati in 1966–67 and in Lotus 49s in the next two years. He scored his first championship victory at Brands Hatch in 1968.

Jo Siffert turned to a March in 1970, with little success, and to BRMs in 1971, winning a second GP. He crashed and died in a non-championship race at Brands Hatch.
World championship races: 97 starts, 68 points, 2 wins: 1968 Britain; 1971 Austria.

Ayrton Senna gained a brilliant first Grand Prix victory in atrocious conditions in Portugal in 1985, when his outstanding car control in a Lotus 97T paid dividends

Shadow DN8, 1977

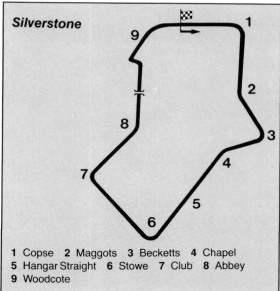

Silverstone

1 Copse   2 Maggots   3 Becketts   4 Chapel
5 Hangar Straight   6 Stowe   7 Club   8 Abbey
9 Woodcote

Silverstone circuit

The venue of more British GPs than any other circuit, Silverstone has four decades of unbroken history a great sense of tradition.

The runways and perimeter track of a Second World War bomber training base were first used officially for racing in 1948, and a Grand Prix was run in October that year, on a 3.67-mile/5.89 km circuit which used both main runways. Villoresi won the only GP run on that circuit in a Maserati, at 72.28 mph/116.32 kmh. In 1949 a 3-mile/4.83 km circuit using the perimeter track was introduced; with minor

modifications that is the circuit which is so well used today.

The first change, in 1950, was the elimination of a chicane at Club Corner, which cut the lap length to 2.972 miles/4.782 km. In 1952 the pits were resited, to the exit side of Woodcote corner instead of the entry, and the length was eased to 2.9 miles/4.67 km. Scaffold-based stands had meanwhile sprouted and remain a characteristic of the place. The pits were rebuilt for 1964 following serious accidents, rebuilt again for 1975 as the demands of top-flight racing changed, then rebuilt again for 1987. All the time other facilities were developed, including a complex of small factory units. As for the track, there was an outcry when one of the most spectacular fast corners in racing, Woodcote, was slowed with a chicane in 1975. That only disappeared in 1987 as an acute left-right was built on the run in to Woodcote and the pits access road.

The very first world championship Grand Prix, won by Farina, was held at Silverstone in 1950.

The International Trophy was the longest-lived of post-1945 non-championship races, and it was often memorable: Vanwall's first victory in 1956; Graham Hill's desperate last-corner effort to beat Jim Clark in 1962 and Jack Braham's narrow victory over Hill in 1964. Jackie Stewart's first F1 victory in the following year. Hunt's first in 1974. In 1977 it became a European F2 championship race and since 1985 has been an F3000 race.

Lap distance: 2.969 miles/4.762 km since 1987.
Lap record: 153.06 mph/246.27 km/h by Nigel Mansell in a Williams, 1987.

The airfield origins of Silverstone are obvious in this 1987 shot from the north – the pits straight is nearest the camera, Stowe is in the distance.

Shadow DN8, 1977

The formal preliminaries for the 1952 British Grand Prix at Silverstone: the cars are paraded to their grid positions (nearest are an A-type Connaught and an HWM, followed by a Cooper-Bristol). Silverstone's present layout of pits and main grandstands dates from that year, when they were resited after the exit from Woodcote corner. The track still follows the same line, the pits have undergone several transformations, but that line of stands still faces them, although those next to the rudimentary tower in 1952 are now topped by commentators' boxes, the Dunlop tower is much more substantial, and high debris fences line the bank

South African Grand Prix

First run in 1934 and revived as a *formule libre* event in 1960, the South African Grand Prix became a world championship round in 1962. That first race decided the outcome of the championship which Graham Hill finally won after Jim Clark retired.

The first three championship GPs were run at East London, as was the non-title race in 1966. The first GP at Kyalami fell to Pedro Rodriguez in a Cooper-Maserati, and Jim Clark's victory a year later was his last in a Grand Prix. Jack Brabham's 1970 win was his last in a GP; the following year Mario Andretti won his first GP in South Africa.

During a period of political skirmishing in 1981 FOCA ran the race as a non-champion-ship event for ground-effects cars; Ferrari and Renault stayed away, and Alan Jones won a race in which all 19 starters had Cosworth engines. The following year a drivers' strike, over a super-licence contract was temporarily resolved and the race run after one practice session. Turbo Renaults dominated it, ironically as the president of Regie Renault threatened to reconsider his company's commitment to racing because of such scandalous behaviour. The series ran without a break from 1965 to 1985, for although finance might have been difficult in some years, backers were always found – this was after all a supremely desirable event to be staged in South Africa.

Venues and winners (world championship GPs)

1962	East London	G. Hill	BRM
1963	East London	J. Clark	Lotus-Climax
1965	East London	J. Clark	Lotus-Climax
1967	Kyalami	P. Rodriguez	Cooper-Maserati
1968	Kyalami	J. Clark	Lotus-Ford
1969	Kyalami	J. Stewart	Matra-Ford
1970	Kyalami	J. Brabham	Brabham-Ford
1971	Kyalami	M. Andretti	Ferrari
1972	Kyalami	D. Hulme	McLaren-Ford
1973	Kyalami	J. Stewart	Tyrrell-Ford
1974	Kyalami	C. Reutemann	Brabham-Ford
1975	Kyalami	J. Scheckter	Tyrrell-Ford
1976	Kyalami	N. Lauda	Ferrari
1977	Kyalami	N. Lauda	Ferrari
1978	Kyalami	R. Peterson	Lotus-Ford
1979	Kyalami	G. Villeneuve	Ferrari
1980	Kyalami	R. Arnoux	Renault
1982	Kyalami	A. Prost	Renault
1983	Kyalami	R. Patrese	Brabham-BMW
1984	Kyalami	N. Lauda	McLaren-TAG
1985	Kyalami	N. Mansell	Williams-Honda

Southgate, Tony 1940–

A prolific designer, Tony Southgate began his career with Lola in 1961, briefly moved to Brabham, went back to Lola to become involved in the Ford GT40 and Lola T70 projects. He played a major part in the design of the 'Hondola' which John Surtees drove as a Honda to win the 1966 Italian GP, and in a rather roundabout way thus saw 'his' first F1 car win its first race.

His Eagle Indy design did win its first 500 in

Shadow DN8, 1977

1968, but when Gurney gave up his GP programme Southgate joined BRM as chassis designer, to design the P153 and the P160 before his next move, to Shadow. His stay there was broken by a short spell with Lotus R & D.

When Arrow was formed by Shadow defectors he went with Oliver and Rees, as design director, and took his number two Dave Wass with him. His promising FA1 design had to be abandoned when legally established as too similar – 40 per cent of the components were identical – to his last Shadow. He designed its replacement, the A1, very quickly, then had to adapt it as a ground-effects car in 1979.

Southgate left Arrows suddenly at the end of 1980, and designed two Theodores. He was involved as a consultant with the Osella FA1E; the chassis of which were built by Auto Racing Technology Ltd., a company set up by Southgate and John Thompson, well known for his fabrication work for numerous teams. Southgate was a consultant on several designs, then in the middle of the decade moved sideways to design endurance cars, notably Jaguars.

Spa-Francorchamps circuit

One of the great circuits of Europe, Spa was completely restructured in 1976–78 yet retains many of the features, and importantly the character, of the old circuit. The Belgian circuit remains one of the most severe challenges for a racing driver. The original roughly triangular circuit in the wooded Ardennes hills some 50 miles/80 km south of Liège was first used in 1922 and was the venue for the first Belgian racing car GP in 1925. It was improved through the years, although no road improvement could offset the notoriously variable local weather, and suddenly-wet stretches of road remained one of the great hazards of Spa.

The eventual length of this circuit was 8.76 miles/14.1 km. When it was last used for a Belgian GP, in 1970, Chris Amon set the F1

record at 152.07 mph/244.74 km/h and Pedro Rodriguez won at a record-shattering 149.94 mph/241.31 km/h.

The Belgian GP returned to Spa in 1983, to a new shorter circuit, with a new pits and start line before the la Source hairpin. The stretch up to les Combes remained from the old circuit, but then a sequence of corners led into the new section with fast bends leading back to Stavelot picking up the old circuit again and to the fast stretch back to the pits, broken by a ridiculous chicane nicknamed 'the bus stop'.

The new circuit was resurfaced to combat aquaplaning in 1985, and the work was completed only ten days before Grand Prix practice. Under the pounding of racing cars it started to break up, and the meeting was cancelled and rescheduled to be run four months later, uniquely in GP history.
Lap distance: 4.358 miles/6.949 km. Lap record: 132.517 mph/213.260 km/h by Alain Prost in a McLaren, 1987.

Spanish Grand Prix

A race with ancient origins and a fragmentary history, which has been run on classic street circuits and sterile autodromes, the Spanish GP was a championship race 17 times between 1951 and 1987. The first was run for touring cars in 1913, and won by Carlos de Salamanca in a Rolls-Royce.

The event was a championship round on Barcelona's Pedralbes circuit in 1951. That year's GP was the last race, and the last victory, for the legendary Alfa Romeo 158/159.

When it was revived again in 1954 it saw a great battle, with 14 changes of lead at the line and it witnessed the promise of the Lancia D50 demonstrated by Ascari. Mike Hawthorn finally won in a 'Squalo' Ferrari.

A non-championship Spanish GP (won by Clark in a Lotus 49) in 1967 introduced the Jarama autodrome as the venue once Montjuich Park at Barcelona had been ruled out, until another lapse after 1981. A 1986 revival at the Jerez autodrome attracted a miniscule crowd, so that the race seemed almost a TV exercise.

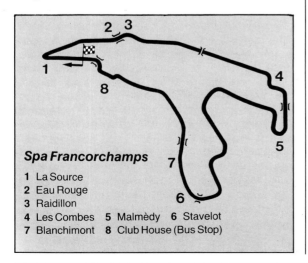

Spa Francorchamps
1 La Source
2 Eau Rouge
3 Raidillon
4 Les Combes   5 Malmèdy   6 Stavelot
7 Blanchimont   8 Club House (Bus Stop)

Venues and winners (world championships GPs)

1951	Pedralbes	J.-M. Fangio	Alfa Romeo
1954	Pedralbes	J. M. Hawthorn	Ferrari
1968	Jarama	G. Hill	Lotus-Ford
1969	Montjuich	J. Stewart	Matra-Ford
1970	Jarama	J. Stewart	March-Ford
1971	Montjuich	J. Stewart	Tyrrell-Ford
1972	Jarama	E. Fittipaldi	Lotus-Ford
1973	Montjuich	E. Fittipaldi	Lotus-Ford
1974	Jarama	N. Lauda	Ferrari
1975	Montjuich	J. Mass	McLaren-Ford
1976	Jarama	J. Hunt	McLaren-Ford
1977	Jarama	M. Andretti	Lotus-Ford
1978	Jarama	M. Andretti	Lotus-Ford

Shadow DN8, 1977

Right: The 1986 Spanish GP finish was the closest in championship history, when Ayrton Senna in a Lotus (left) beat Mansell to the line by 0.014 second. The Williams driver was closing fast, and metres past the flag he was in front!

Below: Eau Rouge at Spa, at the bottom of the drop past the old start/finish line, before the circuit climbs to crest a ridge at les Combes. Mansell, Piquet and Alboreto lead the 1987 Belgian GP field on the first lap

1979	Jarama	P. Depailler	Ligier-Ford
1980	Jarama	A. Jones	Williams-Ford
1981	Jarama	G. Villeneuve	Ferrari
1986	Jerez	A. Senna	Lotus-Renault
1987	Jerez	N. Mansell	Williams-Honda

Spirit

One-time March F2 team manager John Wickham and ex-McLaren and March designer Gordon Coppuck set up Spirit Racing to contest Formula 2 in 1982 with the Honda-powered 201. The following year Honda entrusted their turbocharged RA163 F1 engine to Spirit for a half season of race proving. A 201 was converted into an inelegant F1 car which made its race debut in the hands of Stefan Johansson in the British GP. The mechanical combination came out of its six-race programme well, with a 50 per cent finishing record, but Honda decided to go with Williams in 1984.

Spirit received some compensation, sufficient to cover the switch to Hart engines for 1984 but not to underwrite a race programme, so accepted drivers with sponsorship. Mauro Baldi drove in the first six races, twice placing 101Bs eighth, Huub Rothengatter for the next seven (best placing eighth at Monza), then Baldi for the last two. The cars were uprated to 101D specification for 1985, but the team folded after three GPs, when one of the few assets, a tyre contract, was sold to Toleman. Spirit reappeared in 1988 with Wickham running a Reynard F3000 team under the old name.

sponsorship

Grand Prix racing remained free of the 'taint' of commercialism for a surprisingly long time, although it was used to demonstrate manufacturers' technical superiority and sometimes as a vehicle for nationalist pride. In the early years of the world championship teams and drivers were contracted to suppliers, there was a gentlemanly system of success bonuses and victories by cars using such-and-such a product were duly advertised. Very occasionally an indication of backing appeared on a car, as when Ascari drove an F1 Ferrari in Italian regional events with the name of a quasi-medicinal product on its bonnet.

In the mid-1950s Jack Brabham attempted to run a Cooper as a Redex Special, but the racing authorities squashed that upstart notion very quickly. However, by the second half of the 1960s some of the traditional backers such as Esso had withdrawn and GP costs were soaring. Tobacco company sponsorship of secondary races and championships was accepted. Inevitably full sponsorship came, in 1968 with Lotus running cars in the colours of John Player's Gold Leaf brand of cigarettes and entered by Gold Leaf Team Lotus, which meant that there was little the authorities could do.

Perhaps the major surprise was that the Lotus example was not followed until 1970, when Yardley sponsored the BRM team, although there were rashes of decals on other cars and pathetic attempts to restrict the area of advertising on cars.

The practice soon became general, Ferrari — which in reality had enjoyed sponsorship longer than any other team — being the last to succumb as 'Fiat' was fairly discreetly emblazoned on the red cars, together with a collection of other badges.

Drivers' overalls perhaps carried a club badge in the 1950s, then possibly a small fuel or tyre company badge. Awareness of drivers' value as billboards grew with clothing and helmets becoming available for advertisements.

In 1971 the British Grand Prix was the first world championship race to incorporate a sponsor's name in its title when Woolmark backed the race.

Stebro

Unusual in that it could be rated a Canadian GP car (albeit a hopeless venture), the Stebro comprised an F Junior chassis with a 1.5-litre engine. Peter Broeker qualified it for the last position on the 1963 US Grand Prix grid and was classified as a race finisher — some 22 laps down.

Stewart, Jackie 1939–

John Young Stewart was the first complete professional driver of the modern age, with a quite outstanding racing record, always intensely competitive, a model in his promotional and other work for the sport and his backers, then and now and a vigorous safety campaigner.

He became serious about racing in 1962, was tested by Ken Tyrrell, signed to drive for him in

Jackie Stewart in Tyrrell 003 in the 1971 French GP, which he won from pole position

Shadow DN8, 1977

Jackie Stewart

Formula 3 and won all but two of the F3 races he started in 1964. Before the end of that year he had raced in Formula 2, and at its end drove a Lotus in the non-championship Rand GP, standing in for Jim Clark. His car let him down in the first heat, but he won the second – his first Formula 1 victory.

The next season he was number two to Graham Hill in the BRM team, and came sixth in his world championship debut race, the South African GP. He won the Silverstone International Trophy, and at the end of the summer he narrowly took the Italian GP from Graham Hill, the first of his 27 championship victories.

Stewart led the BRM team in 1966–67, but he stayed with Tyrrell for Formula 2, and when Ken moved on to Formula 1 Jackie went with him. A minor accident in an F2 race briefly interrupted his progress, but in 1968 he won three GPs, and at the cloudy, rain-soaked Nürburgring he won the German GP by no less than four minutes.

In 1969 he was supreme. He defended his world title in 1970 with Tyrrell's stand-in March and then the first Tyrrell car, but suffered too many engine failures. He regained the championship in 1971, but had another down season in 1972 with a stomach ulcer. He went into 1973 determined to win a third championship, as he had decided to retire at the end of the season. He was totally successful, won a then-record 27th Grand Prix (in Germany) and

put in some outstanding drives. That last season ended on a harrowing note, as his Tyrrell team-mate and nominated successor François Cevert died in a practice accident at Watkins Glen. Jackie did not start in that race, which would have been his 100th Grand Prix.

Jackie Stewart retired, but not to rest. He works tirelessly on promotion much of the time with firms he had been associated with in his racing days, such as Ford.

World championship races: *99 starts, 360 points, 27 wins: 1965 Italy; 1966 Monaco; 1968 Netherlands, Germany, USA; 1969 South Africa, Spain, Netherlands, France, Britain, Italy; 1970 Spain; 1971 Spain, Monaco, France, Britain, Germany, Canada; 1972 Argentina, France, Canada, USA; 1973 South Africa, Belgium, Monaco, Netherlands, Germany.* ***World champion:*** *1969, 1971, 1973.*

Streiff, Philippe 1955–

After a conventional French path towards GP racing – school sports cars, Formule Renault, Formula 3 (French champion in 1981), more sports cars and Formula 2 with AGS in 1982 – Streiff was Renault's F1 test driver in 1983, which earned him a first GP drive, in Portugal in 1984. His principal 1985 commitment seemed to be to F3000, but late in the season he drove four races with Ligier (scoring his first world championship points with a rather fortunate third place at Adelaide) and also drove a Renault-engined Tyrrell in the South African

GP. His first full F1 seasons were spent with Tyrrell in 1986–87, and in 1987 he was runner-up to his team-mate Jonathan Palmer in the Jim Clark Cup, then moved to AGS for 1988. *World championship races* (to end of 1987): 38 starts, 11 points.

supercharger

This is an engine-driven forced induction system which feeds a fuel-air mixture into cylinders under pressure – the more that can be forced in (within reason) the more an engine will burn and the greater the power it will produce. However, a supercharger absorbs power in its drive, so the return in greater power tends to diminish, and in the 1970s the turbocharger was preferred. The last distinguished Grand Prix car with a supercharged engine was the Alfa Romeo 158/159, raced in the world championships in 1950–51. Ferrari tried a Brown Boveri Comprex supercharger in the 126C in 1981, but the car was not raced with it and the KKK-turbocharged version was preferred.

Surtees, John 1934–

'He tried to do too much' could well be an epitaph for John Surtees' Grand Prix career, and some of the activities he should have left to others detracted from his driving. For the seven-times motor cycle world champion was a brilliant champion driver, talented and brave.

In 1960 he started racing cars – F Junior (with Tyrrell) and F2 (in his own Cooper-Climax) and in four Grands Prix, with Lotus (in his second Grand Prix, the British, he finished second). In 1961 his GP mount was a Yeoman

Credit Cooper and his best placings were two seconds. For 1962 he drove a Lola, often recalled as merely 'promising' but which he used to gain fourth place in the championship.

His first year with Ferrari, 1963, brought the same overall result, but he also had his first GP win, in Germany.

Surtees drove Ferraris to the championship in 1964, fortunes slipped in 1965, and the follies of the team manager probably cost Surtees and Ferrari the championships in 1966. He left the team after two races and turned to Cooper.

He spent the next two years racing Hondas and trying to persuade the Japanese to adapt to working in the GP world as it was. He won an Italian GP with the hefty V-12 Honda, then left for BRM and a season of frustration in 1969. By that time Team Surtees was taking shape and as soon as it had a GP car he drove it. After 19

Left: John Surtees, still the only man to have won world championships on two wheels and four

Below: Jackie Stewart and John Surtees in the non-championship 1965 International Trophy. Both were great Grand Prix drivers and their cars, BRM V-8 and Ferrari V-8, were both outstanding. One seldom sees such combinations side-by-side through Silverstone's Copse Corner nowadays

Shadow DN8, 1977

races in Surtees, 1970–72, he gave up driving. Appropriately, his last race was the Italian Grand Prix, for *il grande John* was held in the highest esteem in Italy.
World championship races: 111 starts, 180 points, 6 wins: 1963 Germany; 1964 Germany, Italy; 1966 Belgium, Mexico; 1967 Italy. **World champion: 1964.**

Surtees

Team Surtees grew out of John Surtees' association with Lola, when for example it ran Lola sports cars, and in the late 1960s he decided to set up as a constructor. A series of neat cars followed, never quite in the top category as far as Formula 1 was concerned. The first was the TS5 in 1969, successful in F5000 and in the equivalent American Formula A.

Surtees moved into Formula 1 in 1970 as an entrant (with a McLaren), and then as a constructor-entrant. He drove his TS7 in its British GP debut race, scored the first points for his marque in Canada, and won the non-championship Oulton Park Gold Cup. That was an encouraging start for his straightforward TS7 Cosworth-powered car, with its distinctively angular lines. The TS9 which followed was evolutionary, lighter and late in 1971 revised with side radiators; it served through into 1973.

John Surtees in one of his angular and economical TS9s. The corner is the banked Karussel at the Nürburgring and the race the 1971 German GP, in John's last full season as a driver

By that time John Surtees had retired from driving to take on team management and other burdens. But in team driver Mike Hailwood he had a fellow spirit; Hailwood won the F2 championship for Team Surtees, and nearly won a Grand Prix for it, in Italy in 1971 in his first race with the team.

The TS14 was a less attractive car, built to the 1973 deformable structure requirements. Hailwood and Pace showed it to be so-nearly a challenger for top honours. The TS16 for 1974 was less convincing, and shortage of funds showed in slow development and a lack of good results. In 1975 a single-car team was run.

The TS19 was perhaps the last Surtees to show real promise. Designed by John Surtees and Ken Sears, it was a small, light, practical car for a small team. It was very reliable and Jones and Lunger built up a good finishing record and Alan Jones scored points with it, as did Brambilla in 1977, when the cars had revised bodywork.

The TS20 followed similar lines in 1978, when Brambilla scored just one point, in Austria. It was Team Surtees' last championship point. John was disillusioned and at odds with FOCA colleagues and although a ground-effects TS21 was built he withdrew from racing.
Constructors' championship: 1970 8th; 1971 8th; 1972 5th; 1973 9th; 1974 11th; 1976 10th.

Suzuka circuit

Honda's circuit near Nagoya, built to designs by John Hugenholtz and opened for international racing in 1961, was the venue for the revived Japanese Grand Prix in 1987.

Suzuka has a variety of corners and curves in its sinuous and undulating lap and is unique among major circuits in having a crossover (inevitably likened to a slot-car racing layout). It is relatively narrow – but with one of the widest pits lanes in racing – with a surface varying from smooth to bumpy.
Lap distance: 3.67 miles/5.91 km. **Lap record:** *126.21 mph/203.072 km/h by Alain Prost in a McLaren-TAG, 1961.*

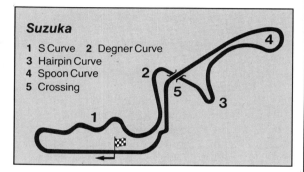

Suzuka

1 S Curve   2 Degner Curve
3 Hairpin Curve
4 Spoon Curve
5 Crossing

Swedish Grand Prix

This was a championship race for only six years in the 1970s, at Anderstorp. There was little racing tradition in the country, although the Cannon races at Karlskoga in the early 1960s were F1 events, and three Swedish GPs were run for sports cars at Kristianstad, 1955–57.

The first championship race in 1973 seemed set for a Swedish victory, as Ronnie Peterson led until a puncture put him out in the closing laps; Fittipaldi and Stewart both seemed likely winners, but at the end Hulme took the flag after a rugged recovery drive. The only victory for the six-wheeled Tyrrell P34 was in Sweden in 1976. 50,000 spectators watched Niki Lauda score a controversial win in the Brabham BT46B 'fan car' in 1975 – if, as had seemed possible, that victory had been over-ruled, then Patrese would have won in an Arrows, and that outcome would also have been unique.

Winners (world championship GPs)
1973	D. Hulme	McLaren-Ford
1974	J. Scheckter	Tyrrell-Ford
1975	N. Lauda	Ferrari
1976	J. Scheckter	Tyrrell-Ford
1977	J. Laffite	Ligier-Matra
1978	N. Lauda	Brabham-Alfa Romeo

Swiss Grand Prix

Five championship races were run at Bremgarten near Berne in the 1950s with results generally to seasonal form, except in 1952 when Ascari, who was to dominate the season, was absent at Indianapolis.

Racing was banned in Switzerland after a disastrous accident in the Le Mans 24-hour race in 1955. The sixth championship Swiss Grand Prix was run at Dijon in France in 1982 following a non-championship Swiss GP held there in 1975, which was won by Regazzoni in a Ferrari.

Venues and winners (world championship GPs)
1950	Bremgarten	G. Farina	Alfa Romeo
1951	Bremgarten	J.-M. Fangio	Alfa Romeo
1952	Bremgarten	P. Taruffi	Ferrari
1953	Bremgarten	A. Ascari	Ferrari
1954	Bremgarten	J.-M. Fangio	Mercedes-Benz
1982	Dijon	K. Rosberg	Williams-Ford

Talbot

The big Talbot-Lagos with 1930s sports car origins were familiar in the first two championship seasons. They were obsolescent, with a 4.5-litre pushrod ohv straight-six, producing up to 275–280 bhp in 1950, but reliable and economical. So their drivers' tactic was to go through a 500 km Grand Prix with, at most, one stop for fuel. In the first championship season they achieved honourable top-six placings – Louis Rosier was third in Switzerland and Belgium in 1950, and he managed to finish fourth in Belgium in 1951.

Tambay, Patrick *1949–*

Tambay fitted the popular image of a Grand Prix driver perfectly – he was handsome and articulate, a top-flight skier as well as a brave racing driver. He started racing in 1971 when he was the first champion in the *pilote Elf* scheme for French drivers. *Formule Renault* seasons followed, leading to Formula 2 in

Tambay's first drive for the Talbot Ligier team was with a JS17 in the 1981 French GP at Dijon. He retired early

1974–76 and to CanAm which he was champion in 1977, with six wins in eight races.

Tambay's first Grand Prix start was in Britain in 1977, with an Ensign, and in the German GP that year he scored his first championship point. He was with McLaren in 1978–79, returning to CanAm in 1980 to win that championship again.

He drove six races for Theodore in 1981, scoring a single point, then jumped at the chance to drive for the 'more competitive' Ligier team – and failed to finish in the next eight races. In 1982 he took Villeneuve's place at Ferrari, and won the German Grand Prix. With Ferrari again in 1983 he won at Imola but Ferrari replaced him in 1984, and he joined Renault for two modestly successful seasons.

The big-buck Haas-Lola (née Beatrice) team contracted him for 1986, when he worked hard for little reward. His name did not appear on the 1987 entry lists.

World championship races: 114 starts, 103 points, 2 wins: 1982 Germany; 1983 San Marino.

Tauranac, Ron *1925–*

Tauranac's cars were always sensibly engineered and although he was never rated an innovative designer he introduced practical novelties such as adjustable anti-roll bars and was into the development of 'wings' before most.

Jack Brabham tempted his compatriot Ron Tauranac away from Australia and his Ralt specials to become his partner in Britain in 1960. That year Tauranac designed and largely built himself the MRD F Junior car that was to become Brabham BT1. It was his first formula car, and the BT2 production version of it sold well. 1962 brought BT3, Tauranac's first Grand Prix car.

Ron Tauranac's reputation for conservatism probably stems mostly from his long adherence to space frames, but in the early days of monocoques this was practical, for customers could easily repair a space frame. When the regulations required it, for his Indianapolis Brabham and the later Formula 1 cars, he produced monocoque cars.

His last Brabham F1 design before Jack pulled out was the 1971 'lobster claw' BT34, so named because of its twin radiators flanking a nose aerofoil. At the end of 1971 Tauranac sold MRD to Bernie Ecclestone. He came back to racing to set up the Ralt company, reviving the name that derived from his and his younger brother's initials. He was occasionally a consultant in Formula 1 (he designed the Trojan, with Patrick Head) but with Ralt concentrated on production cars and running highly successful works teams in the second-level categories, F2 and F3000.

Tec-Mec

Designer Colotti was committed to a successor to the 250F at Maserati when the company abandoned racing , and although a car laid out on the same lines (but with a light space frame and all-independent suspension) was passé in the rear-engined era one was built by Tecnica Meccanica. It eventually started in the first world championship US Grand Prix in 1959, where it completed eight laps. Thereafter it was run as a *formule libre* special in Australia and then found its way to the Donington racing car museum.

Tecno

The Pederzani brothers built some very successful karts, F3 cars and F2 cars at Bologna in the late 1960s and early 1970s. When Martini agreed to back a Formula 1 project the Pederzanis went ahead, but not with a straightforward Cosworth kit car which could have been within Tecno capabilities – after all, Luciano Pederzani was an engine designer.

The Tecno PA123 which appeared in 1972 was not handsome, and its engine was a noisy flat-12, initially used as a stressed member. Modifications to engine and chassis continued through 1972 (Tauranac lending his expertise, Southgate and others being approached for theirs). Tecno recorded six starts in GPs and Galli was still running at the end of the Austrian race.

Alan McCall was commissioned to design a chassis for 1973 and so was Gordon Fowell. There seemed to be promise in the McCall car, as Amon placed it sixth in Belgium, but the point gained there was the only one a Tecno car ever won. The Fowell-designed car with its Thompson-built chassis appeared at Silverstone that year, where Amon drove the McCall alternative. The last appearance for both vehicles was at the Osterreichring, after which the brothers and their backers abandoned the whole sorry affair.

Theodore

The extrovert and energetic Far Eastern entrepreneur Theodore ('Teddy') Yip financed several racing ventures, including F5000 and F1 entrants, before launching his own team. His equally extrovert associate Sid Taylor was manager, while quiet Ron Tauranac designed their first Cosworth kit car, the TR1.

In the Silverstone International Trophy in 1978 Rosberg beat a good field in quite atrocious conditions but elsewhere could not even qualify the TR1.

Yip bought redundant cars from the Wolf team and then acquired the Shadow DN12s.

Tony Southgate was commissioned to design a Theodore ground-effects car, TYO1, which was first raced at Long Beach in 1981 where it was placed sixth by Tambay. In 1982 its TYO2 successor was not competitive.

In 1983 Yip amalgamated Theodore and Ensign, which he had supported in the past and which had a typically neat car. The season started well, but worsened as there was little cash for test and development work on Bennett's N183 design.

Yip tired of Formula 1, and its political disagreements added to those within the team, so for 1984 he shifted his attention to CART racing, and took Morris Nunn with him to the US tracks.

Token

This was another of the hopeful small-scale British projects of the 1970s, initiated by Ron Dennis (later the McLaren supremo) and Neil Trundle, who were unable to finance it and passed it over to Tony Vlassopoulo and Ken Grob. Ray Jessop penned an angular Cosworth kit car, which was driven in a brief race debut by Tom Pryce in the 1974 Silverstone International Trophy, then showed well in the Belgian GP until another driver knocked it out. Ian Ashley drove it to finish 14th in the German GP and 13th in Austria, after which it was seen only as a Safir in two British non-championship races in 1975.

Toleman

Directors of the Toleman vehicle transport company raced at club level in the early 1970s, backed a very successful F Ford 2000 team in 1977 and moved into Formula 2 with an ambitious programme built around cars of their own make. Toleman-Hart drivers Brian Henton and Derek Warwick dominated the 1980 F2 championship.

Ted Toleman decided to enter the 1981 Grands Prix with a Toleman car. This TG181 was designed by Rory Byrne and John Gentry, used the first all-British turbocharged engine, which Toleman commissioned from Brian Hart, and ran on Pirelli tyres, then untried in F1. The programme was restricted by a tight budget, and the first season was one of hard learning – Henton and Warwick managed to qualify a TG 181 to start only once each, and only Henton finished a race, tenth in the Italian GP.

For 1982 the team had the TG181G and late in the season the TG183, which had two very large and distinctive radiators flanking the rear of the slim carbon-fibre monocoque. The cars qualified to start in 11 of 1982's 14 Grands Prix.

The flat-bottom TG183B looked most inelegant with two large rear aerofoils, but it promised well in early-1983 tests, and qualification was hardly a problem. Results were slow to come, but a mid-season change from Garrett to Holset turbochargers helped, and in the Dutch GP, the team's 39th, Warwick at last scored points with a Toleman by finishing fourth.

The TG183Bs served on into 1983, driven by Senna and Cecotto until Cecotto crashed at Brands; Johansson took his place. In a significant mechanical change at the start of the 1985 European season Toleman abandoned the uncompetitive Pirelli tyres for Michelins. Senna came very close to a remarkable victory at Monaco. The TG184, which used some TG183 parts with greatly improved Hart engines, showed real speed on straights as well as in corners (Byrne always produced good-handling chassis). At the end of 1984 Senna went to Lotus and beyond that in 1985 opened with a crisis, with an unsponsored white TG185 on old tyres. Eventually, in the spring the Spirit team's tyre contract was 'transferred' to Toleman. Teo Fabi drove very precisely, and gained Toleman's first pole position at the German GP, but the cars were unreliable.

In 1985 the cars ran in Benetton colours, and for 1986 the whole equipe was bought by Benetton, and the cars were entered and run as Benettons.

Constructors' championship: 1983 9th; 1984 7th.

Trintignant, Maurice *1917–*

Maurice Trintignant had a long and honourable Grand Prix career, seldom in the best of cars.

The Frenchman started racing in 1938 and in the first four world championship seasons he drove Gordinis, scoring his first points with a fifth place in France in 1952, a year when he also won five non-championship races. In 1954–55 he drove the generally outclassed Ferraris, scoring a rather lucky first GP win in a 625 at Monaco in 1955.

In the following seasons he drove Vanwalls, Ferraris, a BRM, a Maserati, the post-war Bugatti and then in 1958–59 Rob Walker's Coopers, winning his second Monaco GP in 1958. He then drove for a variety of teams, in a variety of cars, picking up points here and there until the German Grand Prix of 1964, when he placed his independent 1962 BRM fifth, and then retired.

World championship races: 82 starts, 72½ points, 2 wins: 1955 Monaco; 1958 Monaco.

Trojan

Trojan had built McLaren production sports-racing cars and chairman Peter Agg tentatively entered the racing car business for 1974, Ron Tauranac designing the T102 F5000 car and the

Talbot Lago 4.5 litre, 1948

Above: The Toleman TG183B of 1983 driven by Bruno Giacomelli at Silverstone, with Watson about to pass

Below: Turbocharger fires were spectacular, but seldom did great damage. In the 1987 British GP, Andrea de Cesaris was to pull his Brabham off the track before the next bend (Boutsen in a Benetton is leading the Italian driver)

related T103 F1 car.

The T103 was built down to a modest budget, and was consequently conventional. Driven by Tim Schenken, it started in six GPs and finished in three (placing tenth in Belgium and Austria). That exhausted the budget.

turbocharger

This is a compressor driven by a small turbine rotated at very high speeds by an engine's exhaust gas, used to boost the fuel-air mixture forced through the induction system. Unlike a supercharger, it requires no mechanical power to drive it. Turbochargers run at over 100,000 rpm, and in considerable heat – hence the frequent spectacular turbo failures in Grands Prix in the 1980s and the need for intercoolers on racing installations, as heated air loses density and that begins to defeat the objective.

A major problem was the delay between the driver opening the throttle, the engine picking up speed and the exhaust flow speeding up the turbo, although throttle lag was largely overcome by the late 1980s.

The usual suppliers of turbochargers used in Formula 1 were KKK (Kühnle, Kopp and Kausch) and Garrett AiResearch.

Engine power outputs became excessive in the mid-1980s, and the cost of turbo technology grew alarmingly, so measures were taken to restrain it. Fuel restrictions had little effect after the first season, as teams learned fuel efficiency, so preset pop-off valves (issued by FISA) designed to open if a pressure of 4-bar (2.5 in 1988) boost was exceeded were used to curb the power of turbo engines in 1987–88 as a preliminary to a complete ban in 1989.

tyres

Until the 1960s racing tyre technology was comparatively simple, with widths changing

little through the years of front-engined cars. Dunlop's R1 type lasted from 1946 until 1958, admittedly with some overlap in the second half of the 1950s as R3-R5 came in. Through the 1960s tyres looked increasingly squat as the profile changed, and tread widths increased from about 4 inches/100 mm (front) and 4½ inches/110 mm (rear) early in the decade to 9½ inches and 11½ inches/240 and 290 mm wide, front and rear. Tubes lasted until 1967.

Dunlop also introduced rain tyres, with the R6 where 'high-mu' rubber was as important as tread. From that time compounds became more and more significant. True slicks came in 1970, appearing smooth and with no tread they provided a larger 'contact patch'.

Pirelli, Engelbert and Continental had dropped out by 1958 leaving Dunlop the sole supplier until the two American giants Firestone and Goodyear came to Grands Prix in the mid-1960s. That brought on the first costly tyre war, and led Dunlop to quit F1.

By 1973 Goodyear had the upper hand. Then in 1977 Renault joined the F1 ranks, and their turbo car ran on Michelin radial tyres. The radial concept steadily took over, so chassis designers had to adjust as different types of tyre led to changes in car behaviour (radials even 'grew' less than cross plies at high speeds). The first GP victory for a car on Michelin radials was in Argentina in 1978, when Reutemann won in a Ferrari.

Qualifying tyres, with very soft and sticky compounds, good for maybe one or two really quick laps to record a good grid time, were the subject of ineffectual action, as officials worried about speed differentials. Tyre-change pit stops became a feature of racing, too, out-lasting the fuel stops which occurred simultaneously (the idea being to race with tyres too soft to last a full race distance, to gain 'grip' advantages).

Not for the first time, Goodyear announced an intention to withdraw in 1980, and Michelin did so. Avon briefly entered the field, supplying fairly simple tyres in a very restricted range, then Pirelli came back in 1981, spent a lot in efforts to catch up with 1980s technology, was eventually rewarded when a Brabham won the 1985 French GP and withdrew at the end of 1986. By that time, typical sizes were 15 inches/380 mm front and 15–16 inches/380–405 mm rear for the turbo cars, the relatively narrow rears hanging over from development for wing cars. Goodyear, incidentally, committed to radials in 1984. When Pirelli gave up Goodyear had the monopoly and supplied common tyres for racing, an economy and fair deal for teams.

Tyrrell

Ken Tyrrell has a fine record of achievement in racing and has proved to be one of the great stayers in the Grand Prix world. He has always shown an exceptional ability to talent spot drivers. He has battled on when a decline followed success, often with minimal backing

Stewart and Cevert in Tyrrell 006s leading the 1973 Swedish GP. This was not one of the better races for the team that year, Cevert placing third and Stewart fifth, while Denny Hulme (following the blue cars) won

Talbot Lago 4.5 litre, 1948

The first Tyrrell, the simple 001, before its debut in the Oulton Park Gold Cup in the late summer of 1970. Behind the unusually wide nose aerofoil, radiator air was exhausted through two vents on either side of a spine which split the airflow around the cockpit surround. Jackie Stewart and Ken Tyrrell look pleased with the outcome of designer Derek Gardner's secret labours

and sometimes self-financed.

Tyrrell raced a Cooper-Norton in the 500 cc Formula 3 of the 1950s, and at the end of that decade recognized that others could make better use of his Formula 2 Cooper. So he turned entrant: in the early 1960s he ran the works Formula Junior Cooper-BMC team — among his drivers was John Surtees — and for a while managed the Cooper GP team.

The Tyrrell Racing Organization was set up in 1963, and for his 1964 Formula 3 programme Tyrrell signed a young Scottish driver, Jackie Stewart. That partnership endured, for although he drove for the BRM team in his first F1 seasons, Stewart continued to race Tyrrell Coopers and Matras in F2.

Tyrrell had long been ambitious to enter Formula 1, and when he saw the DFV-powered Lotus in 1967 he ordered engines for the following season, before he had a car. For 1968–69 Tyrrell supplied expertise, engines,

transmissions and personnel — above all, Jackie Stewart — while Matra supplied chassis. Stewart won nine GPs in those two seasons. Matra was taken over by Chrysler's Simca company, ruling out any further use of Ford-associated engines, so Tyrrell embarked on his own car, meanwhile running March 701s early in 1970.

Tyrrell's 001 was designed by Derek Gardner, following the Matra pattern. Flaws were ironed out for 1971. When 002-4 were built — closely similar, so that they might have had a single type number. Best-known was 003, driven by Stewart to win six GPs and the championship that year, while his team mate Cevert won in the USA.

In his second-generation Tyrrells, 005-6 of 1972, Gardner set out to produce smaller, lighter and more responsive cars. These were built around a slab-sided monocoque with deformable side sections in 1973 to meet the new regulations. The 1972 record was 'only' four GP wins, partly because Stewart was ill. He was fit in 1973, when he won five GPs and another championship title in 006/2. Francois Cevert was killed at the end of the season and Stewart retired, so Tyrrell had to build his team anew around Scheckter and Depailler. 1974's 007 (real type numbers from here on) was in a direct line of development and the team remained competitive: Scheckter won three GPs in 1974–75.

Gardner went ahead with plans for a revolutionary car for 1976 with four small wheels at the front to improve aerodynamic penetration, cornering and braking, and to reduce lift considerably. From the cockpit back P34 was entirely conventional. In that it kept Tyrrell in the front line (and Scheckter won a GP in a P34) the experiment was successful but the competitive edge was soon dulled, particularly as Goodyear directed their development work to conventional-size tyres. So the little wheels of the P34s were pushed out as track was increased, and in 1977 the cars had rather portly new bodies — they looked overweight, and indeed they were. Obviously the experiment was going no further, Gardner left, and Maurice Phillippe took his place.

He came up with the conventional 008, built around a very shallow monocoque. Depailler won the Monaco GP with it in 1978, but there was no development life in the design as ground-effects cars set a new pace. For 1979 Phillippe came up with a near-replica of the Lotus 72, Tyrrell 009, which served on into 1980. The team's fortunes were in decline and 010 with its distinct similarities to Williams FW07 was no more successful.

The slump seemed to continue in 1981, when budget restrictions delayed the fixed-skirt 011 until mid-season. Development went well and in 1982 Alboreto used it very effectively

and rounded off the season with a victory at Las Vegas. The 011 design was adapted as a flat-bottom car for 1983 while the smaller and neater 012 was prepared, with a moulded carbon-fibre chassis. Meanwhile, Tyrrell continued to use Cosworth DFV, then DFY, normally-aspirated engines and in the US Grand Prix at Detroit in 1983 Alboreto scored the last victory for a 3-litre Cosworth-powered car. Without a turbo prospects for 1984 seemed bleak, even though Brundle was a splendid second in Detroit and Bellof was third at Monaco. However, after the Detroit race, an 'illegal fuel additive' was detected and although Tyrrell explained this FISA banned his team from the championship. FISA lifted their ban after legal action, but an unpleasant taste of 'politics' lingered.

In 1985 Tyrrell had to join the turbo faction to stay in GP racing and Phillippe designed 014 for the Renault engine. The German GP was his last race with a Cosworth car for a while. Tyrrell cars had won 23 championship races with Duckworth's V-8s between 1971 and 1983.

The mid-1985 Tyrrell 014 was the team's first purpose-built turbo-engined car, designed to take the Renault EF4 or later EF15 V-6. It was mechanically conventional. It finished in a scoring place only once, Capelli's fourth in the last race of the year relieving gloom.

The 014s served for the opening races of 1986, followed by the 'all-new' 015 representing, claimed Ken, the team's largest investment in a new car. It was promising, but lack of testing meant that small problems lingered. The drivers' relative lack of experience, and accidents, compounded problems. Between them Brundle and Streiff scored 11 points. Tyrrell turned with relief to the new 3.5-litre normally-aspirated class in 1987, committing his team to the Ford Cosworth DFZ derivative of the DFV/DFY engine. The design of the new car, 016, was entrusted to chief engineer Brian Lisles — much of the work was attributed to the CAD/CAM equipment of Tyrrell's Data General sponsor — while Maurice Phillippe was given a 'responsibility for special design projects'. The car was effective in the hands of Jonathan Palmer and Philippe Streiff. By the autumn the Colin Chapman Constructors' Cup for this class of car was safely in Tyrrell's hands, while before the last race Palmer had clinched the Jim Clark Cup and Streiff was runner-up.

The 017 for 1988 had low lines, achieved by modifying the DFZ, with a high airbox reminiscent of the early 1970s. Palmer was joined in the team by Julian Bailey and both had handling problems before Palmer scored at Monaco.

Constructors' championship: 1971 1st; 1972 2nd; 1973 2nd; 1974 3rd; 1975 5th; 1976 3rd; 1977 5th; 1978 4th; 1979 5th; 1980 6th; 1981 8th; 1982 7th; 1983 7th; 1985 9th; 1986 7th; 1987 6th.

United States Grand Prix

An American Grand Prize series was run from 1908 until 1916, and as the early races were contested by some of the top international drivers the American GP is the oldest after the French.

In 1959 the first world championship race in the USA was run at Sebring, and in 1960 the GP was run at Riverside. In 1961 the US Grand Prix was moved to Watkins Glen, its venue until 1980, although from 1976 it was called the US Grand Prix East, as the US Grand Prix West was established at Long Beach.

This second GP was run from 1976 until 1983, and meanwhile the thread of the original race had effectively been picked up at another venue, in the running of the US Grand Prix (Detroit) on an indifferent street circuit from 1982. Two other events that they were championship rounds had meanwhile come and gone: the US Grand Prix (Las Vegas) in 1981–82 and the US Grand Prix (Dallas) in 1984.

Venues and winners (world championship GPs)

1959	Sebring	B. McLaren	Cooper-Climax
1960	Riverside	S. Moss	Lotus-Climax
1961	Watkins Glen	I. Ireland	Lotus-Climax
1962	Watkins Glen	J. Clark	Lotus-Climax
1963	Watkins Glen	G. Hill	BRM
1964	Watkins Glen	G. Hill	BRM
1965	Watkins Glen	G. Hill	BRM
1966	Watkins Glen	J. Clark	Lotus-BRM
1967	Watkins Glen	J. Clark	Lotus-Ford
1968	Watkins Glen	J. Stewart	Matra-Ford
1969	Watkins Glen	J. Rindt	Lotus-Ford
1970	Watkins Glen	E. Fittipaldi	Lotus-Ford
1971	Watkins Glen	F. Cevert	Tyrrell-Ford
1972	Watkins Glen	J. Stewart	Tyrrell-Ford
1973	Watkins Glen	R. Peterson	Lotus-Ford
1974	Watkins Glen	C. Reutemann	Brabham-Ford
1975	Watkins Glen	N. Lauda	Ferrari
1976	Watkins Glen	J. Hunt	McLaren-Ford
1977	Watkins Glen	J. Hunt	McLaren-Ford
1978	Watkins Glen	C. Reutemann	Ferrari
1979	Watkins Glen	G. Villeneuve	Ferrari
1980	Watkins Glen	A. Jones	Williams-Ford

United States Grand Prix (Detroit):

1982	Detroit	J. Watson	McLaren-Ford
1983	Detroit	M. Alboreto	Tyrrell-Ford
1984	Detroit	N. Piquet	Brabham-BMW
1985	Detroit	K. Rosberg	Williams-Honda
1986	Detroit	A. Senna	Lotus-Renault
1987	Detroit	A. Senna	Lotus-Honda

United States Grand Prix (Las Vegas):

1981	Las Vegas	A. Jones	Williams-Ford
1982	Las Vegas	M. Alboreto	Tyrrell-Ford

United States Grand Prix (Dallas):

1984	Dallas	K. Rosberg	Williams-Honda

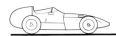
Tyrrell 016 was a straightforward car which dominated the normally-aspirated category of the 1987 Grands Prix

Vanwall

Industrialist G.A. (Tony) Vandervell was a supporter of early BRM endeavours, until he saw that they were never going to defeat the Italian teams. So he set about the job himself, with his Vandervell Racing Team, which gained experience with a 4.5-litre Ferrari Thinwall Special.

The 'Special' appellation was kept for the first Vanwall (from Vandervell and Thinwall, the trade name of Vandervell engine bearings.) Vandervell was also a director of Norton, and the engine that took shape under Leo Kusmicki followed motor cycle practice in many ways. In effect, it comprised four separate cylinder barrels spigoted to a crankcase (a light alloy version of a Rolls-Royce military engine crankcase) and cylinder head.

The first chassis was built by Cooper on Ferrari lines, and four more cars on traditional lines followed for 1955, when there were many setbacks but Harry Schell won four minor British races.

Outwardly the 1956 Vanwalls were far from traditional. Consultant Colin Chapman had designed a new chassis frame and de Dion rear end, while retaining the coil spring and wishbone front suspension. At his suggestion Frank Costin designed the body with sleek and

Right: Stirling Moss in a Vanwall throws an arm high to acknowledge the flag at the end of the 1957 British Grand Prix at Aintree. He had taken it over from Tony Brooks, who was not completely fit, to record this historic first championship race victory for a British car

aerodynamically efficient lines, very distinctive on this high car, with flush intakes and four protruberances to disturb the airflow.

Stirling Moss, driving as a guest, won the 1956 Silverstone International Trophy, while Schell matched the Italian cars in some GPs before falling victim to unreliability. That was by no means overcome in 1957, when Moss and Brooks drove Vanwalls, and shared the winning car in an historic British GP victory. Later in the season Vanwalls won the two championship races run in Italy.

They were effective again in 1958, despite early misgivings about the performance of the engines on petrol. Tony Brooks won the 1958 Belgian, German and Italian Grands Prix, Stirling Moss the Dutch, Portuguese and Moroccan Grands Prix, and Vanwall took the constructors' championship.

By that time, Vandervell was no longer fully fit, and he had to cut his work load. As an anti-climax, Vanwalls were run occasionally – and a rear-engined car was built for the short-lived Intercontinental Formula in 1960, and raced once. A great British team went out with a whimper.

Constructors' championship: 1958 1st.

Veritas

Ernst Loof built sports cars and single-seaters with reworked BMW 328 engines from 1947, and produced some F2 cars at his shops at the Nürburgring. These ran in some 1952–53 championship races, Veritas or Veritas-Meteor cars accounting for 15 starts and 5 finishes. Their best placing was achieved by Riess (another BMW special constructor) who was seventh and last in the 1952 German GP.

Villeneuve, Gilles *1952–82*

The youthful French Canadian made a sensational debut in Grands Prix in July 1977, showing exceptional talents in a McLaren at Silverstone. But for a faulty instrument which cost him time in the pits he would have finished in the top six in his first Grand Prix, at a circuit new to him. He came to it as a past Snowmobile World Champion, F Ford and F Atlantic driver in Canada.

That British GP was his only McLaren drive. Ferrari entered him in two end-of-season races, and he spun out of the Canadian GP and crashed out of the Japanese GP. In 1978 he was in effect Niki Lauda's replacement at Ferrari, still learning. He had accidents, scored his first points in Belgium and won his first Grand Prix, in Canada. Villeneuve was a dutiful number two to Scheckter in 1979 – he drove to win, never just to place, made mistakes, raced fearlessly and sometimes a little foolishly.

Ferrari did not provide him with the most competitive equipment in the early 1980s, but he continued to drive with enormous elan, and won at Monaco in 1981, rewarded for his hard driving in an awkward car as Jones' Williams faltered. He won another victory against the odds in the next race, when he made a typically brilliant start in Spain, exploited the power of the 126CK engine and compensated for its appalling handling.

Gilles Villeneuve at Monaco in 1979 in a Ferrari 312T4, as his many admirers remember him, pushing very hard despite the condition of his left front tyre

He died after an accident in practice for the 1982 Belgian GP.

World championship races: 67 starts, 107 points (101 net), 6 wins: 1978 Canada; 1979 South Africa, US (West), US (East); 1981 Monaco, Spain.

von Trips, Wolfgang 1928–61

German Wolfgang Graf Berghe von Trips – 'Taffy' von Trips – raced sports cars in the mid-1950s, and in 1957 drove a Ferrari in his first Grand Prix, in Argentina. That year he finished third in the Italian GP.

He drove in six GPs for Ferrari in 1958, scoring nine points, but apart from starting at Monaco in an F2 Porsche he raced in only one world championship event in 1959. However, he drove a full programme in 1960.

In the first 1.5-litre season, 1961, von Trips won the Dutch and British Grands Prix and seemed poised to clinch the championship at Monza – he would have been the first German to take the title – only to be killed as he crashed after colliding with Jim Clark's Lotus.

World championship races: 27 starts (twice in an F2 category), 56 points, 2 wins: 1961 Netherlands, Britain.

Walker, R.R.C.

Rob Walker was the pre-eminent private entrant of the world championship era, running a succession of front-line cars for leading drivers.

His R.R.C. Walker Racing Team cars were painted a patriotic Scottish blue. Outstanding wins by Stirling Moss in Walker cars included the 1958 Argentinian Grand Prix, a triple first in world championship racing: for a rear-engined car, for Cooper, and for an independent entrant. Moss also drove Walker Coopers to victory in the 1959 Italian and Portuguese GPs, and a Walker Lotus 18 to win in Monaco and Germany in 1961. Maurice Trintignant won the 1958 Monaco race in a Walker Cooper. In the late 1960s Walker cars were co-sponsored by Jack Durlacher, and when Jo Siffert drove a Lotus 49 to victory in the 1968 British GP it was the last in a championship race for a private car. The team continued with sponsorship into the 1970s, finally with Team Surtees.

Rob Walker then turned to enlightened journalism.

Warwick, Derek 1954–

Talent did not seem enough to bring this British driver victories, and through seven seasons with promising teams that failed to deliver, Derek Warwick tried hard but was an unlucky driver. He first raced karts and stock cars, moved into F Ford in 1975 and on to Formula 3 in 1977 and 1978, when he was British champion. Formula 2 followed, and in 1980 he was championship runner-up, driving for the Toleman team.

He stayed with Toleman as it moved into its first difficult year in Formula 1, in 1981, and did not qualify to start until the last race of that season. The next year promised better and in 1983 he scored his first points, in the Dutch GP.

For 1984 Warwick joined Renault, was quick in testing and in practice, and twice finished second in GPs. In 1985 Renault was in decline and Warwick ended the season with only five points. He missed the first races in 1986, but then he took de Angelis' place with Brabham, to drive the difficult low-line BT55. In 1987 he drove for the apparently resurgent Arrows team, to score just three points. He stayed with Arrows in 1988, when he scored as many points in the first race.

World championship races (to end of 1987): 84 starts, 40 points.

Watkins Glen circuits

The revival of road racing in the USA started on a 6.6-mile/10.6 km circuit of streets and local roads at this little resort in New York. After a fatal accident in 1952 a shorter circuit of roads outside the village was used, then in 1956 the closed circuit came into use. This had a lap of 2.3 miles/3.7 km, the record for which was set by Ickx in a Ferrari in 1970, at 131.97 mph/210.98 km/h, and it was extended in 1971, when the pits were moved to before the turn known as 'the 90'. It was demanding, with fast corners, a chicane before the main straight, a drop (the Chute) followed by a left that led onto the circuit extension and a climbing right before an infield section and the start/finish line.

The general area is delightful but the circuit amenities pleased nobody. The Glen was last used for a Grand Prix in 1980.

Lap distance: 3.37 miles/5.43 km. *Lap record:* 129.248 mph/207.998 km/h by Alan Jones in a Williams, 1980.

Watson, John 1946–

Most unusually, this British driver never raced in Formula 3, moving from small sports cars in Irish racing to Formula 2 in 1969. Chevron F2 drives in 1972 led to a contract for F2 and F1 with Bernie Ecclestone.

His F1 debut was in the British GP in the Hexagon March 721 when he came sixth in a non-championship race at Brands Hatch late in

1972 and his next F1 outing, in a BT42 in the 1973 Race of Champions, ended in a crash. Two months later he was racing again, and made his GP debut in the British race. He had a full season with a Hexagon Brabham in 1974 and despite the handicap of driving a car designed for Goodyears on Firestone tyres he scored points, his first at Monaco. Watson joined Surtees for a 1975 season cut short with cash starvation, drove a Lotus in the German GP, then took Donohue's place with Penske team.

The 1976 season brought him his first GP victory, in Austria. He spent the next two seasons with Brabham-Alfas, then moved to McLarens for the rest of his Grand Prix career, 1979–83, and the one last race in 1985. The years with Barnard's brilliant MP4 in its Cosworth-engined form were most rewarding for Watson, above all perhaps in his 1981 British GP victory. Towards the end of 1983 he drove the TAG-engined MP4, then quite suddenly his fruitful relationship with Marlboro-McLaren was terminated: Alain Prost was signed to join Niki Lauda for 1984.

He had one more F1 drive, and then settled into endurance racing in the following seasons. *World championship races: 152 starts, 169 points, 5 wins: 1976 Austria; 1981 Britain; 1982 Belgium, US (Detroit); 1983 US (West).*

Weslake

As an engine man Harry Weslake concentrated on areas such as gas flow, but the Weslake plant could design and build complete engines. For 1966 a 3-litre F1 engine was undertaken for Anglo-American Racers, the Eagle team, to be dubbed Gurney-Weslake. First run in the summer of that year, it was a V-12 (72.8 × 60 mm, 3997 cc), for which 364 bhp at 9500 rpm was claimed at the time. That was none too generous, and the assumed development potential in the design was hardly realized (412 bhp at 10.000 rpm was later quoted).

A revised version of the V-12 was essayed in the early 1970s, for sports car or F1 use. Brabham even built a car, the BT39, for this engine, but after tests the project was dropped.

In 1987 Weslake Developments at Rye set up an advanced competition engines subsidiary (WRACE), to 'prepare design concepts for a naturally-aspirated Grand Prix engine for 1989'.

Williams

Frank Williams overcame great odds to become pre-eminent in Grand Prix racing, gratifying a passion that lasted through bleak periods and a crippling road accident in 1986. He first saw a Grand Prix at Silverstone in 1958 and 21 years later watched one of his own cars win a Grand Prix for the first time, at the same circuit.

Williams came into racing as a driver, but soon turned to being an entrant combined with some racing components wheeler-dealer activities: in 1967 Frank Williams (Racing Cars) Ltd was established and in 1968 he ran a Formula 2 Brabham BT23C for Piers Courage. They moved up to Formula 1 with an ex-works Brabham BT26 and were rewarded with two second placings in 1969 – many so-called works teams plod through season after season without achieving such a record. An arrangement to run de Tomaso cars in 1970 added status to the fledgling team's record. Sadly Courage was fatally injured in one of the de Tomasos in that year's Dutch GP.

Williams saw out the season, then ran March cars for two years. With backing from Politoys the first Williams car, Politoys FX3, took shape, appearing in 1972 rather than 1971 when it might have scored points.

The Len Bailey design was modified for 1973, when the FX3Bs were run as Iso-Marlboros until new cars designed by John Clarke were completed. These IR01-04, or FW01-03, cars were not competitive, but a Dallara revamp as FW04 was more promising and Jacques Laffite drove one into second place in the German GP, precious points ensuring Williams' continuing FOCA membership. The 18 other Williams' drivers in 1973–76 achieved little.

Williams joined forces with Wolf for 1976, initially running Hesketh 308Cs as Williams FW05s, but the only fruitful partnership was with ex-Lola engineer Patrick Head. When Williams and Wolf parted company, Head went with Williams. In 1977 Williams ran a March 761 and although it was a barren year for results he formed an association with Saudi Arabian businessmen and the FW06 designed.

This was a handsome little car, competitive but less than reliable. It was outclassed by ground-effects cars in 1979. At the 1979 Spanish GP Williams ran the FW07 for the first time; at Silverstone Clay Regazzoni won Williams' first Grand Prix in it and Alan Jones won four Grands Prix with it later in the season.

The FW07 looked similar to the FW06, and in the detail of its make up there was nothing out of the ordinary, but it was a rare consistent ground-effects car, and Jones was strong enough to exploit it. In 1980 he drove FW07Bs to take the drivers' championship while Williams won the constructors' title. With the FW07C in 1981 Jones was runner-up to Nelson Piquet but Williams was champion constructor again.

The back end of the FW07 was carried over to 1982's FW08, a small and light car. Much aerodynamic work was done in Williams' own wind tunnel – an indication of how far the

Williams FW06, competitive with all but the Lotus wing cars in 1978, but let down by unreliability

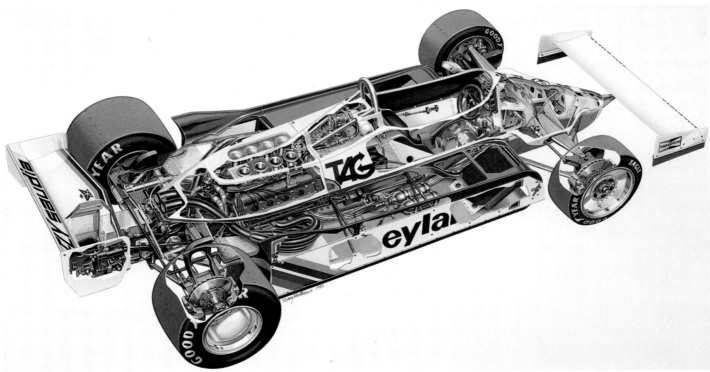

Championship Williams, the FW07

team had come since the struggles to get one low-cost Politoys built. Keke Rosberg drove FW08s to just one victory in 1982, but he took the drivers' championship. A flat-bottom derivative, FW08C, was outclassed.

In 1983 McLaren ran the MP4 with a turbo engine designed and built by Porsche, but underwritten by the Franco-Saudi Techniques d'Avant Garde (TAG) company, which had been introduced to race sponsorship by Frank Williams. Williams could have used these en-

gines, but only as a second customer, for having set up the TAG-Porsche project McLaren obviously had first claim to the equipment. Williams looked elsewhere.

In the autumn of 1983 FW09 was running, with a Honda turbo V6. It was less elegant than its predecessors and suffered handling problems until the longer wheelbase FW09B arrived in mid-season. But it prepared the way for FW10, the first Williams with a carbon-fibre Kevlar monocoque. Honda released E specification engines before mid-season in 1985 and the Williams became the cars to beat again.

Williams' drivers Nigel Mansell and Keke Rosberg won the last three GPs of 1985, then the Finn left for McLaren and Nelson Piquet joined the team, which convincingly won the 1986 constructors' title. Its drivers, with nine race victories between them, were second and third to Alain Prost in the drivers' championship. The 1987 season became a competition between Piquet and Mansell in FW11s, resolved when Mansell was unable to contest the last two races. Their successes meant that Williams quite clearly won the constructors' championship before the final race, just failing to equal McLaren's record points score of 1984.

It was by any yardstick an outstandingly successful season, crowning the partnership between Williams and Honda, yet the Japanese company chose to place their turbo engines elsewhere in 1988. Williams turned to normally aspirated Judd units for the FW12, which also featured a transverse six-speed gearbox which as in some other 1988 cars was mounted in front of the rear axle line, in the interests of agility. Mansell was number one driver, backed by Riccardo Patrese.

After an unhappy half-season with Judd engines, Williams looked to Renault power units for the rest of the 1980s.

Constructors' championship: *1973 10th; 1974 10th; 1975 9th; 1978 9th; 1979 2nd; 1980 1st; 1981 1st; 1982 4th; 1983 4th; 1984 6th; 1985 3rd; 1986 1st; 1987 1st.*

Above: Williams FW11B, the dominant car of 1987

The low Judd-engined Williams FW12 was first raced in the 1988 Brazilian GP, when it proved to have very high cornering speeds in the hands of Mansell and Patrese. Early race performances were disappointing

Williams FW11B, 1987

Williamson, Roger *1948–73*

A one-time British kart champion, Williamson moved into Formula 3 from saloon racing in 1971, and was backed by Tom Wheatcroft in F3, then in occasional F2 drives in 1972. He continued in F2 in 1973, and Wheatcroft hired a March 731 so that he could confirm his undoubted talents in Formula 1. He was eliminated in the infamous 1973 British GP multiple accident then qualified 17th at the Dutch GP, where he was killed in a crash.
World championship races: 2 starts.

wing car

This was a racing car that used the airflow beneath it to promote downforce. Air was passed through the flanks (alongside the monocoque, hence the desirability of slim monocoques) which were sealed to the track surface along their outside edges by 'skirts', to larger venturi where a low pressure area was created to 'suck' a car to the track. This also called for very rigid suspension and wing cars became very unpopular with drivers despite the high cornering speeds made possible. They were banned in 1980, when 6 cm ground clearance was required, although the ban was circumvented by lowering suspension systems. The flat-bottom requirement of 1983 was more sensible, and enforceable.

Wolf

Austrian-born Canadian oil industry equipment entrepreneur Walter Wolf came into racing at the end of 1975, picking up the Hesketh cars and team equipment, and rescuing the Williams team at the price of taking a controlling interest. The Hesketh 308Cs were redesignated Wolf-Williams FW05 and in spite of the best efforts of designer Harvey Postlethwaite and drivers Ickx, Leclère and Merzario the team had an abysmal season.

In a complete reorganization for 1977 Peter

The Wolf WR1 was a workmanlike Cosworth kit car, raced with considerable success by Jody Scheckter in 1977

Zakspeed ZAK 841, 1985

Warr was attracted away from Lotus to become team manager, Jody Scheckter engaged as sole driver, Postlethwaite designed a new, wholly conventional Cosworth-engined car (Wolf WR1, with chassis WR2-4 to follow) and Frank Williams resumed his independence.

Scheckter drove the WR1 to a debut race victory in Argentina, won at Monaco (the 100th victory for the Cosworth engine) and won in Canada.

The 1978 Wolf WR5-6s were ugly wedge cars, overtaken by ground effects: Scheckter's best results were second places in Germany and Canada. Postlethwaite's ground-effects WR7-9 was never properly developed, beset by problems with aerodynamic balance and suspension and short on straight-line speed. James Hunt was the team's driver until he abruptly retired after seven races; Keke Rosberg took his place but managed only two finishes, and no points. Wolf was disillusioned and turned his back on GP racing.

Constructors' championship: 1977 4th; 1978 5th.

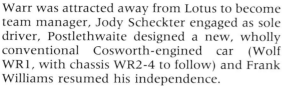

Youngest drivers

The youngest driver to qualify to start in a championship GP was New Zealander Mike Thackwell, who was 19 when he drove a Tyrrell to the grid for the 1980 Canadian race. A start accident led to the race being restarted and as Thackwell had to hand over his car to a teammate he is not the youngest driver to have started in a championship GP.

The youngest drivers to start in championship GPs were Pedro Rodriguez and Chris Amon, both 19 when they ran in the 1961 Italian and 1963 Belgian GPs respectively; they were also the youngest drivers to score points, in the 1962 Belgian and 1964 Dutch GPs respectively.

The youngest drivers to win championship GPs were Bruce McLaren at 22 when he won the 1959 US Grand Prix; Jacky Ickx, 23 when he won in France in 1968 and Emerson Fittipaldi, 23 when he won the French race in 1970. The youngest driver to win a championship race was Troy Ruttman, who won the 1952 Indianapolis 500 at 22, when it was a scoring round.

Zakspeed

Erich Zakowski came to Formula 1 with a high reputation earned in other racing categories, notably with Ford saloons, and the Zakspeed ZAK 841 made a good impression as Jonathan Palmer qualified it to start in its debut race, the 1985 Portuguese Grand Prix.

The carbon-fibre monocoque chassis 841 was designed by Paul Brown, and displayed high-quality in-house workmanship. Zakspeed's own four-cylinder twin KKK turbocharged engine was rated at 700 bhp at 11,500 rpm when the car was introduced.

In that first season the team entered nine races, with only one finish (Palmer's eleventh at Monaco). In its first full season, 1986, matters were a little better. The ZAK 861 was another neat car on evolutionary lines, the engine was rated at 800 bhp and although it was not an easy car Palmer qualified to start in every race, once finishing eighth, in Detroit. A second car gratified sponsors and paid its way, even if the spread of effort was distracting, and Zakspeed ran Dutch driver Huub Rothengatter

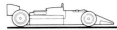

Zakspeed ZAK 841, 1985

in 14 races. Zakspeed ran a two-car team again in 1987, when Martin Brundle took Palmer's place and Christian Danner was the second driver. At Imola Palmer scored Zakspeed's first points when he finished fifth, and the pair recorded several other top ten placings with the ZAK 871s. Piercarlo Ghinzani and Bernd Schneider were contracted to drive the 1988 883s, and found even qualifying problematical. *Constructors' championship: 1987 10th.*

Zandvoort circuit

Williams' 1987 drivers Piquet and Mansell leading at the start of the Spanish GP

Minor street races were run at this modest Dutch seaside resort in the 1930s and a permanent circuit designed by John Hugenholtz in the sand dunes just to the north of the town was opened in 1948, with a meeting organized by the British Racing Drivers Club. It is at the mercy of North Sea weather, and one of the irritants, sometimes a hazard, has been fine sand blowing across the track. The facilities were not really up to 1980s standards.

The start-finish line was two-thirds of the way along a straight, which ended where the 180-degree Tarzan right-hander looped the track back round the confined paddock. A left then turned it to a fast swerving climb, then it dropped down from Hunserug to the daunting Scheivlak. This led to a very fast stretch, slowed in 1978 with a chicane built very quickly with advice from Lauda and Scheckter, and roundly condemned by their colleagues. A mixture of bends and corners then swung the circuit back to that long straight.

Lap distance: 2.64 miles/4.25 km. Lap record: 124.275 mph/199.995 km/h by Alain Prost in a McLaren-TAG, 1985.

Zeltweg circuit

This extemporized circuit was the venue for the first Austrian GP in 1963, although the airfield remained operational and racing facilities were consequently rudimentary. The pattern of taxi tracks and runways used gave an L-shaped circuit. After the championship GP in 1964 it came in for particular criticism for its rough surfaces.

Lap distance: 1.99 miles/3.2 km. **GP Lap record:** *101.57 mph/163.43 km/h by Dan Gurney in a Brabham, 1964.*

Zolder circuit

This circuit in the sandy hills roughly halfway between Brussels and Antwerp was the setting for ten Belgian GPs between 1973 and 1984. It became a Formula 1 circuit as the GP circus deserted Spa and it was politically imperative to have an alternative to Nivelles in French-speaking Belgium.

It was fast, remaining so in spite of chicanes added for the first GP (subsequently there were four chicanes), yet it was often rated 'dull'. Perhaps sombre became more appropriate after Gilles Villeneuve was killed in practice in 1982.

Facilities at Zolder were generally good, by the standards of the 1970s. The fastest lap in 1973 on the 2.622 mile/4.22 km circuit was set by Cevert in a Tyrrell at 110.51 mph/177.81 km/h.

Lap distance: 2.648 miles/4.262 km. **Lap record:** *120.237 mph/193.497 km/h by Arnoux in a Ferrari, 1984.*

The outwardly neat 1985 Zakspeed ZAK 841. Jonathan Palmer worked hard to develop the Zakspeed cars in 1985–86, but did not score points in them

The start at Zandvoort in 1968, when the starter was apparently oblivious of the official standing behind Dan Gurney's Eagle, in front of the two Coopers. He survived. Graham Hill, starting the new Lotus 49 from pole already has his tyres smoking, third-fastest driver Jack Brabham seems to look uncertainly across. (Green light starts – five to seven seconds after the professional starter shows a red light when he is satisfied that the grid has settled after its final pace lap – are now ordained, and are not always perfect. But chaos could often threaten in the days when a Grand Prix was started by a local dignitary or official dropping the national flag, as here)

The hotels and apartments of Zandvoort are in the background, the North Sea is on the other side of the crowded dunes on the right

Author's note

The folly of attempting to force 1.1364 litres into a 0.5682-litre container often lures writers and caring publishers to try to accommodate them. That has happened here, for world championship racing has a rich history. But with a sensible limit on pages, some compromises have been called for. So all the championship events are here and the circuits, the prominent drivers and some who were not so prominent, the leading designers and the marques, but not all their cars model by model or indeed championship table positions outside the top ten — realistically, while umpteenth place achieved by a grid filler on a points table might be important to the team from patron to PR person at the time, in the greater scheme of things it has little significance.

My thanks are due to colleagues in the business and on its fringes, to photographers whose company I have enjoyed and most of all to Cyril Posthumus who set a standard for many aspiring motoring writers and was kind enough to read this manuscript.

DH